Individualizing Gender and Sexuality

Relational Perspectives Book Series

Volume 53

RELATIONAL PERSPECTIVES BOOK SERIES

LEWIS ARON & ADRIENNE HARRIS
Series Editors

The Relational Perspectives Book Series (RPBS) publishes books that grow out of or contribute to the relational tradition in contemporary psychoanalysis. The term *relational psychoanalysis* was first used by Greenberg and Mitchell (1983) to bridge the traditions of interpersonal relations, as developed within interpersonal psychoanalysis and object relations, as developed within contemporary British theory. But, under the seminal work of the late Stephen Mitchell, the term *relational psychoanalysis* grew and began to accrue to itself many other influences and developments. Various tributaries—interpersonal psychoanalysis, object relations theory, self psychology, empirical infancy research, and elements of contemporary Freudian and Kleinian thought—flow into this tradition, which understands relational configurations between self and others, both real and fantasied, as the primary subject of psychoanalytic investigation.

We refer to the relational tradition, rather than to a relational school, to highlight that we are identifying a trend, a tendency within contemporary psychoanalysis, not a more formally organized or coherent school or system of beliefs. Our use of the term *relational* signifies a dimension of theory and practice that has become salient across the wide spectrum of contemporary psychoanalysis. Now under the editorial supervision of Lewis Aron and Adrienne Harris, the Relational Perspectives Book Series originated in 1990 under the editorial eye of the late Stephen A. Mitchell. Mitchell was the most prolific and influential of the originators of the relational tradition. He was committed to dialogue among psychoanalysts and he abhorred the authoritarianism that dictated adherence to a rigid set of beliefs or technical restrictions. He championed open discussion, comparative and integrative approaches, and he promoted new voices across the generations.

Included in the Relational Perspectives Book Series are authors and works that come from within the relational tradition, extend and develop the tradition, as well as works that critique relational approaches or compare and contrast it with alternative points of view. The series includes our most distinguished senior psychoanalysts along with younger contributors who bring fresh vision.

RELATIONAL PERSPECTIVES BOOK SERIES

LEWIS ARON & ADRIENNE HARRIS
Series Editors

Vol. 53
Individualizing Gender and Sexuality: Theory and Practice
Nancy Chodorow

Vol. 52
Relational Psychoanalysis, Vol. V: Evolution of Process
Lewis Aron & Adrienne Harris (eds.)

Vol. 51
Relational Psychoanalysis, Vol. IV: Expansion of Theory
Lewis Aron & Adrienne Harris (eds.)

Vol. 50
With Culture in Mind: Psychoanalytic Stories
Muriel Dimen (ed.)

Vol. 49
Understanding and Treating Dissociative Identity Disorder: A Relational Approach
Elizabeth F. Howell

Vol. 48
Toward Mutual Recognition: Relational Psychoanalysis and the Christian Narrative
Marie T. Hoffman

Vol. 47
Uprooted Minds: Surviving the Politics of Terror in the Americas
Nancy Caro Hollander

Vol. 46
A Disturbance in the Field: Essays in Transference-Countertransference Engagement
Steven H. Cooper

Vol. 45
First Do No Harm: The Paradoxical Encounters of Psychoanalysis, Warmaking, and Resistance
Adrienne Harris & Steven Botticelli (eds.)

Vol. 44
Good Enough Endings: Breaks, Interruptions, and Terminations from Contemporary Relational Perspectives
Jill Salberg (ed.)

Vol. 43
Invasive Objects: Minds Under Siege
Paul Williams

Vol. 42
Sabert Basescu: Selected Papers on Human Nature and Psychoanalysis
George Goldstein & Helen Golden (eds.)

Vol. 41
The Hero in the Mirror: From Fear to Fortitude
Sue Grand

Vol. 40
The Analyst in the Inner City, Second Edition: Race, Class, and Culture Through a Psychoanalytic Lens
Neil Altman

Vol. 39
Dare to be Human: A Contemporary Psychoanalytic Journey
Michael Shoshani Rosenbaum

Vol. 38
Repair of the Soul: Metaphors of Transformation in Jewish Mysticism and Psychoanalysis
Karen E. Starr

Vol. 37
Adolescent Identities: A Collection of Readings
Deborah Browning (ed.)

Vol. 36
Bodies in Treatment: The Unspoken Dimension
Frances Sommer Anderson (ed.)

Vol. 35
Comparative-Integrative Psychoanalysis: A Relational Perspective for the Discipline's Second Century
Brent Willock

Vol. 34
Relational Psychoanalysis, Vol. III: New Voices
Melanie Suchet, Adrienne Harris, & Lewis Aron (eds.)

RELATIONAL PERSPECTIVES BOOK SERIES

LEWIS ARON & ADRIENNE HARRIS
Series Editors

Vol. 33
Creating Bodies: Eating Disorders as Self-Destructive Survival
Katie Gentile

Vol. 32
Getting From Here to There: Analytic Love, Analytic Process
Sheldon Bach

Vol. 31
Unconscious Fantasies and the Relational World
Danielle Knafo & Kenneth Feiner

Vol. 30
The Healer's Bent: Solitude and Dialogue in the Clinical Encounter
James T. McLaughlin

Vol. 29
Child Therapy in the Great Outdoors: A Relational View
Sebastiano Santostefano

Vol. 28
Relational Psychoanalysis, Vol. II: Innovation and Expansion
Lewis Aron & Adrienne Harris (eds.)

Vol. 27
The Designed Self: Psychoanalysis and Contemporary Identities
Carlo Strenger

Vol. 26
Impossible Training: A Relational View of Psychoanalytic Education
Emanuel Berman

Vol. 25
Gender as Soft Assembly
Adrienne Harris

Vol. 24
Minding Spirituality
Randall Lehman Sorenson

Vol. 23
September 11: Trauma and Human Bonds
Susan W. Coates, Jane L. Rosenthal, & Daniel S. Schechter (eds.)

Vol. 22
Sexuality, Intimacy, Power
Muriel Dimen

Vol. 21
Looking for Ground: Countertransference and the Problem of Value in Psychoanalysis
Peter G. M. Carnochan

Vol. 20
Relationality: From Attachment to Intersubjectivity
Stephen A. Mitchell

Vol. 19
Who is the Dreamer, Who Dreams the Dream? A Study of Psychic Presences
James S. Grotstein

Vol. 18
Objects of Hope: Exploring Possibility and Limit in Psychoanalysis
Steven H. Cooper

Vol. 17
The Reproduction of Evil: A Clinical and Cultural Perspective
Sue Grand

Vol. 16
Psychoanalytic Participation: Action, Interaction, and Integration
Kenneth A. Frank

Vol. 15
The Collapse of the Self and Its Therapeutic Restoration
Rochelle G. K. Kainer

Vol. 14
Relational Psychoanalysis: The Emergence of a Tradition
Stephen A. Mitchell & Lewis Aron (eds.)

Vol. 13
Seduction, Surrender, and Transformation: Emotional Engagement in the Analytic Process
Karen Maroda

Vol. 12
Relational Perspectives on the Body
Lewis Aron & Frances Sommer Anderson (eds.)

RELATIONAL PERSPECTIVES BOOK SERIES

LEWIS ARON & ADRIENNE HARRIS
Series Editors

Vol. 11
Building Bridges:
Negotiation of Paradox in Psychoanalysis
Stuart A. Pizer

Vol. 10
Fairbairn, Then and Now
Neil J. Skolnick and David E. Scharff (eds.)

Vol. 9
Influence and Autonomy in Psychoanalysis
Stephen A. Mitchell

Vol. 8
Unformulated Experience:
From Dissociation to Imagination in Psychoanalysis
Donnel B. Stern

Vol. 7
Soul on the Couch:
Spirituality, Religion, and Morality in Contemporary Psychoanalysis
Charles Spezzano & Gerald J. Gargiulo (eds.)

Vol. 6
The Therapist as a Person:
Life Crises, Life Choices, Life Experiences, and Their Effects on Treatment
Barbara Gerson (ed.)

Vol. 5
Holding and Psychoanalysis:
A Relational Perspective
Joyce A. Slochower

Vol. 4
A Meeting of Minds:
Mutuality in Psychoanalysis
Lewis Aron

Vol. 3
The Analyst in the Inner City:
Race, Class, and Culture Through a Psychoanalytic Lens
Neil Altman

Vol. 2
Affect in Psychoanalysis:
A Clinical Synthesis
Charles Spezzano

Vol. 1
Conversing with Uncertainty:
Practicing Psychotherapy in a Hospital Setting
Rita Wiley McCleary

Individualizing Gender and Sexuality

Theory and Practice

Nancy J. Chodorow

Routledge
Taylor & Francis Group
NEW YORK AND LONDON

Routledge
Taylor & Francis Group
605 Third Avenue,
New York, NY 10017

Routledge
Taylor & Francis Group
2 Park Square, Milton Park,
Abingdon, Oxon OX14 4RN

Routledge is an imprint of the Taylor & Francis Group, an informa business

ISBN 13: 978-0-415-89357-2 (hbk)
ISBN 13: 978-0-415-89358-9 (pbk)

Library of Congress Cataloging-in-Publication Data

Chodorow, Nancy, 1944-
Individualizing gender and sexuality : theory and practice / Nancy Chodorow. -- 1st ed.
p. cm. -- (The relational perspectives book series ; 53)
Includes bibliographical references and index.
ISBN 978-0-415-89357-2 (hardcover : alk. paper) -- ISBN 978-0-415-89358-9 (pbk. : alk. paper) -- ISBN 978-0-203-81606-6 (e-book)
1. Gender identity. 2. Sex. 3. Psychoanalysis and homosexuality. I. Title.

BF692.2.C46 2011
155.3--dc22 2011009841

Visit the Taylor & Francis Web site at
http://www.taylorandfrancis.com

and the Routledge Web site at
http://www.routledgementalhealth.com

Contents

Preface

Some books take a long time to write, and by the time you are done, ideas that have barely begun to emerge call for further elaboration and reflection. These ideas emerge piecemeal, in seemingly disconnected, but sometimes also connected, insights about a variety of topics, extensions, and revisions of different parts of the author's thinking. For me, *The Power of Feelings: Personal Meaning in Psychoanalysis, Gender, and Culture*, published in 1999, was just such a book. Written over 10 years, during which time I also published *Femininities, Masculinities, Sexualities: Freud and Beyond*, the book links my three areas of interest and expertise: psychoanalysis, gender, and psychoanalytic anthropology and sociology. I published versions of the chapters in *The Power of Feelings* on gender and on development (development including, of course, the gender-related story of the Oedipus complex) in the mid-1990s, as these chapters were nearing completion, and the larger arguments and overall structure of the book were being consolidated.

As these two books were appearing and for several years thereafter, I was called on to present my thoughts about sexuality and gender in a variety of venues, often with specific foci: women and power; the family; bisexuality; Freud; classical theory; sexual difference; and so forth. All the chapters in the present book are responses to these invitations. They are thus by origin "occasional." As originally presented or published, they were written for conference presentation or for a volume. Published between 1999 and 2005, they follow chronologically and draw upon *The Power of Feelings*, as well as on *Femininities, Masculinities, Sexualities*.

The essays instantiate both continuities and innovations in the trajectory of my work. They exhibit a consistent interest in and attention to theory in itself, in particular, from *The Power of Feelings*, attention to a foundational contradiction in psychoanalysis between general theory and unique clinical individuality. They express a taken-for-granted assumption that psyche and culture are intertwined, perhaps especially in the cases of gender and sexuality. These represent continuities. Reflecting change, I rethink Freud, and I comment on my own previous work. There is more attention to psychosexuality and the psychological experience of the body than was found in most of my early writing, and I address new topics.

The second half of the book includes case material (a change in my writing begun in *The Power of Feelings*), always helpful and grounding to the practicing clinician and, indeed, to any reader. But I also write directly about theory (a continuity). I assume that theory and clinical theory can stand in themselves. My view is that, from the beginning of psychoanalysis, general understandings of the psyche and psychic process filter into the analyst's clinical preconscious and thereby into her clinical work. In this predilection, I follow the late Freud as well as Hans Loewald, whose work has had great influence on practitioners like myself, even though his writing includes only sporadic, not extensively developed clinical examples.

All psychoanalytic writers about gender and sexuality begin, pari passu, from clinical theories and metapsychologies that inform their general psychoanalytic stance, and I am no exception. I have always brought in aspects of psychoanalytic theory and clinical understanding that ground, modify, and extend formulations more exclusively about gender and sexuality. My first forays into the study of gender and sexuality brought the lens especially of British object relations theory. The present volume reflects, although not so explicitly as was the case with object relations theory, both my advocacy of theoretical pluralism and what I have come to consider an American independent, or intersubjective ego-psychological, identity, for which I am most indebted to my reading and rereading of Loewald. The reader will find throughout, especially in the ending synthetic chapters of the book, revisionist applications of ego-psychological concepts like intrapsychic conflict, overdetermination, multiple function, and compromise formation. Here, these are seen through the lens not of ego/structural theory but through the processual, continually differentiating and integrating, image of the individual mind and of two minds in interaction found in Loewald.

Part I, "Theorists and Theory, 1905–2005," begins with Freud, in a foreword to the *Three Essays on the Theory of Sexuality*. Subsequent chapters consider Klein, my own *The Reproduction of Mothering*, and Stephen Mitchell, who wrote on midcentury psychoanalytic writings on homosexuality. It ends with consideration of the postmodern turn in psychoanalytic gender theory. Part II, "Gender and Sexuality in Consulting Room and Culture," begins with specific investigations of contemporary clinical and cultural issues: women and work, women and motherhood, and men and violence. It concludes with reflections on the multiple ingredients and complex processes that compose gender and sexuality in each person. The book's last chapter, "Homosexualities as Compromise Formations," returns us to the first. I begin from Freud's *Three Essays* and elaborate an account of how we observe and experience the individualizing of gender and sexuality in the consulting room.

Because I agree with my analytic colleagues that the analyst's subjectivity and selfhood, which for me include her sociohistorical and cultural context, help to shape her consciousness, I begin this volume with a retrospective account—also invited and occasional—of my own work on women and gender from its earliest emergence in 1970s feminism (and, of course, before) up to the recent past. This chapter serves also as a longer introduction to the collection itself. It situates and refers to everything published herein, and its themes find echo in my concluding summative chapters.

During the entire period of writing the volume's original essays, I had the privilege of both practicing as a psychoanalyst and psychotherapist, learning from my patients, and teaching psychoanalytic theory and clinical technique to graduates and undergraduates, learning from my students (my short essay, "From the Front of the Classroom to Behind the Couch, and Back Again" (Chodorow, 2002b), describes some of this experience). I am still engaged in the former, but not the latter, practice, which, I think, kept me mindful of the need not to take for granted basic assumptions about psychoanalysis. My overview courses were theoretical, and they tended to move chronologically, from Freud to Klein, Erikson, Winnicott, and Loewald, as has most of my writing. Peter Evans, my good friend and then department chair, invited me to teach, as my final graduate seminar, "Chodorow: Theorizing and Theory," thus enabling me to look back carefully with the best readers—engaged students—on all of my work. That rereading has certainly found its way into this book.

At Berkeley, I could teach technique directly, through supervision of psychology graduate students, or indirectly, through a graduate interviewing course in sociology called "Clinical Listening for Social Scientists" and through a course for sociology undergraduates called "Individuality and Society," in which I made the point that the most detailed, fine-tuned rendering of one person's sociocultural-historical situation could not, finally, predict or explain that person's uniquely individual life and life choices. Finally, psychoanalysis and gender came alive in a specialized undergraduate theory seminar. When one student arrived, having read Riviere's "Womanliness as a Masquerade" (1929), and exclaimed, "That's my life!" several others chimed in with agreement. Meanwhile, on reading Freud's "A Special Type of Choice of Object Made by Men," another student enthused, "But Freud is describing the Korean family perfectly! The man gets married so he can bring home a baby to his mother!"

I have made contextual, stylistic, and other editorial revisions to the volume's contributions and have occasionally added references that postdate the original, but I have left the chapters largely to stand as they were. A few clarifying "2011 notes" have been added. There is inevitably some overlap, both in specific formulations and phrasings (the downside of electronic cut-and-paste technique, which makes us so easily able to borrow from ourselves and from others), and in some generally repeated thematic arguments. I was making these arguments in many different contexts: presentations at meetings, contributions to journals and essay collections of different provenance, forwards, commentaries, and so forth. I have for the most part not edited out these overlaps, as the goal of the collection is to make available in one place a number of contributions scattered both because of the nature of article publishing and because my interdisciplinarity and writing for both professional and general audiences have led me to publish in a number of venues. I am hoping thus to make the chapters available to be read and used individually as well as collectively, in classes and study groups, in the context of their origins and topics of inquiry. Situating introductions precede each chapter.

Acknowledgments

A volume long in the making generates much gratitude. I have been very fortunate in the institutional support I have received. A 2001–2002 fellowship at the Radcliffe Institute for Advanced Study was crucial in providing me the time, space, and community in which I could work on several of the chapters that appear herein, as well as in informally facilitating my decision to relocate from Berkeley to Cambridge, and from the academy into full-time clinical work. I thank then-Dean Drew Faust for her welcome invitation and Judy Vichniac, the director of the Fellows Program, for being there in every way from then to now. Recently, I have benefitted by subletting a part-time writing office, also under the aegis of the Radcliffe Institute. Chapter 3 was begun with the support of 1995–1996 fellowships from the Guggenheim Foundation and the National Endowment for the Humanities. A peaceful interlude in 1998 at the Center for the Study of Women of the University of Oslo, initiated by Center Director Harriet Bjerrum-Nielsen, allowed me time to focus and consolidate ideas. Teaching gender and sexuality to candidates at the San Francisco Psychoanalytic Institute helped me to clarify and develop some of the ideas in this book.

Chief of Psychiatry Jay Burke, Director of Residency Training Marshall Forstein, and Director of Psychology Kimberlyn Leary have welcomed me as lecturer in the Psychiatry Department at the Cambridge Health Alliance, Harvard Medical School. Although I am seminar leader rather than presenter-member in the faculty writing seminar at Cambridge, nonetheless I have learned so much about writing through this seminar. I am also grateful to have participated in seminars on sexuality and gender for trainees.

Of personal gratitude, I cannot say enough. Many have contributed both readings of particular chapters and invaluable conversation. Adrienne Harris, who kindly invited me to publish in the present series, is a close friend and colleague. Engagement with Adrienne about the issues herein over the years, specifying and elaborating similarity and difference, as well as collaborative work on journals, panels, and committees that always led to long talks about everything gender-sexual-psychoanalytic, have been crucial in all aspects of my clinical and theoretical formation.

I am indebted to Peter Goldberg and Elizabeth Bott Spillius for early readings of Chapter 3; to Elizabeth Abel and Gabriel Chodorow-Reich for guidance in Chapter 6; to Christine Williams for advice about Chapter 7; and to Victor Bonfilio, my coteacher on sexualities at the San Francisco Psychoanalytic Institute, for understandings of sexuality found especially in Chapters 1 and 11. Gish Jen and Alice Kessler-Harris were during my days at the Radcliffe Institute and are until now walking, thinking, and writing-support partners.

Anything written while I lived in Berkeley, including all the essays in this volume, benefitted from back-and-forth engagement, often during long walks, with Elizabeth Abel and the late Janet Adelman, my personal psychoanalytic, gender-attuned, support network in the English Department; with Carole Joffe and Barrie Thorne, my feminist sociology friends who appreciate the psyche and its complexities; and with novelist Sylvia Brownrigg, who also helped me to find the title of this book. At a recent memorial for Janet Adelman, I was made aware again of how much I owe to a community of psychoanalytic feminist literary scholars who live or spend time in Berkeley, who understood and supported, in conversations and study groups, our collective crossover psychoanalysis and gender enterprise.

Over the years, many colleagues have supported and encouraged these writings. I think of Rosemary Balsam, Ken Corbett, Muriel Dimen, Virginia Goldner, Carol Nadelson, Malkah Notman, and Ethel Person, who have invited, facilitated, and responded to my gender and psychoanalysis articles and presentations. I am grateful, for endorsing whatever I wanted to think and write about, to Bob Wallerstein and his generative seminar for semi-baked ideas, and to Glen Gabbard, Ted Jacobs, Warren Poland, and Wendy Stern, who has also been when I asked her a consummate editor. The late Janine Chasseguet-Smirgel saw through our ostensible differences to our common enterprise, personally invited two of the papers in this volume, and was a valued colleague, reader, and model of intellectual integrity and bravery. Robin Barnes was a needed writing partner as I began to consolidate this volume, and as I complete it, I am extraordinarily grateful to Alexandra Harrison and Ellen Pinsky for incisive, generous commentary and writing community and support. And of course, there are Rachel Chodorow-Reich and Gabriel Chodorow-Reich, who read, challenge, and support all my endeavors.

Kathleen Seltzer has provided invaluable research assistance throughout the completion of this book, making much easier the many demanding tasks involved in finishing it. Her intelligence, flexibility, and patience are commendable, and she has been a pleasure to work with. Routledge editor Kristopher Spring has facilitated every step in the process with intelligence and good humor.

Chapter 1

Psychoanalysis and women from margin to center

A retrospect

For a volume of *The Annual of Psychoanalysis* on psychoanalysis and women, I was asked, along with several other contributors, to write an autobiographical essay on my own professional trajectory in relation to psychoanalysis and women. The chapter traces my writing from the beginning of second-wave feminism, in the late 1960s, through my analytic training and almost to the present, and it alludes to some personal biographical factors that may also have played a role in my intellectual development and the character of my thinking. I suggest that such multiple factors inform all psychoanalytic writings on sexuality and gender.[1]

> I, as a woman, ask in amazement, and what about motherhood?
>
> Karen Horney (1926)

> But, in contradistinction to Freud, we are assuming that the castration complex in female children is a secondary formation and that its precursor is the negative oedipal situation.
>
> Jeanne Lampl-de Groot (1927)

> The reader may ask how I define womanliness or where I draw the line between genuine womanliness and "masquerade" ... they are the same thing.
>
> Joan Riviere (1929)

Psychoanalysts need (at least) two stories—external and historical, internal and psychological—to understand our field, its practitioners, its history,

[1] An earlier version of this chapter appeared in J. A. Winer & J. A. Anderson (Eds.), *The Annual of Psychoanalysis, Vol. 32: Psychoanalysis and Women* (pp. 101–129). Hillsdale, NJ: Analytic Press, 2004. Reprinted with permission.

its theoretical and clinical developments. We find this confluence first in Freud, excluded from the professoriate and research because of Jewishness, whose personal psychology—especially his driving ambition and willingness to engage in and reveal his own self-analysis—combined with his work with patients, early collaboration with Breuer, and studies with Charcot and Bernheim, all these factors together enabling him to discover the methods and theories of psychoanalysis.

Among the classic 1920s and 1930s psychoanalytic contributors to the psychology of women, we find the same confluence. Deutsch, Horney, Bonaparte, Lampl-de Groot, Klein, and others, all these women spoke from within the field, from their unique individuality, and from their psychological response and position as insider-outsiders, at both center and margin: women practitioners in a field that was more welcoming than almost any other but that at the same time put at its core a masculine norm. We find Horney's autobiographical exclamation, Lampl-de Groot's tentative disagreement with Freud (buried, I note, midparagraph 10 pages into her paradigm-shifting article), Riviere's ironic musings. So, too, my own intellectual trajectory is situated in history, in my personal psychology, and in my self-location, historically created and driven from within, at both margin and center.

IDENTITY AND ORIGINS, MARGIN AND CENTER

In the spring of 1969, I went to my first conference on "women's liberation." I was 25 and a budding social scientist about to switch from anthropology to sociology, with an (already greatly overdetermined) interest in child development and the relations of psyche and culture. I had made it my business intuitively to choose an undergraduate field—anthropology—in which there had been an unusual number of prominent women and in which I could actually work with women professors. Influenced by and influencing psychoanalysis in the 1930s, psychological anthropology, my own subspecialty, had even investigated the psychology of gender in culture (Margaret Mead, for example, in the 1920s and 1930s, and my own teachers, Beatrice and John Whiting, in the 1940s and 1950s). However, with few exceptions neither psychoanalysis nor anthropology had in recent years focused on or problematized women or gender.

For me, as for numbers of women of my generation, the women's movement exhilarated and propelled us into awareness. When I entered a graduate program in sociology in the fall of 1969, I wrote what would become my first published essay, "Being and Doing: A Cross-Cultural Examination of the Socialization of Males and Females" (1971). At the time, American feminists had begun to conceptualize and document sexism in political, economic, and familial institutions in terms of men's behavior toward women. Sexism was external, and although the personal was political, this meant that feelings and primary relationships were caused by external forces, not that we needed to investigate their internal constitution and creation.

By contrast to this trend, "Being and Doing" located the origins of male dominance not externally but internally, in men's dread of women and fear of their own internal femininity, and it suggested that men's and women's bisexual identifications were asymmetrical, the man's more threatening. I contrast women's more easily attained feminine identity, based on "being," with men's constantly challenged masculine identity, based on "doing," and I describe a "self-perpetuating cycle of female deprecation" (Chodorow, 1971, p. 41) in which mothers transmit to daughters their own anxieties and conflicts about femininity. The chapter cites only one psychoanalyst, Karen Horney, and its title, "Being and Doing," created in 1969, fortuitously anticipates terms found in Winnicott (1971), whom I had never heard of. I draw idiosyncratically upon a wide range of psychological anthropology, psychology research, and psychoanalytic sociology.

This first publication of mine inadvertently anticipates many of the themes found in subsequent psychoanalytic rethinkings of femininity, as well as constituting a protomodel of my own later work. My argument here, as in many later writings—the intuitively natural mode in which I think, but a mode that has been challenged by my more recent desire to write from within the clinical moment—begins with a single, self-evident, taken-for-granted but previously unnoticed or unstudied feature of the psychic or cultural world and elaborates the consequences of this fact from within.[2] In what would become characteristically Chodorovian fashion, I unabashedly invent theory, putting together observations from different studies and drawing upon evidence and (sometimes apparently contradictory) theories from a variety of fields.[3]

In "Being and Doing," the self-evident observation is that male dominance seems to be universal. I ask: How can we account for this? In my next publications—"Family Structure and Feminine Personality" (1974, written in dialogue and dividing the territory of psyche, culture, and society with Sherry Ortner (1974) who wrote on culture and Shelly Rosaldo (1974) who

[2] Having put things this way, I recognize that my method expresses the principles of ethnomethodology (Garfinkel, 1967), which I learned from my graduate dissertation advisor, Egon Bittner. In this sociological development from phenomenology, sociologists try to unpack the unspoken, unnamed, taken-for-granted rules and processes, the pretheoretical assumptions, that enable social life to move forward.

[3] Many years ago, having just read *The Reproduction of Mothering* (Chodorow, 1978), which in its sociological chapter fuses Marxist Frankfurt School thinking and emphatically anti-Marxist Parsonsian structural-functionalism, Jessica Benjamin exclaimed in a conversation upon the almost blithe way in which I chose synthesis and seemed oblivious to contradictions and incommensurabilities in theories I wished to draw upon. I like to think of myself as in good company: Freud, it seems to me, changed his mind about several key elements in psychoanalysis in an additive fashion (e.g., the changing drive theories, the move from topography to structure) while not giving up his previous conceptualizations.

wrote on society), "Oedipal Asymmetries and Heterosexual Knots" (1976), and *The Reproduction of Mothering* (1978)—I begin from the observation that women mother, a completely self-evident, taken-for-granted fact that at the same time had been hitherto almost theoretically and clinically unremarked (Stoller is the exception here). As is well known, following from this I develop claims that the mother-daughter relationship must be central to female psychology and that the fact that everyone's primary caregiver is a woman must be important to children's gender development and to the relations between the sexes, creating, as I called them, oedipal asymmetries and heterosexual knots. In "Heterosexuality as a Compromise Formation" (1992), I begin from further observations on heterosexuality, noting that it has been taken for granted as normative, not only culturally but within psychoanalysis, and that it has therefore not been studied. I ask: What if we treat heterosexuality as problematic, as we have done with homosexuality and the perversions?

In *The Power of Feelings* (1999b), I begin from clinical individuality—the obvious fact that each person who walks into the analyst's consulting room is unique. In relation to psychoanalysis, I elaborate the claim that our universalistic developmental theories and theories about the content of unconscious fantasies of self and other, including those about gender and sexuality, do not take account of this clinical individuality. Also beginning from basic psychoanalytic principles—the demonstrated existence and effect of dynamically unconscious mental processes, thoughts, and feelings; the fact that meaning comes from within as much as from without—I argue against the taken-for-granted assumption, found in feminist poststructuralism, cultural studies, and social science, that people are shaped culturally and discursively rather than creating their own psyches from within.

Just as with the classical writings on female psychology, there is some implicit autobiographical input in my contributions. I do not think that without a personal analysis, a strong mother and maternal lineage, and early experiences of finding myself a cultural outsider,[4] my writings would have the emotional and affective solidity and resonance that they possess. Yet, in spite of being of the feminist generation who believed that the personal was political and knowledge perspectival, and that the female scholarly "I" should replace the male objectivist view from nowhere, my writings, at least until well into the 1990s, do not begin from a female experiential voice. My voice seems characterized by clarity and confidence, even by a certain courage: "This is what I think, there is no other way I can think, all I can do is present it to you, as directly as possible." When I first presented "Family Structure and Feminine Personality" to a group of feminist

[4] See Chodorow (2002a) where I describe how, as a result of postwar migration, my Jewish family moved when I was 3 from New York to a still traditionally Western, semirural, pre-Silicon Valley, emphatically not Jewish, mid-San Francisco Peninsula.

English faculty in the Boston area in 1972, I was accused of being too confident and "writing like a man": How could I begin so directly, "I propose here a model ... " (Chodorow, 1974, p. 45)? I was shocked, in 1978, upon first encountering *l'écriture feminine*, to find that French feminists such as Irigaray and Cixous believed that traditional language and modes of argument were phallologocentric (Chodorow, 1979).

My voice echoes, perhaps, those no-nonsense, speak-your-mind, midwestern and western pioneer lineage women with whom I grew up, or my Jewish New Yorker mother and aunts, all of whom had been professionals—teachers, librarians, scientists, social workers, musicians—before marriage and some afterward, those women of that prefeminine mystique 1890–1920 birth cohort with higher education and professional participation than those who came before or after them. In my voice, there is also a paternal identification—hence, writing like a man. My father, an eminent professor of physics and applied physics at Stanford and a Silicon Valley pioneer, once told me (at least, this is my screen memory) that while he was not a great theoretical physicist, he had an especial capacity to see linkages and structure—connections among widely disparate scientific theories and discoveries, often heard of years apart—in ways that enabled him to conceptualize comprehensively, leaving nothing out, how these principles and discoveries might all be put together to work perfectly in a new instrument or process.

A traditional stance toward voice continues. In the present period, I find myself uncomfortable with and resistant toward the postmodern locutions and wordplay that became so prominent in academic feminism and the humanities more generally and that, in psychoanalysis, characterizes relational more than classical writing. Thus, although I have written (Chodorow, 1989b) that the great difference between women psychoanalysts of the second and third psychoanalytic generations and feminist psychoanalysts of my generation was that for us the theoretical was personal—that we evaluated psychoanalytic theories of femininity against our personal experience—it is not the case that I explicitly brought in my own personal experience, or shifted voice, in making my theoretical arguments. I begin from experience, from a freedom to challenge, and from a sense that knowledge is perspectival and derived from power, but I have found myself on the classical-modernist side (or somewhere in the middle; see Chapter 6[5]), in psychoanalysis, as in feminism, of a divide about evidence and language (a place perhaps more characteristic of analysts who were trained in the "mainstream" institutes of the American Psychoanalytic Association).

These qualities of invention, starting from the unremarked and taken-for-granted, synthesizing disparate or surprising theories and observations in a not theoretically monolithic, interdisciplinary, almost structural template,

[5] Here and elsewhere, I am referring to chapters within this book unless otherwise noted.

and using traditional approaches and language that are theoretically steeped but quite straightforward, characterize many of my writings.[6] Yet these same qualities, which also gave my work a relative independence—that is, I respond to trends that seem relevant to my thinking and am careful to cite relevant work, but I do not fit easily into a school, probably by conscious and unconscious intention—have meant that my work has always received attention somewhere, but often belatedly, and not necessarily from its intended audience. *The Reproduction of Mothering* was immediately recognized and lauded within the feminist humanities, ambivalently accorded admiration but also widely criticized in my then-exclusive field, sociology, and only noticed within psychoanalysis many years later. Articles that became classics, widely reprinted and cited, were originally rejected by leading psychoanalytic journals for being "not psychoanalysis" (for example, "Heterosexuality as a Compromise Formation") or severely criticized by editorial readers for feminist journals for being intersubjective and reflexive rather than statistical (e.g., "Seventies Questions for Thirties Women," 1989b).

I have not, it seems, wanted to be placed, and others have not wanted to place me. Even as I originated the idea that feminine personality is founded on relation and connection and named women's self in relationship, I am not a self-in-relation theorist, and I have been criticized by those who are for not understanding the mother-daughter relationship (Jordan, Kaplan, Miller, Stiver, & Surrey, 1991). Although I was one of the first American psychoanalysts to make British object relations theory central to her or his theorizing (in 1974, I cite Alice Balint, Fairbairn, & Guntrip; in 1978 also Michael Balint & Winnicott) and have been recognized as a founding American relational thinker (Mitchell & Aron, 1999), I do not consider myself a relational psychoanalyst.

When I was honored by CORST (the Committee on Research and Special Training that enables academics to be trained in the American Psychoanalytic Association), I titled my talk, "Why It Is Easy to Be a Psychoanalyst and a Feminist, But Not a Psychoanalyst and a Social Scientist," and I joked that I had considered calling the talk "From Margin to Margin and Back Again." There, I described the experience in 1979 of simultaneously receiving the Jessie Bernard Award for *The Reproduction of Mothering* from the American Sociological Association and being in a symposium on the book, later published in *Signs* (Lorber, Coser, Rossi, & Chodorow, 1981), in which Judith Lorber observed, "When I read *The Reproduction of Mothering*, I found to my disappointment that it is primarily an exegesis of psychoanalytic theory and therefore, in my eyes, a lesser contribution to the sociology of gender than Nancy Chodorow's earlier, short pieces" (p. 482), and Alice Rossi said, "I was not prepared for so extended an exegesis

[6] I have taken as my model here the sociologist Howard Becker (1986), who writes that the social scientist can choose between writing for the man on the street or for the *gymnasium*-trained European theorist.

of psychoanalytic theory past and present ... what constitutes 'evidence' in Chodorow's book [?] ... does her central insight require the burden of so much psychoanalytic theory?" (p. 493). Only Rose Coser enthusiastically supported my use of psychoanalytic theory in the work.

At sociology meetings for years afterward, I would wander into session after session on gender, feminist theory, or mothering, only to hear someone saying, "We can take seriously five different understandings of sexual inequality (or women's mothering), but Chodorow's individualistic psychology is not one of them." A former student, Michigan professor of sociology Karin Martin, remarked, when we were at the meetings of the University of California Interdisciplinary Psychoanalytic Consortium, that of the faculty present, all the feminists were in the humanities, except me, and all the social scientists, except me, were men.

My sociology colleagues were right to be uneasy. Even as I have drawn upon many theories, my "field" has always been, basically, psychoanalysis. I have always been interested in the complexities of individuality and in studying people, and I think that the absence of serious attention to individuality as a field of study in its own right is a great lack in the academy. I have never studied groups, institutions, organizations, stratification, collective behavior, or any other typical sociological topic, and I do not do research. I came to feminism in the first place partly because it called for an understanding of the psyche.

Yet, even as sociological colleagues were excoriating my individualistic psychology, colleagues in the humanities—in literary criticism, philosophy, and political theory—were writing books and dissertations based on my work. My focus on the mother-daughter internal world and its sequelae opened new vistas for understanding women authors, women characters in women's novels, and imagery, metaphor, and characteristics found in women's writing. My characterization of the female psyche, in terms of relation and connection, and my noting the defensive denial of connection and dependency in men, served as a basis for thinking in moral philosophy and epistemology and for critiques of normal science, classical political theory, and so forth. For many practitioners of these literary and textual-theoretical academic feminisms (at least until the poststructural and Lacanian turn), my work was almost idealized (for some, however, I erred in my purported "difference feminism," or "universalizing and essentializing"). Whether praised and criticized, I was certainly a founding feminist theorist.

THE REPRODUCTION OF MOTHERING

Returning to substance and chronology: After "Being and doing," I became interested in mother-daughter relations and women's mothering, participating in a women's group discussing mother-daughter relations and reading whatever I could find in the psychoanalytic literature. I read the classical (contested among themselves) 1920s and 1930s theories of Lampl-de Groot, Freud, Deutsch, Riviere, Horney, and Klein, which at the time were published mainly in obscure anthologies, along with the lone 1950s and 1960s voices of Chasseguet-Smirgel (1964, 1976), Kestenberg (e.g., 1956a, 1956b, 1968), Stoller (e.g., 1965, 1968, 1976), and the odd, controversial Mary Jane Sherfey (1966), who had argued, in the pages of the *Journal of the American Psychoanalytic Association*, for the existence of the unified clitoral-vaginal orgasm. I found a psychoanalytic mentor, George Goethals, at Harvard, and seminars for graduate students (in a model I wish all institutes would emulate) at the Boston Psychoanalytic Society and Institute (BPSI). BPSI subsequently assigned me to Malkah Notman as dissertation mentor.

Propelled again by an inner search as much as by an external intellectual or political context, I published "Family Structure and Feminine Personality" (1974) and finished my dissertation, which subsequently became *The Reproduction of Mothering*, in 1974.[7] Aged 30, a daughter but not yet a mother, a psychoanalytic sociologist whose first intellectual love had been psychological anthropology but not yet a psychoanalyst, I had, as a feminist during its writing the dubious benefit of the sharp feminist critique and dismissal of psychoanalysis found in de Beauvoir, Friedan, Millett, and others. I could also draw upon a few psychoanalytic feminist books and articles that appeared from 1971 to 1978, during the period from when I began the dissertation to book publication.[8]

Thinking about context is important for psychoanalysis as well as for feminism. As we look back over the development of psychoanalytic thinking about women, and the place that my own work, along with that of other feminists, played in psychoanalysis itself, we can recall what Fliegel calls "the [40-year] quiescent interval" (1986, p. 17) in thinking about women, an interval brought to an end by psychoanalytic feminism, and then, almost in response, by psychoanalysis (e.g., Blum, ed., 1976). These changes did not simply emerge from within psychoanalysis, through the disconfirming of hypotheses and "normal" scientific progress. Rather, theorizing and critique mainly from without came slowly to be accepted from within, leading to major breakthroughs in understandings of gender and sexuality and changes in psychoanalytic attitudes toward mothers. Indirectly, the feminist psychoanalytic project also generated increased attention, revaluation,

[7] Historical note: In 1976, when I signed my contract, my University of California Press editor was uncomfortable with my title, afraid that mothering was too uncommon a word. He thought that we would be better off calling the book *The Reproduction of Motherhood*.

[8] Mitchell's 1971 *Woman's Estate* included a chapter on psychoanalysis; Miller's anthology of classic papers appeared in 1973 and Strouse's comparable collection in 1974, as did Mitchell's *Psychoanalysis and Feminism*. Rubin's brilliant "The Traffic in Women" appeared in 1975, Dinnerstein's *The Mermaid and the Minotaur* and Baker Miller's *Toward a New Psychology of Women* in 1976.

and depathologization of "preoedipal" levels of functioning and perhaps also greater mainstream American psychoanalytic acceptance of relational theories—both native-grown Sullivanian and Horney schools and British object-relations and Kleinian thinking. In addition, feminism as a social and political force propelled greater numbers of women into the professions, and psychoanalytic institutes began accepting more women candidates, so that women now (or once again) form a strong presence in American psychoanalytic societies.[9]

As is well known, *The Reproduction of Mothering* radically rethought the psychology of women on many levels. I begin from the observation that it is not enough, as previous psychoanalytic theories of women had done, to reduce the psychology of women to female sexuality. How could it be, I wondered, after all the advances and transformations in theory that followed the libido-centered *Three Essays on the Theory of Sexuality*—the structural theory that led to the ego psychological focus on intrapsychic conflict, defense, and compromise formation; British object relations and Kleinian theories; our expanded developmental understanding and greater attention, whether Mahlerian, Winnicottian, or Kleinian, to infancy and the preoedipal mother-child relationship—how was it that psychoanalysts, when it came to the subject of women, could write as if such developments in thinking had not occurred?

Looking back, the reader could speculate that I was responding to Freud's self-defense of 1933, when, in noting that his account is "incomplete and fragmentary and does not always sound friendly," he reminds us to "not forget that I have only been describing women in so far as their nature is determined by their sexual function" (p. 135). Many of Freud's contemporaries and followers had tended to follow Freud's lead, or, as Lampl-de Groot, to couch radical extensions and challenges in apparently consonant terms.[10] By contrast, I wanted to consider other determinants of women's "nature," as psychoanalysis had been considering other determinants of the psyche in general. Especially, I had discovered British object relations theory, and I sought to reinterpret female and male development through the lens of the unconscious internal world and self construction, rather than through the lens of a "sexual function" automatically determined by the character of the female body. As I wrote, quite courageously for my age and training, and for the psychoanalytic era itself:

> In what follows, I reinterpret both the traditional psychoanalytic theory of feminine (and masculine) development and psychoanalytic clinical

[9] My research on the history of women in psychoanalysis documents a decline in the proportion of women psychoanalysts in the United States, in contrast to England and continental Europe, during the 1950s through 1970s.

[10] The ways that the early women psychoanalysts chose to acknowledge or occlude their originality and their disagreements with Freud deserve an essay in itself.

> case studies in terms of the developing ego and the growth of relational potential and psychological capacities. The story I tell is for the most part not explicit in these accounts, but can be drawn from them. I apply object-relations theory and the theory of the personal ego to our understanding of masculine and feminine development. ... The object-relations reformulation has not been brought to bear upon the question of gender. Object-relations theorists (like ego psychologists) have hardly begun to address questions concerning differences in female and male ego development, gender differences in object-relational experiences, and the effect these have on the differential constitution of mental structure and psychic life. Psychoanalysts continue to assume a biological and instinctual basis for the sexual division of labor, gender personality, and heterosexuality. Writing concerned with gender has continued to emphasize oedipal, libidinal issues and sexual orientation, has continued to see women as appendages of their libido, has continued to emphasize feminine sexuality, penis envy, masochism, genitality, frigidity, more than object-relations and ego development. My work here is a step away from that trend. (1978, pp. 53–54)

Substantively, *The Reproduction of Mothering* argues that psychoanalysis had not noticed theoretically the import for the psychology of gender of women's being primary caregivers. Moreover, the import of mothers, *as women*, for infantile development had been taken for granted. "Women mother" are the book's opening words.

The book makes a number of interrelated arguments. First, I suggest that we cannot talk about a generic mother-infant relationship because, from the beginning, the mother-daughter and mother-son relationship differ. In response to the mother's sense of gender-similarity and gender-difference, daughters and sons from earliest infancy begin to develop a different sense of self-in-relation—a basic "I" that responds to the mother's unconscious, as well as conscious, gender-inflected senses of and fantasies about her infant. I suggest that these different senses of self are elaborated throughout development, creating a kind of relatedness—one that enables empathy, intuition, and ability to see the point of view of the other—that is more typical of women than of men, and that in turn becomes the foundation for maternal capacities. In a context in which there had been virtually no psychoanalytic recognition of gender differences in the mother-child relation in the preoedipal period (although there had been recognition of a 2-year-old genital phase), I milked a sparse clinical literature to argue for subtle gender differences in portrayals of individual mothers and their children to make my argument.

A reformulation of oedipal and later developmental periods was easier to elaborate, because for psychoanalysts gender had always been located in the oedipal period. I drew upon the classical accounts—of Lampl-de

Groot, Freud, Deutsch, Brunswick, and others—to expand upon the claim that the girl's complete Oedipus complex was more long lasting and more fully bisexual than the boy's, emphasizing that this was because her first love object was a woman. I thus anticipate the view (as I note in Chodorow, 1991a) that Persephone, rather than Oedipus, provides a better mythic model of female development (for elaboration of this position, see Kulish & Holtzman, 1998, 2008).[11] This reinterpretation generated my claim that the female oedipal triangle further propelled maternality in the girl, whose heterosexuality is triangular (mother-father-daughter/child) rather than dyadic, as is more characteristic of men.

In keeping with my goals—to retain psychoanalysis while eliminating sexism—I discovered and drew upon the variety of accounts that made more dynamic sense than Freud's in explaining penis envy: Chasseguet-Smirgel's suggestion that the girl wants a penis to gain autonomy from her overpowering mother; Lampl-de Groot's implication, and Rubin's claim, that the originally matrisexual girl wants a penis to satisfy her heterosexual mother; Horney's argument that the girl's nonvirulent wish to urinate like a boy is replaced by the desire for a penis as an object of (hetero)sexual desire; Klein's and Jones's claim that the wish for a penis is a defense against fear of loss of female organs and female sexuality, both threatened as punishment for oedipal (hetero)sexual wishes.

At a time, then, when there was really nothing in the psychoanalytic literature after Freud's penis-baby equation that could explain maternal capacities or desires, with the exception of Kestenberg's claim that an early inner genital phase foreshadowed in drive terms pregnancy and maternality (Kestenberg, 1956a, 1956b, 1968), *The Reproduction of Mothering* took on both of these problematics: How did maternality develop?[12] Why did women want to become mothers? Furthermore, at a time when mothers and maternal activity were seen exclusively from the point of view of the child—as holding environment, container, seducer or not-seducer, rather than as experiencers and experienced by the child in their own right—the book considered maternal subjectivity, the mother as subject.

[11] Confirming this observation, the classicist Helena Foley (1999) reprinted my "Family Structure and Feminine Personality" among the interpretive essays in her new translation and interpretation of the Homeric *Hymn to Demeter.*

[12] Not that I appreciated Kestenberg's contribution at the time. To the contrary, in my great skepticism about the biological, I was very critical. I now appreciate how original and generative Kestenberg was, not only for her time but also for ours. During my research on early women psychoanalysts, I was brought sharply up against my prejudice when I met Kestenberg and came to understand both what she had been doing and how radical (and isolating) her work was. I consider her one of the three lone voices, along with Chasseguet-Smirgel (1964) and Stoller (1965, 1968), of the "quiescent interval" between the 1930s writings on female sexuality and the feminist revival of interest in the psychology of women.

The impact of *The Reproduction of Mothering* went beyond its understandings of the psychology of women. My writings of the time anticipate and provide part of the groundwork for feminist critiques (like self-in-relation theory and theories of women's voice and morality) of psychologies that favor separation and autonomy over relatedness, but also for the development of relational psychoanalysis and other critiques of classical psychoanalysis. As early as 1974, I claimed that "'ego strength' is not completely dependent on the firmness of the ego's boundaries" (p. 61), and in 1979, I argued that

> separateness is defined relationally; differentiation occurs in relationship ... the child learns to see the particularity of the mother or primary caretaker in contrast to the rest of the world ... adequate separation, or differentiation, involves not merely perceiving the separateness, or otherness, of the other. It involves perceiving the person's subjectivity and selfhood as well. ... Thus, how we understand differentiation—only from the viewpoint of the infant as a self, or from the viewpoint of two interacting selves—has consequences for what we think of as a mature self. (pp. 102–104)

I conclude that "differentiation is not distinctness and separateness, but a particular way of being connected to others" (p. 107).

Yet, even as the book had impact, it also generated critique, particularly among some feminists. Some readers were uncomfortable with my account of the psychology of women, feeling that I romanticized the "difference feminism" outcomes I describe (for more recent commentary along these lines, see Heenan et al., 2002). In my view, these readers seem to pass over the attention I pay to the challenges women face in separating and individuating and to my documentation of difficulties that take different forms in each sex with closeness to the mother—for girls, the threat of overidentification and loss of a separate sense of self; for boys, engulfment and loss of masculinity.

Perhaps because my arguments about the differential constructions of the Oedipus complex are not so easily understandable in non-psychoanalytic terms (you need to know how object relations theory portrays the psychic reality of an unconscious internal object world, rather than simply to understand the intuitively clearer notion that women are relational), such readings also tended not to recognize that the book is about oedipal and not just preoedipal outcomes—the internalized bisexual triangle, the unresolved, un-"smashed to pieces" (Freud, 1925, p. 257) female Oedipus complex, the oedipal asymmetries and heterosexual knots of adult relationships, and the mother's greater "oedipalization" of the relationship to her son than to her daughter.[13] Finally, I describe maternal difficulties in separating and acknowledging the child, as well as the ideological and psychological splitting in attitudes to mothers and fathers that result from mothering:

> Psychoanalytic accounts ... reproduce those infantile expectations of mothers which they describe so well. ... Mothers, they suggest, come to symbolize dependence, regression, passivity, and the lack of adaptation to reality. Turning from the mother (and father) represents independence and individuation, progress, activity, and participation in the real world. ... Girls and boys expect and assume women's unique capacities for sacrifice, caring, and mothering, and associate women with their own fears of regression and powerlessness. They fantasize more about men, and associate them with idealized virtues and growth. (1978, pp. 82–83)

As I make these critiques, I am, like some of the classical women thinkers, at the same time quite dutiful (a dutiful, if challenging, daughter or granddaughter—just as, in arguments with my father, I was always careful to be rational and articulate rather than emotional, and to cite facts to ground arguments). I stay carefully within the lines of and draw capaciously from previous psychoanalytic writing and do not dismiss, except very carefully and with a heavy baggage of elaboration, any of Freud's claims, even about penis envy or the weak female superego. This is part of my work's strength: The theory is complex and multifaceted, but there is little unprocessed rage or feminist outrage, which, in my view, usually detracts from readers' freedom to think. Another way to put this is that the theory was radical, but the writer was not.

I am only intemperate and overly dismissive, as I note in my 1999 preface (see Chapter 4), about the reproductive body. Not yet a mother, swept up in 1970s feminism, I am leery about the possible influence, however clinically and developmentally individual, of libido, lust, physical maternal passion and desire, or for the demands for psychic representation and fantasy of bleeding, breasts, arousal, pregnancy, and lactation (it would be no surprise to a psychoanalyst that I seem to have been from the beginning more intemperate in regard to theories about the body than about anything else that contributes to psychic life). As I note in the same preface, the call for shared parenting at the end gives short shrift to the very psychic developments—of maternal passions, desires, and capacities in women—that the book documents, and that I experienced firsthand within a year of the book's publication. As I have noted recently (see Chapter 8), this call

[13] 2011 note: Perhaps such partial reading still holds. A recent psychoanalytic book (Kulish & Holtzman, 2008) rediscovers the mother-daughter Persephone story, and cites the same classic texts, of Deutsch, Lampl, and others, that I had discussed extensively (though of course without clinical case material, since I was not then a psychoanalyst) in 1978.

has come back to haunt me, in patients, students, and young colleagues who put forth, among other feminist and culturally rationalized defenses against exploring intrapsychic conflicts and ambivalence about motherhood, the claim that they will not have children unless their husbands agree to do half the child care, or the claim that motherhood and work are incompatible in our culture.[14]

STUDYING WOMEN PSYCHOANALYSTS/ BECOMING A PSYCHOANALYST

The Reproduction of Mothering was published in 1978. The main outcome of my thinking in the book was professional development, rather than more writing. I thought at the time, quite rightly, that I had gone as far as I could in clinically and experientially persuasive thinking about the psyche from within, and not just about the contours of the theory from without, without clinical experience and psychoanalytic training, which I began in the mid-1980s. Partially as a result, the 1980s were for me a fallow period. *The Reproduction of Mothering* was still sedimenting into my consciousness as well as into concurrent feminist and psychoanalytic consciousness, and I was immersed in the wonders and rigors of psychoanalytic training (and of being a mother).[15]

Two contributions of this period bear mentioning. First, following upon our observation that feminist thinking about motherhood seemed to replicate the blame, idealization, and enmeshment in primal attachment and fears of abandonment or attack found in both cultural and psychoanalytic thinking, Susan Contratto and I published "The Fantasy of the Perfect

[14] I put this more assertively in an interview (Elovitz & Lentz, 2005). In response to a question about my "call for equal parenting" (Chodorow, 1978, p. 218), I say, "Well, I think you put it exactly right: 'issuing a call.' It was a naïve call, though I know that many people feel grateful to me for having suggested it. ... It is a sort of social engineering call that is really undermined by the heart of the book itself, which is about the development of maternal desires, subjectivity, and capacities, and the importance of the mother-child relationship for both mother and child. The entire argument of the book implies that fathers are not mothers and, as I have done clinical work, and myself become a mother, I know that more strongly than before. The call for 'equal' parenting comes from two sources. ... First, I am of the generation of war babies who were the subjects of all the 'father-absence' studies—fathers were off at war or doing war work, and, after the war, working hard in the beginning of a boom economy, while women were 'returning' to the home. I translated this cohort experience into a political call, but you don't need equal parenting to have men participate in child care. Secondly, this call is characteristic of my political generation—an absolutist claim for how society *ought to be* transformed, without a lot of attention to the subjectivities, feelings, and wishes of the people themselves whose causes we were advocating."

[15] If you look at the vitae of any number of women academics of my generation, you will find that there is often a 10- to 12-year time of low textual productivity that coincides with a time of high familial generativity.

Mother" (1982). We drew upon my conclusions about the mother as subject and Contratto's critique of the prevalence of mother-blame found in the developmental and clinical literature (Contratto, 1980, 1987), along with her extensive clinical experience, to argue that like psychological and psychoanalytic thinking, feminist thinking about the maternal role and maternal activity expressed an unconscious "fantasy of the perfect mother." This fantasy reflected and projected infantile expectations and understandings into psychological assessment and cultural theories.

As Alice Balint had put it, perhaps ironically: "The ideal mother has no interests of her own. ... For all of us it remains self-evident that the interests of mother and child are identical, and it is the generally acknowledged measure of the goodness or badness of the mother how far she really feels this identity of interests" (1939, pp. 93, 97).[16] Contratto and I argue for a more secondary-process view of maternal activity and for a perspective that sees the mother as a subject, rather than an object or cipher to be evaluated in terms of her child. We address reciprocally related tendencies to blame or idealize mothers and to desexualize or oversexualize them, and we locate how a primary process mode of thought and feeling—what we would now call paranoid-schizoid splitting and rage—invades supposedly neutral or empirical conceptions of the mother-child relationship.

Second, perhaps in a tacit search for the reproduction of professional mothering, I undertook in 1980 an interview study of early women psychoanalysts. I wanted to hear, from these women themselves, how it came to be that there were, compared to other professions, so many important women psychoanalysts among the second and third generations (those analyzed by Freud, Ferenczi, Abraham, and others of their generation, and those analyzed by their analysands). I wondered what it was like for these women and, especially, how they came to understand and internalize Freud's theories of femininity, which were such a challenge and insult to women of my generation.

As with my theoretical work, I seem even in this historical and sociological project presciently to have made problematic the heretofore unnoticed and taken-for-granted. When I began the research, there was little published work on women psychoanalysts—in English one full-length study (Carotenuto, 1973) and a few chapters in other books (Roazen's, 1971, section "The Women," with chapters on Brunswick, Anna Freud, Deutsch, and Klein; and Alexander's, 1966, several chapters on individual women). Ten years later, over 25 biographies and autobiographies of individual early

[16] An interesting side note, which I discovered during my research on early women psychoanalysts: Alice Balint and Margaret Mahler were high school friends, and Mahler learned of psychoanalysis though Balint's mother, Wilma Kovacs, who was a colleague of Ferenczi's. Mahler's work on separation-individuation, beginning from the child who is fused with the mother, is consonant with and an elaboration upon Balint's preliminary thinking (Balint died at a young age) about love for the mother and mother-love.

women analysts had appeared, as well as several studies of women as a collective presence in the post-Freudian period. Today, we find plays and films about these women.

In this context, my 80 interviews, just over half with women of the second and third generations and the rest with those who knew them (trainees; sons and daughters who were themselves analysts; colleagues), along with my attempts to gather comparative quantitative data on women in the field, did not continue to promise new in-depth information. More to the point, however, the main result of my research was to precipitate me relatively quickly into psychoanalytic training. I did not, apparently, want to study women psychoanalysts; I wanted to *be* one. I published only a few essays on early women analysts (Chodorow, 1986c, 1989b, 1991b, in English; others translated into French, 1986a, 1999d, and German, 1987) and then moved on.

My data gathering itself tells a story about the sociology and history of psychoanalysis. I began my research shortly after the Masson/Freud Archives and Eissler/Malcolm debacles, and many analysts had felt exploited by Roazen. As a result, several were interview shy and needed convincing, letters of introduction (support from Robert Wallerstein was invaluable in this sphere), copies of my book, and so forth. From my side, I was working within the constraints of social science, where it was necessary to document my claims—impressions would not do—that there were "many" women analysts. However, a number of factors—local institutional organization, the shift of the psychoanalytic center from *Mitteleuropa* to the United States and England, the Nazi destruction of institutes and institutional records, the forced emigration of psychoanalysts themselves—all made statistical data gathering almost impossible. Moreover, several contemporary institutes, along with national organizations like the American Psychoanalytic Association and the British Society, were reluctant and seemingly suspicious when it came to sharing data, for example, lists of training analysts during a particular period, as if membership data called for the same level of confidentiality as that required in the consulting room.

Finally, although I had an intuitive sense of the strong presence of women, intuition did not serve to document, for example, that 30% women practitioners was a high number in 1930s Vienna or Berlin, say, in comparison to something else—the proportion of women lawyers, academics, or doctors, for instance. For my interviewees, 20% or 30%—huge in comparison to other contemporaneous professions—could still feel, as one put it, "not so many."

I was way above my non-statistically-trained head. Yet, I was more or less able to document that, relative to other professions, psychoanalysis in Europe and the United States had an unusually high proportion of women practitioners in the 1920s, 1930s, and 1940s, and that these percentages had stayed high in Europe, especially in Britain, in the 1950s through the

1970s. I could also show that numbers had plummeted in the United States as the émigré analysts began to retire, because the requirement, unique to the United States, that psychoanalysts be physicians, had served as de facto discrimination against women.

Through my research, I learned also of the family culture of psychoanalysis—analytic couples and parent-child lineages that are still with us and that give psychoanalysis something of a craft and guild character. I described, in implicit and explicit contrast to the academy, what I called the several "hats" that psychoanalysts can wear—clinician, teacher, theoretician, writer, institutional mover and shaker—which, along with the sense that psychoanalysis required both a kind of knowledge (about children, families, feelings, the psyche) and stance (listening, empathy, careful attention to the other) that women were particularly likely to have, allowed women not only to participate but also to gain recognition and eminence. Unlike in psychiatry or any other medical, scientific, or academic field, recognition and advancement in psychoanalysis came in the first instance from clinical acumen rather than from research or writing. The field thus recognized that aspect of its practice in which women, often balancing family and work, were as likely to participate as men.

On the matter of the theory of femininity, which was of equal concern to me as the question of what facilitated female participation, my encounter with my interviewees was perhaps the first step in my own rethinking and revaluation. In the reflexive paper, "Seventies Questions for Thirties Women: Gender and Generation in a Study of Early Women Psychoanalysts" (1989b), I came to see for the first time that the views of my own feminist psychoanalytic generation, while partly based on progress in knowledge and theoretical advances, were also partly a product of our own generational location and (lack of) life or clinical experience.

Most stunning, in contrast to feminists and psychoanalysts of the second-wave generation, for whom it was axiomatic that the theoretical was personal, few women of the second and third psychoanalytic generations seemed to—as Freud had explicitly invited them—"enquire from [their] own experiences of life" (1933, p. 135). These women had been, after all, independent and strong enough to get themselves into medical school and perhaps from the United States to Vienna in the 1920s and 1930s; they were political and cultural radicals; they had participated in anti-Nazi work in the 1930s. A few interviewees claimed to hold, as Henriette Klein put it, "secret" theories that challenged penis envy; others observed that what Freud said was nonsense. But more characteristic, in terms of the personal and theoretical, were interviewees like Margaret Mahler, who responded that "it didn't go through [her] brain" to consider Freud's theories in relation to her own life, or Jeanne Lampl-de Groot, who claimed that there was nothing autobiographical in her 1927 observations about the daughter's attachment to her mother. These came entirely from her work with patients.

Yet, by switching generational perspective and thinking from the point of view of an early 20th-century woman, a new view emerged. Penis envy, made into a driving force by Freud only in the 1920s, could not obscure a much more important discovery. As interviewee Ruth Eissler emphatically put it, "For Freud, women were sexual beings, with sexual desires!"

CLINICAL INDIVIDUALITY: TOWARD *THE POWER OF FEELINGS* AND BEYOND

"Seventies Questions for Thirties Women" makes problematic the different views on femininity that women of different generations and trainings can hold. It brought my feminist social scientist's eye to perspectives on femininity held by practitioners and added generation as a feature of specificity to feminist understandings of differences among women. Depending on someone's generation, country of origin, professional background, own mother and family, and personality, she will have her own individualized view.

I had first explored clinical individuality in "Freud on Women" (1991a) and "Heterosexuality as a Compromise Formation" (1992), both included in *Femininities, Masculinities, Sexualities* (1994). My plurals themselves challenged psychoanalysis, which had always written about "the girl," "the boy," "the woman," "the man," "the mother," "the father." Even in Freud, I argue, there is no single clinical femininity, masculinity, or sexuality, but along with him, we have conflated a singularized normativity and clinical plurality. "Rethinking Freud on Women" notes that, although we can take several stories from Freud, we have tended to read only the story that charts the well-known tortuous path to normative femininity.

Freud was faced with the many individual heterosexual and homosexual women he had in treatment, including his own non-traditionally feminine daughter and several of the early women analysts, as well as with the profession he created, in which he and his colleagues encouraged a large number of women, some of whom had their own ideas about femininity. In his writings, you find the individual women he describes in the *Studies on Hysteria* (Breuer & Freud, 1893–1895), in "Dora" (Freud, 1905a) in "The Psychogenesis of a Case of Homosexuality in a Woman" (1920), and in other writings—all the "sexual beings with sexual desires"—who cannot be reduced to a singular "woman." You find in his later theorizing that clinical women tended to fall into three, rather than one, typical developmental trajectories, three typical patterns, only one of which is the path to "femininity." This is how Freud *wants* women to turn out, and he calls it "femininity" to make his point. Similarly, as I argue in "Heterosexuality as a Compromise Formation," the divide heterosexual/homosexual, or straight/gay, does not begin to specify the personally unique constellation of fantasies and desires that go into each heterosexual person's "sexual orientation."

Although it had also theoretical origins, my perspective on the clinical individual came most radically to the fore in my writing and thinking as a result of psychoanalytic training and practice, as I began to ground myself in the view "from behind the couch" (Chodorow, 2003a). As all clinicians know, the individual is immersed in bodily, sexual experience and in affectively charged, psychically organizing (and disorganizing) unconscious fantasies about internal self and other, but psychoanalytic theory, at the same time, tends to generalize and often universalize: You are an ego psychologist, a relational analyst, a Kleinian, a Winnicottian, a Kohutian, a Bionian, a Lacanian, and you see your patients through that theoretical lens.

My thinking about clinical individuality culminated in *The Power of Feelings*. Addressed to both psychoanalysts and academics, the book, as my previous contributions, derived from a simple observation: Of the several women and several men patients I had treated, each person's psyche was unique. What psychoanalysis gives us is a universalized account—an account of the psychobiology of being human—of the functioning of the human psyche, much as, say, cognitive psychology gives us a universalized account of cognition, perception, and so forth. I locate the center of this functioning in the creation of personal meaning, meaning best described as created through transference, fantasy, introjection, and projection. "Experience," whether embodied and biological, cultural and social, or interpersonal and familial, is actively created and individually filtered through these affective, unconscious, meaning-creating capacities and the internal, affect-laden fantasies about body, self, and other that they create. Each of our many theories helps to explain these elements of psychic life in some individual some of the time.

Psychoanalysis, I suggest, argues against determinism. In a dialogue with psychoanalysis, I claim that universalized developmental theories based on the *content* of unconscious fantasy or affect—the universalized accounts we have of gender, for example, or of the necessary interpretation of the body, as in the later (but not the earlier) Freud, or of "Oedipus"—exhibit a misplaced concreteness. What is universal is the demand, because of the powerful salience of bodily experience, or the powerful salience of early family experience, or the powerful salience of being labeled and treated as female or male, that these experiences be given psychic and fantasy representation, but the particular representation that they are given will be set in the context of the individual's overall psychic makeup and functioning. When we call something "oedipal," "feminine," or "oral," it is because we have discovered prevalent *patterns* that characterize the ways that people respond to these meaning-creating demands. When we universalize these, we take away from the activity of the psyche and from clinical individuality.

Our knowledge of patterns helps us to make sense of what we experience clinically. When we recognize something that has previously fit a pattern, we may look for other manifestations that have, in our experience, hung together with that pattern (I employ this formulation in Chapters 4 and 8). That everyone is unique and that we can also find patterns in psychic life indicates, further, a need for theoretical pluralism rather than theoretical exclusivity and embattlement. Different theorists tend to address different aspects of psychic functioning and fantasy and different constellations of patients. *The Power of Feelings* is theoretically inclusive (what I call *both/and* rather than *either/or*), drawing especially from Loewald, Klein, Winnicott, and Erikson. I take from these theorists Loewald's generative syncretism and his radical claim that ego and reality, self and other, drive and object, and primary process thinking and language are all developmentally emergent from a proto ego-self; Klein's focus on projection and introjection—what she calls the "doubling" or filtering of external experience through unconscious fantasy and internal experience (1940; see also Chapter 3); Winnicott's attention to the internal, private, true self and to transitionality; and Erikson's serious consideration of how culture and history are transferentially filtered and created by the individual psyche. I bring my argument for the power of feelings and the powers of personal meaning to expanded understandings of gender and culture.

One result of my clinical experience, then, was to enable and require me to rethink the psychology of women, especially two particular characteristics of the thinking that went into *The Reproduction of Mothering* and related early work (see Chapter 4). First, the book falls into a tendency (though I am careful not to universalize) to create a generalized theory. I wrote it in an era of universalistic theory (structuralism, functionalism, Marxism), as well as of classical universalizing psychoanalysis. At the time, we had no postmodernism, poststructuralism, or psychoanalytic pluralism to temper our grand theoretical visions.

In my generalizations themselves, however, I was, in contrast to some of the classical theories, like universal penis envy as *the* driving force in femininity, largely right. It is certainly the case that for virtually all women, the internal and external relation to the mother is developmentally central. The experiences of puberty, menarche, breast development, the potential for pregnancy and motherhood, pregnancy, childbirth, lactation, and motherhood themselves (including adoption or co-mothering a partner's child) are also important in virtually every woman's development. My own solution, as I note earlier, was to think in terms of patterns of development and of psychic femininity: The intrapsychic and intersubjective reproduction of mothering that I describe is certainly a prevalent pattern, but it needs clinical specification for each individual, put in the context of her entire internal life. We will not find it in all patients, but it helps us to have this pattern in mind and to know that for many women, a projective and introjective filtering of the mother-daughter relationship will be centrally constitutive of their sense of female self and femininity (see especially Chapters 4, 8, and 11).

Similarly, both clinical experience and cultural change required, along with the reconsideration of embodied femininity and maternality that I discuss earlier, an expansion of my thinking about sexuality. *The Reproduction of Mothering* discusses sexuality very much in the terms of the later Freud (e.g., 1925, 1931)—that is, more in terms of gender than of sexual desire and fantasy. The active libido of the radical *Three Essays* is neither in these late essays of Freud's nor in my early writings. In a feminist era that was phobic about biological determinism and that advocated political lesbianism and the lesbian continuum (Rich, 1980), sexuality was not thought of as something that erupted asocially out of the body and desire. Rather, it was politically shaped by cultural heterosexism and could and should be politically challenged. Most feminist writing (Rubin, 1975, is an exception here) made sexuality into a political choice or political constraint.

Clinical experience made the actuality and power of embodied sexuality evident, but I was also inspired by my students, whose understandings of sexual object choice were well in advance of anything found in the psychoanalytic literature (see Epstein, 1991; Martin, 1996; Stein, 1989, 1997).[17] My first foray into thinking about sexuality, while attuned to the individuality of desire, had nonetheless some of the character of feminist outrage. I wrote, and named, "Heterosexuality as a Compromise Formation," originally entitled "Heterosexuality as a Symptom," in response to several talks I had heard in which homosexuality was called a symptom.

Once again, the impulse and language were reactive, but the underlying thinking was generative. I tried to figure out what we psychoanalysts knew about the sexual object choice that characterized most of us, most of our patients, and indeed the majority of people in the world—what I called, tongue in cheek, to myself and my friends, "garden-variety heterosexuality." The essay reviews the various criteria by which homosexuality was judged pathological and suggests that these criteria apply equally to some manifestations of heterosexuality and some of homosexuality.

Two implications follow. First, in assessing pathology, some other criterion enters, and must enter, besides the gender of the object in relation to the subject's gender: Neither term adequately specifies anyone's sexual orientation. Second, there must be several homosexualities and heterosexualities. No "heterosexual" man is attracted to all women and to no men, similarly for heterosexual women, similarly for those who are gay or lesbian. I claim:

> Those who are called or who consider themselves heterosexual are, in all likelihood, tall-blond-Wasposexual, short-curly-haired zaftig-Jewishosexual, African-American-with-a-southern-accentosexual, erotically excited only by members of their own ethnic group or only by those

[17]I cite published work, but I was reading this work long before publication.

> outside that group. Some women find themselves repeatedly attracted to men who turn out to be depressed, others to men who are aggressive or violent, still others to narcissists. Some men are attracted to women who are chattery and flirtatious, others to those who are quiet and distant. Some choose lovers or spouses who are like a parent (and it can be either parent for either gender or a mixture of the two); others choose lovers or spouses as much unlike their parents as possible (often to find these mates recapitulating parental characteristics after all, or to find themselves discontented when they don't). These choices have both cultural and individual psychological resonance. (1992, p. 38)

Sexual desire is an individual project and outcome that we learn of, like gender, in the clinical context of fantasy, transference, and descriptions of actual relationships. As I describe this (see Chapter 11), it is composed of a number of constitutive components, including an internal oedipal and preoedipal world, a prevalent personal erotism, organizing fantasies, a sense of gender in relation to sexuality, a filtering of culture, and so forth. It is intertwined with other aspects of psyche, self, and fantasy and can be defensively subordinated to aggression. Gender itself can fade in its presence. My conclusions thus return us again to clinical individuality.

Following from this essay, I was invited to write or present several reflections on sexuality. A new foreword to Freud's *Three Essays on the Theory of Sexuality* (Chapter 2) allowed me to notice how Freud distinguishes "inversion" from "perversion"—deviance in object choice from deviance in aim—both found in all people, abnormal or deviant only when fixation and exclusivity reign. For Freud, I notice, anyone exclusively either heterosexual or homosexual in their fantasy life is abnormal and represses the alternative, and all people's sexuality includes perverse elements. The *Three Essays*, then, anticipate my argument in "Heterosexuality" that there is nothing inherent in the gender of the object relative to the gender of the self that makes a particular sexual orientation pathological.

A public forum that considered homophobia (Hoffman et al., 2000), attended by several hundred at the meetings of the American Psychoanalytic Association, enabled me to begin to elaborate thoughts about sexuality, body, and culture and to begin to consider the "faultlines" of masculinity (Chapter 9). As I put it then:

> What is true, I think, is that the parts of prejudice that are most deep and violent are often cast unconsciously as well as in cultural tropes as bodily and sexual. For instance, when you read the most virulent anti-Semitic tracts, or reflect on lynching of blacks in the South and the accusations of interracial rape or sex that often preceded these lynchings, it is sexual and bodily imagery that stands out. In recent years, we notice that rape and even more brutal and violent attacks on women

> are instruments of war, especially in ethnic wars and in dictatorships that engage in kidnapping and torture. Men also kill other men who perform abortions, although whatever the hate involved here—and I do think it is extreme—we still have to notice that this is done with a single bullet, rather than with prolonged brutal torture, as in the case of violence against homosexuals.
>
> What seems to be the case is that there is a huge psychic faultline around the sexual body in relation to masculinity. Images of a man having sex with other men, a black man having sex with a white woman, a woman who is sexual without having a baby, are for some men extremely threatening. (Hoffman et al., 2000, p. 23)

Finally, I was asked to contribute to an issue of *Studies in Gender and Sexuality* that featured Stephen Mitchell's groundbreaking early critiques of psychoanalytic treatment of homosexuality (Chapter 5) and to a special issue of the *Revue Française de Psychanalyse* on the "homosexualities"—a plural that would not have been found 10 years earlier (Chapter 11). There, I extend my discussion of Freud's *Three Essays*, noticing that Freud gives us an account of gender-bending and fluidity that rivals that of any postmodern theorist: Everyone is homosexual and heterosexual, masculine and feminine; the most "masculine" man can be gay, the most "feminine" man heterosexual; both heterosexuality and homosexuality involve the "tyranny" of one object and aim.

I began my graduate work in 1969 with an intuition that psychoanalysis gave us a primary vehicle for understanding gender and its discontents. Forty years later, clinical (as well as life) experience has deepened and transformed my understanding of men and women, masculinity and femininity, sexuality and desire, and, more generally, of psychic life and how we study this. The lens that best captures what clinical experience has given me, one that I continually return to in this essay and throughout my recent writing, is that of clinical individuality. It is a lens generated by experience, by "listening to" rather than "listening for" (Chodorow, 2003a), and it is given specificity by my reading and following of many theories of mind and theories of technique. Listening to the patient, rather than listening for manifestations of a particular theory or documentation of a particular belief, whether about the operation or contents of the mind or about the analytic relationship, respects clinical individuality, in matters of gender and sexuality and in the rest of psychic life.

Part I

Theorists and theory, 1905–2005

Chapter 2

Freud's *Three Essays on the Theory of Sexuality*

A reading

> In the late 1990s I was invited to write a foreword to a new paperback edition of the *Standard Edition* translation of Freud's *Three Essays on the Theory of Sexuality*. The book was being published for a lay audience—for college classrooms and the general reader. My remarks, though brief, introduce my reflections on a classic work that underpins and still contributes today to our understanding of sexuality and gender. I bring great appreciation to Freud's founding text, awe at some of his brilliant insights, puzzlement at some of his claims, and amusement at some notable lacunae. We cannot think or write psychoanalytically about sex and gender without beginning from the *Three Essays*. For me, immersion in this preface integrated my attempts since the early 1990s, including my rethinking of my own and others' early writings on Freud, to return to psychosexuality and the body. It enabled further writings on sexuality and bodily maternality.[1]

Sexuality is one of the oldest clinical and theoretical problems in psychoanalysis and one of the most perplexing. We know that sexuality in all its forms—as drive, passion, physical sensation, way of relating, identity, behavior, fantasy—is unique among human experiences and central to life. Yet this same sexuality in all its forms remains for psychoanalysts, as for everyone else, basically mysterious, as we try to define it and describe its contours and significance. Psychoanalytic thinking on the subject begins with Freud's original and threatening *Three Essays on the Theory of Sexuality*—uneven, internally contradictory, puzzling—and extraordinary.

It is always a pleasure to see Freud's mind at work, to admire the style of his rhetoric and the elegance of his prose, regardless of what he is writing about. Here, characteristically, Freud begins from what "we" have traditionally believed: from the "popular opinion" that the sexual instinct

[1] An earlier version of this chapter appeared in J. Strachey (Ed. & Trans.), *Three Essays on the Theory of Sexuality by Sigmund Freud* (pp. vii–xviii). New York: Basic Books, 2000.

is "generally understood to be absent in childhood" and to awaken only at puberty, and that it is "revealed in the manifestations of an irresistible attraction exercised by one sex upon the other" (1905b, p. 135). Further, our beliefs arise from our "habit of regarding the connection between the sexual instinct and the sexual object as more intimate than it in fact is" (p. 147). Also characteristically, Freud subsequently marshals every argument and all the evidence in his power to puncture these conventional assumptions. These arguments and evidence form the heart of the *Three Essays*. As he will elaborate, prepubertal childhood sexuality does, indisputably, exist. Men are, demonstrably, attracted to men, as women are to women. Both empirical observation and clinical investigation reveal that "the sexual instinct and the sexual object are merely soldered together" (p. 148).

Freud ends not with certainty but with diffidence. On almost the last page of the work, typically forthright about the limits to his knowledge, he says

> We are not in a position to give so much as a hint as to the causes of [such] temporal disturbances of the process of development [as precocity and other variations among individuals in the timing and duration of the different elements of childhood sexuality]. A prospect opens before us at this point upon a whole phalanx of biological and perhaps, too, of historical problems of which we have not even come within striking distance. (p. 241)

Freud's arguments for continuity among all forms of adult sexuality and for infantile sexuality as on a continuum with adult sexuality are surely among the most salient elements substantively and rhetorically in the *Three Essays*. They were among the most challenging to convention in Freud's time, and even today, they are hardest, unconsciously if not consciously, to embrace. Freud addresses these arguments in his first two essays.

Freud's first essay addresses "The Sexual Aberrations." He opens this essay by questioning assumptions widely taken for granted (in his day and in ours, even among many psychoanalysts) about sexual object choice, specifically about the radical difference between homosexuality and heterosexuality. He claims that there is continuity rather than discontinuity between homo- and heterosexual object choice, in that everyone has both homosexual and heterosexual libidinal attachments in his or her unconscious. Heterosexual object choice, he argues, is just as restricted in choice and aim as homosexual. Both, Freud points out, involve a "tyranny" of one object and aim. Expanding on this observation in 1915 (Freud continued to add to the *Three Essays* until well into the 1920s), Freud says, "The exclusive sexual interest felt by men for women is also a problem that needs elucidating and is not a self-evident fact based upon an attraction that is ultimately of a chemical nature" (1915 footnote, p. 146).

In Freud's view, we cannot find a single homosexuality that can be contrasted with a single heterosexuality. Rather, we find great variability among the homosexualities (as I note in Chodorow, 1992, Freud, as a consequence of his focus on the sexual aberrations, has ironically much less to say about the heterosexualities than the homosexualities). While Freud does not say, as many contemporary commentators would wish that he did, that all sexual orientations are equally normal or healthy—indeed, he makes clear in the third essay, "The Transformations of Puberty," that the desirable developmental path leads to heterosexual object choice with coitus as a final aim—he does not think that heterosexuality and homosexuality are different in kind or in their developmental trajectory in the individual. Moreover, in keeping with his goal of making all sexual outcomes developmentally contingent, Freud suggests that heterosexual object choice, instead of being innately determined, is generally helped along by family process as well as by laws that proscribe homosexuality.

Freud makes a different kind of argument for the "normality" of the perversions, which he defines mainly by aim rather than by the sex of the object in relation to the self. In particular, the perversions employ organs other than the genitals in the final sexual act, and they sexualize non-human objects, as, for example, in fetishism. In his section on perversions, Freud also identifies what he calls the "component instincts"—the pairs, sadism and masochism and scopophilia and exhibitionism—whose exclusivity of aim can also be criterial in defining perversion.

As with homosexuality, perversions exist on a continuum with normality for Freud, and he in two ways folds in an assumption that defines perversion in relation to a normative heterosexual coital aim. First, on a behavioral level, many activities that count as perversions are quite normal when part of the process leading to heterosexual coitus: "Most of these extensions ... are rarely absent from the sexual life of healthy people" (p. 160). Considering the component instincts, for example, Freud notes that looking and showing are often integrated into sexuality, whereas voyeurism and public exhibitionism are perversions. Freud reminds us further that on the level of arousal and fantasy, any organ can come to function as an erotogenic zone. Thus, in cases of both component instincts and erotogenic organs, it is not content but "exclusiveness and fixation" that distinguish a perversion from "normal" sexuality (p. 161).

Second, on a psychological level, perversion and neurosis are two sides of the same psychic formation. Freud concludes, radically, that those who are conflicted about or condemn sexual desires that they define consciously or unconsciously as perverse or abnormal may repress them and constitute neurotic symptoms in their place: "Neuroses are, so to say, the negative of perversions" (p. 165). Symptoms themselves originate from the repression and transformation not only of normal sexuality but also of perverse aims and component instincts. The unconscious fantasies underlying the symptoms, as well as the symptoms themselves, reproduce or mimic these perverse forms—as when masochism is transmuted into something moral and the person constantly engages in self-punishment and verbal self-flagellation, or when sadistic anal desires are expressed in attacking and attempting to destroy the creations of others through ridicule or mental demolition or transformed into compulsive withholding and orderliness.

Even more radically and astonishingly, Freud in this Nietzschean moment connects neurosis and civilization—a connection that he develops further, especially in his later works on group psychology, religion, civilization, and artists and their art. Thus, Freud is already telling us in 1905 that all that is highest and best in human civilization—creativity, religion, art, order, and progress—depends on reaction formations and sublimations that result from psychic transformations and displacements of sexual aims and interests. There is continuity rather than discontinuity, then, among all forms of adult sexuality—heterosexual and homosexual object choice, perverse and non-perverse sexual aims—and among all the transformations of sexuality—perversion and neurosis, sexuality and the creative mind, sexuality and all those social and cultural practices that make up civilized life.

Freud's second essay, "Infantile Sexuality," advances beyond the argument he and Breuer make in the *Studies on Hysteria* (1893–1895) for the centrality of sexuality in the etiology of the neuroses, beyond his subsequent affirmation in *The Interpretation of Dreams* (1900–1901) that when he refers to sexuality, he is talking about infantile sexuality. This second essay, originating a developmental theory that is now foundational to and taken for granted by most psychoanalysts, specifies exactly whence sexual wishes arise.[2] They come from innate psychobiological propensities beginning from birth that combine with family experience.

Freud describes both childhood and family as seething arenas of sexuality and sexual curiosity, and he investigates at some length the various forms of infantile sexual behavior (which he insists, of course, on calling sexual), including thumb-sucking, sensual sucking, nursing, and anal and genital masturbation. He names the polymorphous perversity of childhood, in which different parts of the body can bring erotic gratification through different behavioral modalities—sucking, skin contact, touching and being touched, masturbation—but none of these has erotic primacy.

[2] Specifically notable among those added after the original 1905 publication are sections on developmental phases that we now take for granted. For example, although Freud writes about orality and anality in the perversions and in infantile masturbation throughout these essays, the section, "The phases of development of the sexual organization," in which Freud names the oral and anal-sadistic phases and points to the diphasic nature of sexual development, was not added until 1915, following upon his 1913 paper, "The Disposition to Obsessional Neurosis." Freud does not name the phallic phase until his 1923 paper on "The Infantile Genital Organization."

In this second essay, Freud points out that in spite of and in contrast to the fluidity and lack of synthesis of aim in childhood sexuality, childhood sexual object choice is singular and relatively fixed, especially during the oedipal phase (we notice here a blind spot in Freud's consistent inability to recognize the mother of infancy, the preoedipal mother as a sexual object of special importance, or—I return to this later—to distinguish autoerotism and erotism directed toward the mother).[3] He shows further how the latency period is crucial in instituting "civilized" reactions to sexuality—reactions of disgust, shame, and moral condemnation—all of which figure centrally in the genesis of neurosis as well as in the reaction formations and sublimations of culture and high culture.

Here was Freud, then, in 1905, describing childhood masturbation and childhood sexual curiosity and insisting that, just as there are continuities between perverse and normal, heterosexual and homosexual, genital and non-genital sexuality, there are also continuities between child and adult sexuality. Here was Freud, further, claiming that mothers—in mid-19th and early 20th-century iconography and ideology as pure, almost, as children—are themselves complicit in fostering this childhood sexual development. But, Freud reassures them, mothers should not be horrified by their complicity: It is the very sexuality that they foster in their children that will enable these children, in adulthood, to love and to work.

Children are sexual, the mother-child relation is sexual, and childhood sexuality is different from but continuous with adult sexuality. The relations between perverse and normal, heterosexual and homosexual, perverse and neurotic or sublimated, all can be found in the expression and development of sexuality from childhood. All sexuality is like in kind, originates in childhood, and is related in manifold ways: "Not only the deviations from normal sexual life but its normal form as well are determined by the infantile manifestations of sexuality" (p. 212).

The cultural and personal threat of the essay on "Infantile Sexuality," perhaps an even greater threat than that of "Sexual Aberrations," continues to the present, notwithstanding the complacent presumption that now, well after the end of the Freudian century, its postulates are widely embraced. People—many contemporary therapists, ordinary citizens, our patients, we should not exempt analysts themselves—are still, in spite of conscious claim, skeptical about the unconscious. Their skepticism seems to center today, as over 100 years ago, on the existence and transformational residues of childhood sexuality. People still believe that if they have no conscious memory of particular experiences of childhood sexuality, then those experiences did not occur. Turning to conscious memory or family mythology, they wonder

[3] On this, see Sprengnether (1990), but see also Freud's own claim about the mother's breast in the *Introductory Lectures*, "I can give you no idea of the important bearing of this first object" (1917, p. 314).

how a girl could want a penis if she never saw one, or how a boy could fear castration if he never saw the female genitals. They are sure that they never knew until at least latency and maybe later, when they learned through friends or reading, of the genital difference between the sexes or of the role of sex in reproduction. They do not remember sexual fantasies about parents, wanting one parent and finding the other in the way.

Clinical experience may also elicit an opposite observation: A patient's active approach in therapy or analysis to childhood sexual memories, images, and feelings may be rooted in knowledge about the centrality of sexuality to psychoanalytic theory, but this conscious focus masks less conscious (or equally conscious but disavowed) disbelief or skepticism. Sexuality in general makes people uneasy and anxious, and Freud's proposal of infantile sexuality makes people especially uneasy and anxious—over a century since its unveiling.

Freud's third essay, "The Transformations of Puberty," undoes to some extent the radicalism of the first two. Here, he melds the insights found in his first two essays, about the stages of infantile sexuality and childhood sexual behaviors and about the wide varieties of sexual object choices and aims, into a more normative developmental schema that leads, in the desirable case, to consolidation of genital heterosexual object choice in adolescence. "Tyranny" of aim and object for all sexual orientations, for example, cedes place to "one of the tasks implicit in object-choice is that it should find its way to the opposite sex" (p. 212). Freud worries not only about the dangers of sexual inversion, but also we find here his differential valuation of the genital experience of men and women. The section also gives us reflections on the attractions and dangers of fore-pleasure in relation to end-pleasure. Yet it is also in this section, as he investigates object choice, that Freud gives us one of his most insightful developmental observations: that "the finding of an object is in fact a refinding of it" (p. 222).

One reading of Freud's *Three Essays* traces these essays through their specific substance. In its most general contours, Freud's argument connects all forms of sexuality, connects sexuality to the non-sexual realms of individual and social life, and documents the existence and development of childhood sexuality. Throughout, Freud shares other importantly generative insights—not, however (as in any great work, or any work that is great to think), without leaving some contradictions and lacunae in their wake.

First among Freud's specific insights, in evocative power as well as in accuracy, is his account of the genesis of adult object choice—the remarkable, beautifully, and simply put claim that "the finding of an object is in fact the refinding of it," or as he puts this more fully, if less evocatively, in a 1915 addendum: "The innumerable peculiarities of the erotic life of human beings as well as the compulsive character of the process of falling in love itself are quite unintelligible except by reference back to childhood as being residual effects of childhood" (p. 229). Freud's insight here illuminates our entire literary corpus, the sociology and anthropology of love, family, and kinship, and our clinical and personal experience.

Freud here also makes a profound and prescient, if indirect, contribution to social theory, as he explains why the social prohibition on incest—so much the focus of a particular era's sociology and anthropology—is so intensely invested psychologically. Simply put, everyone's original object choice is incestuous and parental (extending to siblings as well). Freud suggests that an evolutionarily developed latency period conspires with reinforcing moral precepts and social rules to turn the child, after puberty, toward non-incestuous love objects. As Freud also notes, however, and as literature, sociology, anthropology, and clinical and personal experience attest, the incest taboo, even if it succeeds for the most part in modulating behavior, does not succeed in wiping out incestuous fantasy and desire.

Second among Freud's generative insights is the simple but persuasive theory he lays out concerning the relations of the organic and the psychological: his pivotal developmental and clinical conception of the "complemental series." Throughout the *Three Essays*, Freud is wrestling with the question of constitution and experience. How is it that the same constitution can result in different sexualities? How can the same experiences have different effects? How do we explain developmental outcomes—in current parlance, how do we choose between or reconcile essentialism and constructionism? Freud claims that whereas the organic or physiological givens vary by individual, everyone is born with some innate disposition or "constitution." Everyone also has "accidental experiences" arising in his or her family, sometimes involving trauma.

Constitution and accident interact. Freud tells us that "the relation between the two is a co-operative and not a mutually exclusive one. The constitutional factor must await experiences before it can make itself felt; the accidental factor must have a constitutional basis in order to come into operation" (p. 239). While accidental experiences in early childhood will have a more determinative effect than later experience, Freud hypothesizes that constitution and experience play off against each other throughout. Thus, a strong constitutional propensity needs less experience to have its effect, and, by complement, intense experiences can offset the near absence of constitutional propensity and produce the same impact. Any particular sexual outcome will be the result of both constitution and experience. Neither alone can predict outcome.

Third among Freud's generative insights in the *Three Essays* is his description of the inextricable but complicated relationship between sexuality and gender. Indeed, these writings have spawned a veritable gender and sexuality industry, beginning early in the history of psychoanalysis and continuing into contemporary psychoanalysis, feminist psychoanalysis, psychoanalytic feminism, and gay, lesbian, and queer theory. Here again, Freud makes explicit what "everyone" supposedly knows: that gender and sexuality are not the same thing but cannot be separated one from the other; that body image and sexual experience relate in complex ways to sense of gender; that there is no one-to-one correspondence between sexual (or gendered) anatomy and sexual (or gendered) object choice. At the same time, of course, Freud claims the opposite: There is an inescapable connection between anatomy and sense of gender; the castration complex comes with having a penis in boys; penis envy comes with not having a penis in girls.

Three Essays on the Theory of Sexuality is in no way a seamless whole. The contradictions that surface, contributing to its curious or baffling spots and its unevenness, explain, I believe, some of the crucial developments and remaining difficulties in post-Freudian thought. To begin, the reader notices (at least this reader—who has written both appreciatively and critically about Freud's later-developed account of femininity—notices) a particular asymmetry that prevails throughout the *Three Essays* whenever women and men, or boys and girls, are noticed. On the one hand, Freud definitely begins from a male norm: Girls' sexuality before puberty is "of a wholly masculine character," libido is masculine, and possession of the penis is central to boys and girls (p. 219). On the other hand, Freud in these essays pays scant attention to males, an asymmetry and differential that, with rare exception in psychoanalysis, continues almost to the present. Thus, for example, in the section "The Differentiation Between Men and Women," Freud is entirely preoccupied with how it is with girls and women, both in their development and in their adult sexuality. Freud is fascinated and absorbed with understanding women and femininity much more than with men and masculinity, a fascination that begins with the *Studies on Hysteria* and "Dora" and presages his whole oeuvre through "Analysis Terminable and Interminable" (1937). In this context, a tacit comparison to men and assumed masculine norm is barely acknowledged.

Passing over the taken-for-granted in order to focus on the seemingly abnormal or pathological extends to other normative assumptions and reminds us further of the patchwork character of these essays. Thus, just as Freud pays little attention to (normative) masculinity in comparison to femininity, these three essays on the theory of sexuality pay scant attention to "normal" sexuality in comparison to the sexual aberrations. Regarding childhood, Freud did not develop his full theory of infantile sexuality until later, yet it is nonetheless notable that he begins the work's second essay, "Infantile Sexuality," not with thumb-sucking, masturbation, and the infantile erotogenic zones, all subsequently discussed, but with a nod toward infantile amnesia followed by a section on latency.

More surprising, finally, is a relative absence of psychological theorizing, of any real attention to the mind, in the work, especially when compared to Freud's intense interest here in body and behavior. We notice when Freud, supposedly a psychoanalyst of the mind, spends pages as a sexologist in long, puzzled ruminations on the exact physiology of stimulation, sexual arousal, excitation, and discharge. We notice when he reminds us, as if we do not already know, that the external and internal genitals take final physiological form at puberty, or that the stimulation of the erotogenic zones from without both provides pleasure and generates further sexual tension. In his pages on "The Primacy of the Genital Zones and Fore-pleasure" and "The Problem of Sexual Excitation," we find over and over stunningly and bizarrely mundane statements of the obvious—albeit filtered through Freud's quirky and original mind. Nevertheless, we are fascinated even here, as Freud takes us step-by-step through the solutions to straw-man problems—for instance, his curious claim that sexual excitation is so bewildering because of our "complete ignorance."

Freud's understandings of repression, neurosis, character, and sublimation link the biological-physiological aspect of sexuality to psychic life, but you would barely know this from a reading of the *Three Essays* alone. Freud is, I think, both somewhat unaware of and determinedly disingenuous about his intentions, which are, finally to use this study of physiological sexuality to underpin his psychological theory of the pleasure principle. He is pointing to the physiological basis of his claim that tension release is the central goal of human functioning, and he wants (elsewhere more than in these essays themselves) to draw our attention to the role of internal, mental forces (fantasy and wish) in generating sexual excitation or tension. However, Freud's key section, "The Libido Theory," that makes such unrecognized intentions manifest, was not added until the 1915 version of the work. It is only then that Freud blended his physiological discussion into libido theory, as he claims that his earlier "hypotheses" about the chemical basis of sexual excitation can now be understood in terms of libido—that special energy that is qualitatively different from other forms of energy underlying mental processes.

Similarly, Freud is interested in infantile sexuality not so much in itself as because its various forms, through regression and fixation, condensation, displacement, reaction formation, and symbolization, generate varieties of neurosis and character, especially the hysterical, phobic, and obsessional, as well as feeding into adult sexualities of all sorts. Here again, Freud displays the same fascination with body and behavior that characterizes his investigation of sexuality in general. Even in the section on fixation that concludes the *Three Essays*, where we find Freud returning to the account of childhood sexuality and its significance that is for him the chief contribution of this work, we discover regrets, about our lamentable lack of biological, not of psychological, knowledge.

Throughout these essays, then, Freud's interest in how, exactly, physiological sex works and how the sexual body develops seems a passion in itself, not to be subsumed under his interest in the mind. Indeed, I believe that Freud's obsession with the actual body (or body parts and their function) and with actual sexual behavior and excitement, rather than with mind, desire, wish, and fantasy, may also contribute to and rationalize popular resistance to and disbelief about childhood sexuality and about psychoanalysis.

We find another contradiction, more explicit than, but partly explicable as a consequence of, Freud's obsession with biology, physiology, and behavior in this ostensibly psychoanalytic work (on this contradiction, see also Marcus, 1975). In his section, "Infantile Sexuality," Freud writes eloquently about the infant at the breast, noting that "no one who has seen a baby sinking back satiated from the breast and falling asleep with flushed cheeks and a blissful smile can escape the reflection that this picture persists as a prototype for the expression of sexual satisfaction in later life" (p. 182). Toward the end of the work, he tells us, "A child sucking at his mother's breast has become the prototype of every relation of love. The finding of an object is in fact a refinding of it" (p. 222). Thumb-sucking, he contends, is derivative of and a substitute for this primal experience. The breast is the first sexual object, and autoerotism, following after, provides "a second erotogenic zone, though one of an inferior kind" (p. 182).

But Freud makes equally strong assertions that infantile sexuality is originally autoerotic. Immediately following his panegyric to the infant at the breast, he tells us that the "three essential characteristics" of infantile sexuality include that "it has as yet no sexual object" (p. 182). As he puts this same contradictory conclusion in his 1915 addendum, he says, "The characteristics of infantile sexual life which we have hitherto emphasized is that it is essentially autoerotic (i.e., that it finds its object in the infant's own body)" (p. 187). Adult sexuality requires, then, the gathering together of infantile component instincts, the primacy of one (i.e., the genital) erotogenic zone, and object finding, which is and is also not a refinding.

Beginning in these *Essays*, and continuing into his later work, then, Freud makes mutually exclusive claims for the primacy of the breast and the primacy of autoerotism, and of course, these two claims are foundational sources for competing psychoanalytic theories. In "On Narcissism" (1914), when he is interested not only in sexual pleasure in the self or the mother but also in the primary ego state of being narcissistic or object-related, Freud asserts that the child has originally two objects, himself and the mother who feeds him. These two mutually exclusive claims, sexual pleasure in the self, sexual pleasure in the mother, and later, both at the same time, are left to stand, unresolved.

Now, whether the infant is originally libidinally attached to an object or not, and whether she gets erotic satisfaction from another or herself—indeed, whether humans are initially connected to others, so that forms of connection need explaining but not connection itself—is a pivotal question. Its extensions have separated drive theorists from object relations theorists for many years—Fairbairn's "libido is object-seeking" against Freud's "libido is pleasure seeking," ego-drive theory against relational theory, beliefs about what kinds of unconscious fantasies constitute psychic reality.

Furthermore, it has implications for conceptions of human possibility, politics, and society (on this, see Chodorow, 1978, 1979, 1985, 1986b).

Psychoanalysts continue to write clinically about sexuality, and many elements in the *Three Essays* have been elaborated, challenged, or revised. Female development has been studied and rethought creatively and with great depth, most basically, as Freud's claim for the universality of envy has been countered by arguments for a primary genitally based femininity located in the female body and to a lesser extent by a focus on internal psychobiological femininity—pregnancy, inner genitality. Some have questioned Freud's account of male sexuality as well. Analysts have argued that the first genital phase takes place in the second year of life rather than the third or fourth, and our understandings of the homosexualities, as well as of what we still call the perverse and perversions, have been extensively revised.

French psychoanalysts in particular, like Chasseguet-Smirgel, McDougall, Laplanche, and Green, along with the Israeli Ruth Stein, have continued to make sexuality central to their thinking and writing, defining its nature, exploring further the perversions, and describing the forms of perverse thinking in the rejection of gender and generational difference that deny and distort reality and undermine genuine creativity, even as sexuality itself is less attended to, except in its exceptional forms, in American psychoanalysis and hardly at all in British and other continental traditions. Across psychoanalytic cultures, some individuals and some traditions continue to adhere to Freud's original views—homosexuality is a perversion; castration definitionally divides masculinity and femininity—whereas for others, there is no such thing as a sexuality that is innately perverse, or perversion is a mind-set and a way of thinking, with little reference to the body at all.[4] Others ignore sexuality altogether.

At the same time, psychoanalytic commentators note these days that the place of sexuality in psychoanalysis has been inappropriately diminished and remains hard to determine. None of these elaborations, critiques, or revisions is comparable in scope or depth to the theoretical and clinical developments that have extended and transformed so many other aspects of the Freudian corpus, and none of these latter developments itself offers us a general theory of sexuality. Neither the ego psychologies of Anna Freud, Hartmann, Arlow, or Brenner, the interpersonal and relational theories, Kleinian theory, the British object-relations tradition, nor self psychology have generated a serious challenge to the *Three Essays* or any kind of

[4] 2011 note: Much has been written on sexuality since I wrote these words, especially by relational psychoanalysts like Corbett (2009) and Dimen (2003). Yet, the distinctions I make remain alive and were particularly noticeable at a panel on perversion chaired by the late Ruth Stein at the 2009 meetings of the International Psychoanalytic Association, where beliefs ranged from perverse is a way of thinking, to no sexuality is innately perverse, to castration = homosexual preoccupation = perverse = femininity.

revisionist analogue. Only occasionally do writers make sexuality as a general feature of psychic and psychobiological life (as opposed to the sexualities, which have, of course, been addressed by a number of feminist and gay and lesbian writers) a central point of interest. Indeed, it is probably Freud himself who came up with the major revision of his work when, in *Beyond the Pleasure Principle* (Freud, 1920a), he introduced the death drive and argued that it limited the role of libido and sexuality in the psyche.

Psychoanalysts also continue to be interested in development from infancy throughout the life cycle. We have directed attention to attachment, affective development, self- and emotional development, cognitive development, meaning making, the interaction of developmental lines, the extension of developmental stages past puberty, the move from paranoid-schizoid to depressive position, the idea of the transitional object and transitional space. But with the exception of a few specific challenges, the 1905–1923 developmental theory of sexual phases and infantile sexuality has either been tacitly relegated to a place of secondary importance in the overall schema of development or it has been left fundamentally unchanged.

The literary critic Steven Marcus writes in his 1975 introduction to the *Three Essays* that no other theory has come along to replace Freud's and that no theory "resembles it in explanatory power" (p. xli). He is surely right. But he writes also about the "coherence and integrity" of the ideas put forth in the *Three Essays*, and here he is surely wrong. These essays, though fertile, are (as he also notes) completely fragmentary. And burdened as they are by Freud's riveted attention to physiological experience, behavior, and development as well as by that fragmentation, the *Essays* themselves are at least partially responsible for the curious lack of cohesion in psychoanalytic thinking about sexuality and the diminution of its role in our investigations.

Still, the topic of sexuality pervades psychoanalytic thinking, just as it pervades contemporary culture. Psychoanalysts, like other therapists, are interested clinically in actual sexual behavior, in sexual orientation, in desire, passion, and lust, that is, in sex as sex. We are interested in body image and sexual identity. We are interested in childhood sexual development, in order to understand both children and adults. All these issues are intertwined with gender identity and the sense of gender. This is the ground covered in the *Three Essays*, in sections on the sexual aberrations, on libido theory, on the component instincts and erotogenic zones, on the differences between men and women, and on childhood sexuality and its transformations and outcome in puberty.

Psychoanalytic thinkers in all fields are of course interested in sexuality in the mind as well as the body—in conscious and unconscious sexual fantasy, in erotic transference and countertransference, in perverse thinking as well as perverse behavior. We are interested, as was Freud, in sexuality as a basic foundation—in drives, libido theory, neurosis, and character and in the idea of libido/Eros, in all its transformations and substitutions, as a basic motivating force in psychic life. And psychoanalysts, like Freud, pay attention to cultural definitions and redefinitions of sexuality, sexual orientation, and gender, because these so centrally affect practitioners and their patients, in relation to both their behavior and their conscious and unconscious fantasies. Psychoanalysis itself has led ordinary people to have different ways of thinking about their sexuality. And of course, no practitioner can work without being continually aware of the anxiety sexuality can evoke, in him- or herself as well as in the patient—anxiety deriving from thinking and fantasizing about sexuality, acting sexual, or addressing childhood sexuality, about erotic transference and countertransference, about one's own body integrity and sexuality.

Freud's thinking about these sexual matters of mind, being, and body is foundational to and shapes our thinking about all of them today, but it is ironic that so many of the roots of our thinking can barely be uncovered in his one work most exclusively focused on sex. Yet, even as other parts of Freud's oeuvre devote more attention to a number of these matters, none of them, nor our contemporary culture, can be understood without reference to these essays. Comprehensive, with unevenness, and with remarkable flashes of brilliance, the *Three Essays on the Theory of Sexuality* still require persistence, imagination, and openness to the unfamiliar on the part of the reader, but they tell us what sex is all about.

Chapter 3

From subjectivity in general to subjective gender in particular

Rethinking Melanie Klein, "Mourning and its relation to manic-depressive states"

In the late 1990s, Donna Bassin initiated a book of commentaries on classical contributions to the psychology of women. I stretched her invitation to meet my own current interests, choosing, not a paper about women, but a theoretical paper by Melanie Klein. During the 1990s, I, along with several other members of the San Francisco Psychoanalytic Institute, became involved in learning about Kleinian theory and technique. Our training had centered on a resistance-focused ego psychology and Freud, with some excursion into San Francisco-based control-mastery theory, also derived from ego psychology, and into a Loewaldian intersubjective ego psychology developmental perspective. Comparative theory and technique, so prominent in American training programs today, were scarcely considered. Thus, when several of us had the opportunity to study with contemporary Kleinians in supervision groups, we welcomed it. Working with our British visitors brought an opportunity to study Klein in depth and to apply Kleinian theory to our own work. I could have selected a number of other Kleinian papers: the point was, I wanted to write about what a Kleinian understanding of gender might look like.

I had cited Klein on gender in previous work, but here, I chose to consider how fundamental Kleinian concepts—splitting, projection, introjection, projective identification—could themselves enhance our understanding of these matters. Retrospective volumes like the present one are always children of their times. Whereas it was relatively novel for Americans to write or think about Klein in the 1990s, Kleinian psychoanalysis is today as commonly (perhaps more commonly) attended to as ego psychology and relational psychoanalysis—though presentations on gender and sexuality themselves often exhibit a surprising lag time and fidelity to early formulations.[1]

[1] An earlier version of this chapter appeared in D. Bassin (Ed.), *Female Sexuality: Contemporary Engagements* (pp. 241–250). Northvale, NJ: Aronson, 1999. Reprinted with permission.

Klein is not an immediately obvious choice if the writer wishes to consider classical papers on female sexuality. Klein wrote few papers exclusively or primarily on female psychology, and differences between the sexes and anxieties and conflicts about being gendered and sexual do not seem especially central to the Kleinian project. Contemporary Kleinians have not shown much interest in or contributed to recent psychoanalytic considerations on gender or sexuality; their developmental attention, as well as their attention to the clinical situation, have been elsewhere.[2] Yet I knew, when invited to write on a classical paper, that reading Klein and the contemporary Kleinians had deeply influenced my ability to think and work clinically, both substantively to understand my patients' unconscious fantasies and to understand the analytic situation and process. I wanted to think about Klein and gender.

Kleinians give us an account of a psyche in process, continually active and changing. Klein brings conviction to a phenomenological-experiential sense of inner reality: The analyst can talk to her patient in Kleinian terms, for example, pointing out how they put their own warded-off feelings or different aspects of themselves into her, noting their refusal to think or make connections or their attempts to deaden and make meaningless their interactions with the analyst. Freud's writings before the consolidation of the structural theory—for example, the cases, the dream book, his theoretical attempts in "On Narcissism" (1914), say, or in "Mourning and Melancholia" (1917), to grasp what he found clinically—these also portray a psyche in process. But as a result of the ego-psychological reliance on the structural theory, there has been in the Freudian legacy a tendency to conceptualize a fixed psyche enacting structural givens (see Chodorow, 1996a). If the therapist talks to patients in the terms of ego psychology, he invites them to observe their inner workings as objective processes.[3]

Perhaps my being drawn to Klein for the clinical understanding of women and psychoanalysis is peculiarly biographical. Previous to becoming a clinical psychoanalyst, I had thought extensively about the psychology

[2] Implicit noticing of gender, specifically of the normative heterosexual couple, is found in contemporary Kleinian writing in an interpretive emphasis on the child's refusal to accept parental intercourse and the sexual exclusivity of the parental couple, as this extends to interpretation of particular transference situations in which the patient by extension tries to undermine the intercourse of ideas in the analyst's mind. A refusal to allow the analyst to think may be a way of warding off the envy or feelings of loss that come from recognizing that someone important can do things without you, and an inability to think together with the analyst may be engaged to prevent unconscious associations to the primal scene (see, for example, Britton, Feldman, & O'Shaughnessy, 1989).

[3] 2011 note: My claim here will puzzle readers, who know that for years I have argued for and identified myself with what I have named *intersubjective ego psychology*. It is a critique with which I now both agree and disagree. I am still critical of ego psychologies that focus too much, as I see it, on the rational ego, self-observation, and observation of defenses, but I would now make the same criticism about the constantly active, moment-to-moment, contemporary Kleinian interpretive focus on defense.

of women and had formulated many expectations, understandings, and insights. As I read the recent literature, or as I reread the classics, then, I was looking less for further knowledge about the *content* of psychologics of gender (prevalent unconscious fantasies, self-other constructions, sexual senses of self, body experiences, and fantasies) and more for insight into how to help patients' unconscious senses of gender, body, and sexuality emerge, as well as into the ways that gender is related to other elements of the internal world and unconscious fantasy. According to my current understanding, gendered subjectivity—all elements of anyone's psychology of gender—is part of psychic functioning in general. To understand this psychology, we need the best possible general psychological theory and the best possible understanding of clinical process. We need to move beyond those theories that base their psychologies of gender on a search for gender differences and a comparison of men and women or that reduce gender psychology to one element (whether genital, relational, or anything else). We need a theory that can point us toward and help us to understand the clinical individuality of gender. For this understanding, Kleinian theory promised to be helpful.

As I was considering Klein, I kept in mind that some of the British object-relations theorists, who had so influenced me when I first became interested in psychoanalysis and gender, could be thought of as neo-Kleinians. Klein's focus on the object provided the initial grounding for British object relations theory, and many British independent analysts were influenced by Kleinian theory and technique, even as they revised and expanded upon these and disagreed with some major Kleinian claims. Such recognition on my part may have been virtually impossible in the early 1970s, given the proscription of Kleinian theory, and lack of knowledge of British object relations thinking, in American psychoanalysis.

Klein gives us several useful formulations directly concerning the psychology of women and men. In her paper, "Early Stages of the Oedipus Conflict" (1928), she discusses a "femininity-phase" in both sexes. She describes a "femininity complex" in boys that includes male envy of female reproductive organs—"organs of receptivity and bounty" (p. 190)—that is of equal virulence, but more obscured and displaced, than the castration complex in girls. She notices the girl's dread of the mother (arising out of her anxiety that her mother will attack and destroy her) as well as of the father, and she shows how all these processes have consequences for the boy's and the girl's superego formation.[4] *The Psycho-Analysis of Children* (1932) contains chapters on the differential effects of early anxiety situations on boys and girls (see also Klein, 1945, 1955). In "Envy and Gratitude"

[4] As I notice in 1989, psychoanalytic feminist rethinking of the psychology of women would have been greatly advanced if we had taken this paper and other early Kleinian writings as seriously as we took contemporaneous Freudian writings.

(1957), Klein returns to women's envy or idealization of the penis and of men, and she traces the roots of this envy and idealization not to something self-evidently superior in maleness or masculine genital equipment but to conflicts, envy, and anxiety in a girl's relation to her mother. In "Envy and Gratitude," Klein also discusses male envy of the breast and other feminine attributes (pp. 199–201). Unlike Freud, then, Klein provides an account of envy and idealization of the other gender that applies to both sexes and that has a dynamic and developmental explanation.

The usefulness of Klein's writings, however, goes beyond her specific attention to girls and boys, men and women, or subjective psychological gender. As we now know, the psychology of gender and sexuality themselves includes every element that goes into how someone unconsciously and consciously fantasizes about and creates her senses of gender, well beyond psychological body centering or what I once called (1991a) normative woman in the developmental theory. In terms of this broader definition, which notices gender wherever it is found, the substantive content of Kleinian theory must be seen as completely gendered. All the important psychological processes of human life—projective and introjective processes, fantasies of goodness and badness, splitting, envy, and reparation—center originally around the maternal breast (moreover, of course, in Kleinian theory the breast is much more than a part of the maternal anatomy). An infant does not know that her or his mother's breast comes with female gendering, but learning about gender and unconscious gender fantasies eventually comes to include this knowledge. It is also striking that in discussing gender differences and female sexuality and psychology, psychoanalysts classically focused entirely on the genitals, virtually ignoring the presence or absence of the anatomic breasts. Breasts (*the* breast, as if there is typically only one) are noticed from the point of view of the nursing child, but hardly as a psychosexual organ important to women themselves.[5]

In this broader context, then, Klein's account of the consequences of a child's (both a girl's and a boy's) fantasies about and terrors, fears, desires, or envy of the good and bad breast, described most powerfully in "Envy and Gratitude," must be seen also as indirectly gender-related, tying unconscious fantasies about women to one of our most destructive intrapsychic and interpersonal emotions. As Klein and other writers note, these fantasies, based on envy, can also generate some of the deepest threats to clinical work

[5] In contrast to the classical psychoanalytic literature, the anthropological literature suggests that weaning, a new sibling, and the transition from babyhood have more widespread traumatic import for both sexes than learning about genital difference (e.g., Briggs, 1971; Levy, 1973; Whiting & Whiting, 1975). Moreover, when ethnographers describe a sex that is preoccupied psychodynamically with envy, anxiety, fear about its own gender, and a need to repudiate cross-gender identifications, it is always the male, who is, like the generic baby, too enmeshed in his early tie to his mother and too uncertain about how to achieve a successful masculinity (e.g., Gregor, 1985; Herdt, 1981; Whiting, Kluckhohn, & Anthony, 1958).

and to the analyst's sense of well-being. If Klein is right here, then, patients of both sexes engender their analysis when they destroy either a female or a male analyst's interpretations because their envy and projective fantasies make them unable to accept good from another. As Klein has put it, "The capacity to give and to preserve life is felt as the greatest gift and therefore creativeness becomes the deepest cause for envy" (1957, p. 202).

It is not surprising, I think, that this breast-centered, mother-centered, general theory written by a woman would be a promising approach to understanding psychoanalysis and women, whether or not Klein spends much time directly discussing female psychology. Nor is it surprising that the clinician would need Klein (among others) to understand transferences toward a woman analyst (at the very least). Yet, the import of Klein's theories for a psychology of gender and sexuality goes well beyond breasts, the mother's insides, or the primal scene. Klein's understandings of body configuration and gender-related fantasy certainly describe aspects of gendered and sexual subjectivity, but these elements can be understood only in the context of other, perhaps more basic, Kleinian concepts. As Klein gives us an account of the creation of subjectivity in general, we are able to see the processes that go to create subjective gender in particular.

Klein's account of the intertwining and mutual creation of inner and outer worlds founds the Kleinian contribution. Her concept of projective identification describes how people endow the external world with unconscious meaning, animating or tinting this world with emotional and fantasy meaning. Such concepts describe specifically how individuals experience and appropriate cultural gender, how they make personally meaningful cultural beliefs, stories, and fantasies. Unconscious fantasies help any individual to locate herself among these cultural beliefs and stories: I think here of a patient whose unconscious masochistic fantasies, developed in relation to her father, help fuel an addiction to Gothic romances and to images of herself as originally the mousy and finally as the triumphant woman. Gender for the individual also has a particular affective tonality, generated projectively by unconscious fantasies created through interaction with particular kinds of mothers and fathers. Experiencing a depressed mother, for example, may lead a woman to lend a diffuse depressive tonality to her unconscious sense of female self. Reciprocally, children understand the unconscious messages about gender transmitted by parents through introjective identifications that filter these messages through unconscious fantasy and that introjectively take in fantasied aspects of the parent. Such unconscious messages include, for example, recognition and confirmation, or envy and disparagement, of the child's gender, body, and self as well as the parent's own complex unconscious senses, feelings, and fantasies of self and gender.

Although they were not developed with the psychology of gender specifically in mind, then, Kleinian concepts of projection and introjection help specify the psychic processes that create gendered subjectivity. Similarly, the Kleinian account of psychic positions helps us to understand how anyone creates their gender (see also Sweetnam, 1996). For some people, or during some periods of analysis, gender may be created more in paranoid-schizoid terms. Male and female will be radically split, the one good and the other bad, one's own or the other's gender repudiated and denied. Still in paranoid-schizoid fantasy, unconscious gender will become imbued with destructive envy, or one or the other sex becomes experienced in terrifyingly persecutory terms. Alternatively, gender may be created in more depressive terms, not dominated by persecutory anxiety and defensive splitting but with a rueful sense that something must be given up, something acknowledged, in the complex wholeness of one's gender.

By extending Klein's theory to an understanding of gender in these ways, we begin to imagine how such shifts might occur throughout life and transferentially in relation to gender, creating the extensive complexity of any individual's unconscious sense of gender and gender fantasy. We can evaluate personal meanings of gender, sexuality, and body in terms of their dominant character as rigidly split or integrated and in terms of their dominant associated affects and affective tone. We can explore the leading anxieties and defensive patterns and processes that create gender, as well as the creative and constructive elements that may animate, enliven, and enrich it.

The Kleinian concept of reparation (1937) provides another ostensibly non-gendered concept of relevance to the psychology of gender. I am thinking here of the many developmental theories that consider separation from and rejection of the mother, along with turning toward or idealizing the father, as necessary developmental tasks for both sexes. As I and others have noted, a felt need for separation from and repudiation of the mother contributes to the installation of male-dominant heterosexuality and to psychological, social, and cultural male dominance (symbolized in psychoanalytic talk of the primacy of the phallus, the phallic world of difference, the name of the father, and so forth—almost as if theory here mirrors the child's putative developmental task). In turn, this rejection and repudiation deeply affect how many women feel as mothers and how we conceptualize (and blame) mothers clinically.

The view that this transfer of idealization and attachment is a necessary developmental task contributes to the difficulty so many writers seem to find in holding evenhandedly in view the subjectivity of both mother and child. As I note earlier, Klein herself describes clearly and forcefully the repudiation of feminine identifications and maternal dependency in both boys and girls. She also describes the potent envy and fantasied destruction of the breast that lead to overvaluation of the penis and father. Yet in neither case does she suggest that such processes are necessary, and in both she describes them as defensive—growing out of anxiety.

In contrast to a developmental account that seems to require repudiation of the mother, Klein's work on manic-depressive states (1935) implies another goal. The main achievement of depressive-level functioning is the ability to create the mother as a whole person (to create a whole breast) with good and bad aspects, rather than fantasying mother, breast, and self as composed of split, fragmented, unintegrated good and bad bits. In the depressive position, as one recognizes that his or her destructiveness and rage have been directed against a whole object, there is guilt and a wish to make reparation. According to this understanding, one could argue that the often developmentally found and even, in classical psychoanalysis, advocated rejection of the mother and turn to the father is a paranoid-schizoid solution to the felt need to separate. For both sexes, a non-misogynist, non-mother-repudiating psychological solution to fear, hatred, or rejection of the mother and envy of her breast may be, not idealization of the father, but depressive-level reparation toward the mother.

Indeed, I believe that coming to terms with the internal and external mother is a major developmental project and a lifelong internal process for most women (for most men as well). My clinical experience only substantiates this claim, which I first articulated in 1978, although I have also become much more aware through clinical work of the great individual variation and complexity in such processes. Fantasy reparation toward the whole object, whether it be through decreasing envy, direct recognition of one's own destructiveness, or a lessening of a protective idealization of one's mother, that has itself, in turn, covered genuine acknowledgment of her real limitations and one's own rage at these, all these enable a sense of separate self based neither on the destruction of the mother nor on the severance of the connection to her.

My point here is not that this reparative project describes women rather than men, but that it solves for both sexes the implicit mother rejection in much psychoanalytic theory and practice. (I would make a similar point about coming to terms with the internal and external father. Insofar as this is done mainly through comparison of him with the mother and radical choice making, this is a more paranoid-schizoid process. Insofar as his different aspects are engaged, appropriated, mourned, or rejected in relation to the father himself, the achievement is more at the depressive level.)

Klein developed the concepts I have been describing over many years. Among these papers, Klein's "Mourning and Its Relation to Manic-Depressive States" (1940) covers many clinical and theoretical themes succinctly and with moving eloquence. Cited infrequently in comparison to several of Klein's other papers, not part of the main psychoanalytic corpus on mourning, this paper nonetheless gives us in detail an account of how inner worlds are built and rebuilt in development, in life, and in analysis. Klein describes with particular clarity, through her brilliantly concise concept of "doubling," the relations among inner and outer worlds, and she documents specifically how a sense of inner aliveness depends upon the aliveness of the outer world, as well as the reverse. Klein provides in this paper an account, summarizing her earlier work, of how the psyche can shift rapidly from paranoid-schizoid to depressive states and back again.

Klein's topic in "Mourning and Its Relation to Manic-Depressive States" is initially actual mourning for actual loss (her own included), but her account draws from and is extended to her understanding of internal loss as a more general phenomenon in psychic life. She begins from recognition that from early infancy, all development and all change involve loss. Both the acknowledgment of the loss and the acknowledgment that one has survived it constitute a substantial psychic threat. Extending Freud's "Mourning and Melancholia" (1917), Klein argues that the loss of inner or outer objects brings several challenges. Such a loss must be endured without denial, a collapse into an internal sense of deadness, excessive guilt, complete destruction of the lost object and turning all its good aspects into bad, and without hatred for abandonment. Any of these internal processes leads to paranoid splitting. On the other side is the danger of manic omnipotence, as feelings of triumph over the other and an elation at surviving also reflect splitting and denial.

These general processes have direct relevance to the psychology of women and gender (not negligibly, the autobiographical case of Mrs. A also provides a powerful early psychoanalytic account of maternal subjectivity). Especially, we can fruitfully apply Klein's account specifically to what happens for many women as they attempt to come to terms with their mother (see also Loewald, 1979, on the developmental necessity of parricide, triumph, and atonement). Here, too, women find themselves in a precarious balance between depressive sadness, reparation, and "progress in integration" (Klein, 1957, p. 233) on the one hand and on the other a pull toward paranoid-schizoid triumphant mania and elation at surviving her.

In this mania and elation, however, if the continued internal connection to the mother is denied, it eventually comes back to haunt. I have described elsewhere (Chodorow, 1999b) what I call "weeping for the mother," which I have found especially in my women patients whose active professional, personal, and sexual lives contrast sharply with the lives of mothers who are trapped in classically patriarchal marriages. Difficulties in the successful resolution of many guilt-laden or envious transferences, perhaps especially those characteristic of some woman analyst-woman patient pairs, also often involve issues of mourning and conflicts about surviving and triumphing over the other.

I have come to believe that we need to look at individuality in the psychology of gender and to move beyond generalizing and universalizing claims about *the* woman and *the* man. Klein's substantive theory can be read as a universalizing developmental theory as well as a universalizing symbolic theory about the meaning of the breast. But her clinical guidance toward particularized introjective and projective fantasies and shifting transferences and her understanding of the critical lifelong battle between paranoid-schizoid and depressive ways of functioning both point us toward a clinical method that can uncover individuality in gender fantasies and transferences and varied levels of integrated or unintegrated gender. With such a theory, we are not always focused on the meaning of the genital, the meaning of a particular parent, or the comparison of males and females. Indeed, at this point in time, a psychology of gender that does not begin from overgeneralizations or reductionist claims about gender difference is consonant with both clinical observation and feminist theory.

Chapter 4

The Reproduction of Mothering

Reconsiderations

Twenty years after its first publication, *The Reproduction of Mothering* was reissued with a new preface. In it, I restate what I see as the main contribution of the book—its psychodynamic and developmental account—and I suggest why it has had enduring appeal. I respond to criticisms or areas of unease about the book articulated by feminists, social scientists, and psychoanalysts, including my own 25-years-older self. In particular, I consider my attitudes toward the psychobiology of maternality and my original surrounding of the argument in a more sociological context than I believe it warrants or that I would now propose. I point to tensions faced by feminists, psychoanalysts, and other proponents of liberatory change, between psychological understanding and social and political advocacy.

In an abstract for this preface, which was published simultaneously as a separate contribution, I say: "*The Reproduction of Mothering* attracted readers from a wide variety of backgrounds—ordinary women seeking to understand themselves; psychoanalysts and psychotherapists; feminist scholars from a range of disciplines including literature, philosophy, political theory, sociology, and anthropology; and social and cultural theorists. These reflections address all these readers" (2000b, p. 337).

As I jump in the present volume from commentaries on Freud and Klein to a commentary on myself (and then on my contemporary Stephen Mitchell), I need to remind readers that I am in no way suggesting that this specific lineage defines the territory of psychoanalytic thinking.[1]

It is rather daunting to look back on *The Reproduction of Mothering*, published just over 20 years ago and conceived when I was about half my cur-

[1] An earlier version of this chapter appeared in *The Reproduction of Mothering* (2nd ed., pp. vii–xvii). Berkeley: University of California Press, 1999. Reprinted with permission.

rent age.[2] The book has certainly come to have a life of its own, and this life must be due to some enduring or immediately recognizable truths that it conveys to readers. At the same time, it has certainly been subjected to many critiques, indeed, has even been taken as the paradigmatic case of problematic feminist theorizing. People will ask: Do I still hold to the account I put forward? Where would I modify the account? As I reflect upon *The Reproduction of Mothering* now, I bring to it the stance of a psychoanalyst as well as that of the feminist sociologist and former anthropologist who wrote it. It must also be especially relevant to reconsider reflexively a theory that is so definitely and centrally generational and developmental since I myself have moved generations and developed.

The book's title says it all: It is about the reproduction of mothering—but in the intrapsychic and intersubjective sense, not literally. The enduring contribution of the book, I believe, is in its understanding of important aspects of female development and the dynamics of the female psyche. In particular, I investigate the mother-daughter relationship and how women create and re-create this relationship internally. It is a cyclical process that I break into at the daughter's birth, but developmental outcomes in the mother already situate that birth and subsequent development and give it characteristic features. Implied and elaborated to a greater or lesser extent in this account of the mother-daughter relationship and its lodging in the female psyche are comparative claims: women in comparison to men (the female self and psyche in comparison to the male psyche, femininity and masculinity, mothers and fathers) and, more specifically, the mother-daughter in comparison to the father-daughter and mother-son relationships.

The central terrain of *The Reproduction of Mothering*, that is, is that of the individual psyche. I characterize the female and male psyches especially in terms of an unconscious internal world and a conscious and unconscious sense of self, and I describe how this internal world and sense of self are formed developmentally, mainly through unconscious communications between mother and child. I am elaborating typical gender differences in the formation of one version of what psychoanalysts mean by the ego, or "I"—the ego that is formed and modified through internal object-relations. In Freud's view, this "I" is the precipitate of abandoned object cathexes or an ego upon which the shadow of the object has fallen. In Klein's and Fairbairn's views, not entirely unrelated to Freud's, it is an internal ego-object world formed through projection and introjection driven by the anxieties and guilt associated with unconscious fantasies. This internal world is shaped as the child unconsciously creates rudimentary pictures of herself in the world and copes with anxiety and other unpleasant affects, but it is more basically and originally simply how we come into being as a self—as the psychoanalyst Hans Loewald puts it (see, e.g., Loewald, 1951), how we

[2] 2011 note: "20 years" here refers to the time of the new preface (1999c), not today (2011).

originally differentiate and individuate ourselves as creatures with drives, a sense of what is external and what internal, and a sense of ourselves in relation to our primary others.

Specifically, in *The Reproduction of Mothering* and the anticipatory article that preceded it, "Family Structure and Feminine Personality" (1974), I make the claim that women experience a sense of self-in-relation that is in contrast to men's creation of a self that wishes to deny relation and connection. I also make the claim, broadly, that the mother is very important in the daughter's psyche and sense of self, such that core psychological and interpersonal experiences for women can be understood in terms of this internal mother-daughter lineage. Mothers, I argue, by virtue of their gender (whatever the individualized conscious and unconscious fantasy and emotional casting they give to this gender) experience daughters as, in a certain sense, like them, and sons as, in a certain sense, unlike. Reciprocally, girls and boys themselves appropriate and transform these unconscious maternal communications through their own intrapsychic capacities for fantasy, their own defensive reactions to anxiety and guilt, and their own desires, passions, and impulses.

Chief among the conscious outcomes of these processes are the ways in which many women feel intuitively connected to others, able to empathize, and embedded in or dependent upon relationships, on the one side, and on the other many men's counterphobically asserted independence and anxiety about intimacy if it signals dependence. Another outcome is many mothers' senses of maternal self, as well as ways that fathers' experiences of paternal self are, typically, different from those of mothers. I also claim to explain some of men's well-documented greater preoccupation with masculinity and fear of being unmasculine, in contrast to women's lesser preoccupation with basic femininity, and the widespread, almost universal ways in which this greater preoccupation with masculinity is culturally and politically elaborated or expressed.

I argue further that we need to look at the different object-relational configurations of the masculine and feminine Oedipus complex, not only in terms of the constitution of traditionally described gender identifications and sexual orientation but also, centrally, in terms of how the relation to the mother becomes so entangled in, and even constitutive of, women's desires to become mothers and the quality of their maternal affects and identifications. Many women may experience what feels like a drive or biological urge to become mothers, but this very biology is itself shaped through unconscious fantasy and affect that cast what becoming pregnant or being a mother means in terms of a daughter's internal relation to her own mother. I thus theorize maternal subjectivity—mothers' unconscious and conscious experiences of being a mother, of having a connection to a child or to children.

These insights, elaborated extensively in the main part of the book, struck a chord for readers, especially women readers. These included readers who were simply trying to understand themselves and had a sense that the classical psychological and psychoanalytic theories that privileged separateness and autonomy over connectedness and empathy did not speak to their reality and values, women who knew that their mothers as well as their fathers were extremely important in who they thought they were, and even more specifically, those who found that the psychoanalytic legacy of Freud, in which women saw themselves primarily as failed men, was not an adequate description of their experience or basis for imagining a desirable femininity.

Part of the usability of these insights, I think, was that there is no simple valuation of the outcomes I describe. Although *The Reproduction of Mothering* is very much a generalizing book, describing typical aspects of many women's and men's psychic life and of mother-daughter relationships, it is possible to see the female self-in-relation either in terms of potential or actual strengths or in terms of typical problems, say, in claiming enough autonomy or agency or in feeling enough separateness. Similarly, the mother-daughter relationship as I describe it is clearly a passionate and central one, helping to form one core of women's lives, but I also point to ways that the mother-daughter relationship may overwhelm and invade both the mother's and daughter's psyche. That is, I revalue, without idealizing, both female psychology and the mother-daughter relationship that helps to found it.

These same insights proved useful to people in many different fields. Literary critics drew upon them as they tried to understand female (and male) characters and narratives, especially mother-child relationships in both canonical literary works and in the recent vast contribution by women writers of many races, ethnicities, and nationalities, who often centered their fiction in maternal experience and in the converging and diverging stories told by mothers and daughters. Investigators of women's voice and morality, as well as feminist philosophers, ethicists, and legal theorists, looked to my account of women's relationality and its development to help explain their own findings about how women reason morally and to underpin their arguments for what a desirable morality, ethics, or legal reasoning might be.

Psychoanalysts and therapists drew from the work to understand their patients, to counter classical psychoanalytic views of female development, and as a basis for further theorizing and investigation of female psychology. The book also anticipated the development of American relational psychoanalysis and American interest in object relations and Kleinian theory. Others interested in gender in history or women's biography or oral history could use, even if they modified or disagreed with them, some of my claims. For all these people, and many others, it was also important that I provide a well-formulated critique and alternative to classical psychoanalytic views of femininity, while I remain firmly psychoanalytic and draw from the same classical psychoanalysts that I critique.

Several features of the book become clear as I summarize its core insights and impact. First, the greatest influence of the book seems to have been upon those who think about female subjectivity (or those who think that understanding female subjectivity is central to understanding a gendered society), rather than upon those who focus exclusively on social factors. However, my account of the intrapsychic and intersubjective reproduction of mothering also encompasses an account of the social and cultural reproduction of a male-dominant sex-gender system. As I have noted elsewhere (1989a, 1999b), the book is cast in the form of classical grand theory, as was much of the feminist writing of the time. As such, and much like other contemporaneous feminist grand theories and their grand theoretical functionalist, structuralist, Marxist, and even psychoanalytic (I am thinking of *Civilization and Its Discontents*) forbears, it has a persuasive wholeness that has made it, for many, generatively useful to think with. It insists, as have all my writings since, upon the inextricable interconnectedness and mutual constitution of psyche, society, and culture.

But just as grand theory is both enduringly useful and always problematic, so, I think, the grand theory of the sex-gender system in *The Reproduction of Mothering* is not as elaborated or complex as the account of development and psychological life. Its grand theoretical strengths lie in its articulation of psychological, cultural, and social analysis and its demonstration that such articulation, and especially the central place of psychology within it, are necessary to understand gender adequately. It is, accordingly, not surprising that so many of the people who draw upon the account are interested in subjectivity for its own sake or in the psyche in the culture.

Those whose professional or personal identity comes from arguing for the primacy of society and culture and the autonomy of these from psychology find *The Reproduction of Mothering* less appealing. Accordingly, it has from the beginning been viewed with some ambivalence among feminist sociologists and within my academic home discipline of sociology. On the one hand, the book received an award upon first publication for its contribution to our understanding of women in society, and it was honored by the official review journal of the discipline as one of the 10 most influential books of the past 25 years (Laslett, 1996). On the other hand, sociologists have argued that this work (a work that from my own current perspective may even be *too* socially determinist) focuses too much on individuals and gives too much autonomy to individual agency and psychology. Moreover, although my developmental account very much gives psychic agency and meaning to the child in internal and external interaction with the mother, many readers have been able to read the book as an account of direct cultural internalization and socialization by mothers or conscious identification with them.

Second, *The Reproduction of Mothering* has not only been drawn upon as a founding feminist theory; it has also been extensively subject to critique. Along with the writings of many white American feminists, it has been criticized for generalizing beyond the white Western middle class and for assuming a heterosexual nuclear family form. From the perspective of a later generation of postmodernist-poststructuralist feminists, the book is full of currently tabooed universalizing and even essentializing language about "the girl," "the mother-daughter relationship," and a presumably generic "female psychology." Much of my subsequent writing addresses and moves beyond these critiques about racial–ethnic diversity, sexual orientation, and the place of generalizing in feminist thinking and in psychoanalysis, so I will not repeat my arguments here (see 1989a, 1994, 1999b). But the specific context of writing was, of course, a period when many feminists wanted to document the universality of gender and male dominance as important objects of study (and politics). Given this context, and on review of the text itself, I think that I was by and large quite careful about what could be universalized or generalized in my claims and when I was describing a statistically prevalent rather than a morally normative model (say, of the heterosexual family) whose reproduction and psychological underpinnings needed explaining.

On a general level, I would reiterate that everyone has a psyche that operates in the ways that psychoanalysis describes (through unconscious fantasy, projection and introjection, defenses against anxiety and guilt like repression and splitting, creating an inner world, managing desire and aggression, and so forth). This psyche is part of our human psychobiological makeup. Insofar as such a position argues with poststructuralist-postmodernist claims, this is simply an unresolvable disagreement, in part because my terrain of argument is significantly empirical-clinical, and this is not a terrain on which the poststructuralist-postmodernist theorist engages (though I would also suggest that each of these critics would in everyday life recognize herself as subject to unconscious emotions, fantasies, forces, and meanings in the ways that psychoanalysis describes). Critiques of specific accounts of psychological development or organization for being overgeneralizing or universalizing should not make the mistake of thinking that people from different cultures or different families do not have a psychological life that can be described in terms of these psychical processes and the creation of psychical meanings.

In recent years, I have stressed the clinical individuality of personal gender, including the clinical individuality of any mother-daughter relationship. My point here is that culture, whether it be a hegemonic culture imposed on or internalized by subordinate groups or the particular culture of a specific group, does not determine the personal meaning of gender, the particularity of any mother's unconscious fantasies about her daughter, or the complex particularity of how any daughter images her mother or her mother's gender. Each of these is created with characteristic emotional tonalities for the individual and for the intersubjective pair (individual tonalities which also engage and reshape cultural forms and which may have prevalent features for many members of a particular culture in contrast to another culture).

This unconscious realm of psychical meaning shapes the experience of the mother, of the daughter, and of any relationship mutually created by two individual psychological subjectivities. As *The Reproduction of Mothering* claims, whatever the particular mother-daughter relationship, whatever the uniquely created self and gender of the mother, and whatever the particular cultural inflections of maternality or femininity, both daughter and mother experience this relationship intensely, such that it contributes in profound ways to the creation and experience of self.

Thus, my social scientific colleagues have been uneasy with my attention to the psyche and the individual, and my feminist colleagues are critical of my universalizing and generalizing. Meanwhile, some of my psychoanalytic colleagues, while admiring and drawing from my object-relational account, have also considered me, in my attempt to create an account of female psychology in which women are not appendages to their libido, to have repudiated bodily experience and drives.

I agree and disagree with this critique. In some ways, my critics are right: The book does not pay attention to women's subjective experience of their reproductive and sexual bodies. You have only to know an infertile woman who wishes to bear a child, to look at the lengths to which women will go, the painful and humiliating treatments, and the risks of pregnancy in the mid-to-late 40s, the willingness to bear and care for children on their own rather than not at all, the strong desire to mother, clearly not tied primarily to a relationship to a man, of many lesbian as well as heterosexual women. You have only to listen to mothers, to see that the biological experiences involved, and unconscious as well as conscious fantasies about these, are deeply central to many women's sense of self and one of the central meanings for women of motherhood. This is true for biological mothers, adoptive mothers, stepmothers, and the non-biological mother in a lesbian maternal couple (and this does not mean that all women experience these reproductive and sexual bodies in the same way).

Similarly, the demands of the "drives"—of pleasure, passion, and desire, tied to conscious and unconscious fantasy, as well as to conscious and unconscious experiences of genitality—are clearly central to most women's consciously and unconsciously experienced self and gender. As we have become aware, painfully, from the great epidemic of breast cancer, breasts, as part of body integrity, sexuality, and maternality, are for many women, though for each differently, central to emotional well-being and identity. With the exception of some feminists' reclaiming of an active sexuality for women and critiques of compulsory sexualities, which themselves certainly entail assumptions about innately rooted drives and desires, many feminists still remain uneasy with thinking that bodily experiences are not exclusively culturally or politically constructed.

In the 1970s, however, it was important to challenge the tyranny of biological explanations of gender, and this included (and includes today, insofar as many psychoanalysts still hold such views) a psychoanalytic theory that derived female psychology almost exclusively from reactions to a genital difference in which only presence or absence of the penis mattered (the book acknowledges, albeit critically, because of their continuing genital determinism, those few early theorists like Horney, Klein, and Jones, and later Kestenberg, who developed an alternative theory that became the basis for more recent "primary femininity" accounts of female genitality). I still hold that the psychology of women and men, of femininity and masculinity, is more than a psychology of bodily experience, and that bodily experience is not somehow more fundamental than other contributors to gender psychology.

Further to the point, I believe that *The Reproduction of Mothering* allows us to see bodily experience in psychologically more accurate ways. It seems to be the case that features of genital and reproductive bodily experience, as psychoanalysis suggests, demand psychological elaborating (as well as, perhaps universally, to be culturally inflected and elaborated). Much of this elaborating, however, comes not in an unmediated way from universal features of the body itself, but from the way that each particular body is intrapsychically created and incorporates, beginning from birth, an unconscious relational story that derives in complex ways from experiences of handling and from unconscious messages given both verbally and in body contact.

This intrapsychic creation and incorporation—bodily experiences are always particularized and situated—and cultural stories (themselves given directly, and more significantly, filtered through unconscious and conscious feelings and fantasies of relational others) help explain why all women do not experience their sexual and reproductive bodies, their drives, pleasures, and passions, in exactly the same way. At the same time, these bodies themselves, as well as common features of developmental and interpersonal lives, help to explain why we find some widespread patterns in these experiences.

A latent story of the bodily and drive reproduction of mothering and sexuality, though certainly not explicit in the text, can be developed out of *The Reproduction of Mothering*, especially if we extend its object-relational account in Kleinian directions or even if we insist upon the object-relational components of the Freudian account. As Klein describes it, any daughter, any child, has created herself through unconscious fantasies about the mother's body and insides and about the mother's and her partner's sexuality. My argument would be that bodily experiences and "drives," whether sexual, aggressive, or reproductive, are inflected, and thus personally created, as part of an unconscious fantasy story about these other sexual and reproductive creatures and oneself, and that biological mothering is itself specifically cast intrapsychically partially in terms of this internal, bodily imaged mother-daughter world.

Biological mothering—pregnancy, childbirth, the felt reproductive drive—is filtered and created through the prism of the intrapsychic and intersubjective reproduction of mothering. This is true for women who make the whole range of conscious and unconscious choices, or whose choices are made for them, about becoming an actual mother: I am not, here, prescribing that all women should mother or claiming that all women are intrinsically required to bear children. I am not suggesting that there is something unnatural about a woman who is not a mother or who does not want to be a mother.

Even in this early book, I am careful to point out that I am not describing a universal or essential story but a pattern. As I have been arguing in many of my recent writings, projection and introjection, attempts to manage anxiety and guilt, and those compromise formations that result, shape all interpersonal experiences, bodily experiences, cultural categories, and social processes and perceptions. We can generalize about patterns in these psychological processes, as I do in *The Reproduction of Mothering*, or we can look especially to clinical individuality and personal uniqueness. One informs and enriches the other.

Throughout, whether in dialogue with social scientists, feminists, or psychoanalysts, I am paying attention to psychical reality, to people's creation of an inner world and sense of being. My theory documents the developmental centrality and power of maternal identity for many women and the psychological significance of the mother-daughter, and, more generally, mother-child, realms. I describe problematic features of these psychological processes in the context of a mid-20th-century full-time mothering ideological norm: potentials for lack of individuation in women; expectations of total maternal availability to the child that did not acknowledge other parts of women's lives and identity; difficulties in masculine identity and development; typical tensions in heterosexual relationships. But I also claim that I was describing a reproduction that, mainly, works. The account clearly values, on balance, the psychological qualities that I describe as characteristic of women—the sense of relation and connection versus the repudiation of relation and connection—and I claim that if they become mothers, most women are good-enough mothers, to sons and daughters alike.

This brings me to conclude by noting a major tension that I now find in *The Reproduction of Mothering*, a tension between the book's main contribution, which is an account of the psychological reproduction of mothering, and its political afterword, an argument for equal parenting. If you take seriously that psychological subjectivity from within—feelings, fantasy, psychical meaning—is central to a meaningful life, then you cannot also legislate subjectivity from without or advocate a solution based on a theory of political equality and a conception of women's and children's best interests that ignores this very subjectivity. My psychological story should have enabled me to recognize and acknowledge this tension, but the feminist moment within which I wrote, as well as my own generational location, made such recognition difficult.

I do not mean that many mothers might not wish to share parenting, or, moreover, insofar as I was looking at children's development in a cultural context that had radically different expectations of mothers and fathers, that a call for greater involvement of fathers or men in children's lives did not make sense. This call has certainly been heeded in many families, whether in response to the realities of work, to feminist calls for more male involvement in child care, or to a less-conscious cultural shift in conceptions of men and masculinity. I am certainly not claiming that men cannot or should not be caretakers of children or participate in parenting. Rather, I am noting that the call for equal parenting, while supported by my argument linking mothering and male dominance, was contradicted in consequential ways by my accounts of maternal subjectivity and its centrality for many women and of the correspondingly distinctive character of the mother-child bond.

In critical and liberatory theory and practice, there is always a tension between respecting people's subjectivity and arguing that their subjectivity emerges from problematic social conditions or cultural mandates. For every claim for a universal good, we can find groups or individuals who find that such a claim does not speak to their particular situation but rather appropriates their right to know and speak for themselves. Just as feminists from different backgrounds or what are now called different subject positions have argued that my account cannot be taken without modification to stand for the experiences of women of all races and classes, I think it could be said that my universalizing advocacy of change cannot be taken without modification to stand for the experiences and desires of many mothers. As *The Reproduction of Mothering* makes clear, mothering is not simply another socially created unequal role that can be challenged, like the glass ceilings and discriminatory practices that keep women from achieving in the educational, economic, and political worlds.

Accordingly, a feminist recognition of the centrality of the realm of psychological reality would not have singled out a demand for equal parenting as a social goal—a goal that not only ignored many women's identities, wishes, and desires but that was also easily transformed into a claim for fathers' rights. Rather, it would have focused on a variety of social goals and institutional and political supports that fostered and aided mothers to mother their children and to have a full life (this would include those women who found shared parenting appropriate to their family lives). Nor could I foretell that a culture that advocated full-time mothering and an economy that permitted it for many women would be replaced by workplace practices and economic transformations that erode recognition of the mother-child relationship and often entail that neither mothers nor children have enough time with each other. When we begin from the realm of psychical reality and personal meaning, we are not necessarily also in the realm of abstract justice and social engineering.

In my social vision, I could not fully acknowledge, even as I was describing it, the sui generis level of psychological life and the vast variety of individual patterns of interpreting, creating, and changing reality. Like other feminists, I felt forced to choose between one position that seemed biologically determinist and entrapping of women and another that claimed that women's feelings about mothering and their potentially reproductive bodies were a product of social structure and cultural mandate.

On a more personal level, I believe that I and many feminists of my generation did not in our 20s and early 30s adequately understand how mothering is actually experienced (in all its particularized individual forms), and many of us were ourselves not prepared for the powerful, transformative claims that motherhood would make upon our identities and senses of self. *The Reproduction of Mothering* is written from the daughter's point of view more than that of the mother, even as the kernel of the mother's viewpoint, in the psychological capacities, desires, and identities whose development it describes, can be elicited from within it.

Like psychoanalysts, feminists always have some conception of more and less preferable subjectivities and social practices, but the feminist assumption that all patterns of psychological gender difference that can be linked to inequality need to be overridden seems to me not to recognize that psychology and politics are not always homologous and that, as we imagine fulfilling lives, the relative claims of each are not self-evident. My experiences as a clinician mesh with my theoretical insights into maternal subjectivity. I am now more respectful of the ways in which individuals create their emotional reality and sense of personal meaning and less absolute about how they ought to create these.

Chapter 5

Prejudice exposed

On Stephen Mitchell's pioneering investigations of the psychoanalytic treatment and mistreatment of homosexuality

After Stephen Mitchell's sudden death in 2000, *Studies in Gender and Sexuality* reprinted two prescient articles on the psychoanalytic treatment of homosexuals and homosexuality that Mitchell had written as a young man. Several people responded, and my response, like others, also includes an appreciative and elegiac quality. Although this tone would be natural in writing about someone who died, suddenly, in his early 50s, it is for me as well a mode found throughout all my writings on theorists and theory (see, e.g., Chodorow, 2003d, 2007a, 2007b, 2009). To paraphrase Freud (1917), as we look back on previous contributors, we know whom we have lost, and, to a greater or lesser extent, we are mindful of what we have lost in them. In my abstract for the original article, I wrote:

> Stephen Mitchell's two early papers on the psychoanalytic theory and treatment of homosexuality show characteristic Mitchell qualities: an astounding intelligence, a theoretical syncretism, an unusual ability to fine tune his sense of clinical case examples to particular theories. Surprisingly, they also show a serious commitment to some of the principles of ego psychology. In these papers, Mitchell is perhaps the first analyst to challenge the distinctly unpsychoanalytic pathologizing of all homosexual orientation based on developmental origins characteristic of all sexualities, as well as the distinctly unpsychoanalytic clinical practice of trying to change sexual orientation and behavior in patients rather than helping them to achieve self-understanding and the diminution of conflict. (Chodorow, 2002d, p. 61)[1]

[1] An earlier version of this chapter appeared in *Studies in Gender and Sexuality*, *3*(1), 2002, pp. 61–72. Reprinted with permission.

In 1998, when Victor Bonfilio and I were designing the first course on sexual orientation and sexualities at the San Francisco Psychoanalytic Institute, it turned out that about the earliest and best critique we could find of psychoanalytic pathologization of homosexuality and of analysts' attempts to change sexual orientation through treatment had been written in the late 1970s and early 1980s by the now-eminent, respected, well-published leader of the relational school and founding editor of *Psychoanalytic Dialogues*, Stephen A. Mitchell. Here is Mitchell, age 32 and already a graduate analyst, in his first published paper:

> Unless one begs the question entirely by simply defining homosexuality as pathological, it seems apparent that any determination of pathology must rest not on the presence of psychodynamic factors, nor on the demonstrability of a psychodynamic causation, but on the presence and relative weights of defensive and adaptive aspects in the behavior, the quality of the interpersonal relationships, and the degree of development and integration of the self. To call the outcome pathological because the origins are "pathogenic" is tautological. (1978, p. 259)

He goes on to point to writers who write about homosexuality "as if the latter were, once again, a unified, one-dimensional disease entity" (p. 259).

The wonder of these papers is not how good they are—we know how blessed we were to have Steve Mitchell as a colleague and psychoanalytic innovator—but how Mitchell knew to write them in the mid-to-late 1970s. "Psychodynamics, Homosexuality, and the Question of Pathology" (1978) was published when psychoanalytic approaches to homosexuality ranged from pathologization to condemnation. Mitchell points to how developmental accounts—with their inevitable inclusion of conflict, fixation, and complex object relations—were allowed, in the case of homosexuality, to constitute pathology. Much as Schafer (1974) had noted that Freud's reasoning in understanding female development undermined his own interpretive principles (a method I also tried to follow in Chodorow, 1978), Mitchell shows that psychoanalytic explanations of homosexuality run against psychoanalytic principles: "The recognition of a psychodynamic contribution to the development of a homosexual orientation, or the appreciation of a psychodynamic dimension or meaning in current homosexual functioning, is assumed to imply the pathological nature of the condition" (1978, p. 257).

But Mitchell is more specific. He focuses on two lapses in these accounts. First, the principle of overdetermination—that all behavior and experience condense and express several dynamic meanings—is lost when applied to homosexual functioning. In the case of homosexuality, if any meaning or motive leading to homosexual object choice is found to be conflictual or defensive in any way, this motive or meaning is allowed to stand for the entirety of meaning and motive.

Mitchell also points to the ways that much psychoanalytic reasoning about homosexuality manifests the genetic fallacy and a failure to recognize the operation of secondary autonomy. Here he follows Hartmann (1964), who argued that some ego functions, on the one side, have "primary autonomy," for example, the capacity to postpone gratification in order to avoid pain, or the adaptive functions of perception and cognition. These ego functions are inborn, and they mature, as do the drives, and they can also become, through fantasy and defense, embroiled in conflict. On the other side, some ways of being that originate in conflict and defense can gain "secondary autonomy," a relative freedom from their genetic origins.

The genetic fallacy ignores this possible transformation, retaining "the assumption that a behavior originating out of conflict is inevitably forever linked to conflictual difficulties" (Mitchell, 1978, p. 258). In both the loss of the principle of overdetermination and the genetic fallacy, single factors replace the multiplicity of factors that go into any psychic formation. For the case of homosexuality, the genetic fallacy assumes that, because early relations to parents or preoedipal and oedipal conflicts initially motivate homosexual (as heterosexual, but this is ignored) object choice, such choices cannot come to be what Hartmann calls "functionally independent of their origins [and] protected against regression and instinctualization" (1964, p. xi).

It is not directly relevant to a consideration of Mitchell's writings on homosexuality, but I must admit that I was astonished to read a paper by Stephen Mitchell that drew so centrally, and without special comment, on ego psychology. Mitchell turns out to be a relational thinker who has the whole range of psychoanalytic theory in his bones from the beginning. His extraordinary psychoanalytic erudition is evident even at this young age, as he in passing mentions "developments in psychoanalytic theory" (1978, p. 256) and, in evenhanded review, refers to the expansion of our understanding of psychic forces as a result of the work of Sullivan, Fromm, and Horney, the studies of the ego and non-pathological functioning contributed by Hartmann and Rapaport, and our knowledge of internal object relations gained from Klein, Fairbairn, and the British object-relations school.

Among these theories, this first paper of Mitchell's, if we need to pigeonhole it, is more ego psychological than it is relational. Specifically, Mitchell makes his points not only by arguing that we need to assess the quality of object relations and fantasy in anyone's sexuality, but also, as I note earlier, through arguments drawn from Hartmann, that these object relations and fantasies, whatever their origins, can gain secondary autonomy. Mitchell even draws his example of the genetic fallacy from one of Hartmann's examples—the surgeon whose early sadistic interests may have helped fuel his choice of career, but whose current functioning cannot necessarily be assumed to be primarily motivated by these same interests. Like the ego psychologists, Mitchell is most interested in internal conflict, as he quotes Freud on the "interplay of forces in the mind" (1978, p. 255).

This is not to say that Mitchell is unaware of Freud's ambivalence about homosexuality itself. He notes that the pathologization of homosexuality comes partially from Freud's inconsistent but persistently held views about the normal and desirable development of heterosexual genital primacy and his (sometimes) single-path account of development, regression, and fixation. Theorists, he suggests, make exceptions about homosexuality when they address its secondary autonomy. Unlike other psychic formations that have some secondary autonomy and some engagement in originary conflict, homosexuality is still seen as pathological because of its non-autonomous features and developmental history.[2]

That Mitchell makes an ego-psychological argument is not at all to imply that he defends the ego psychologists themselves, as his second paper on psychoanalysis and homosexuality makes clear. In "The Psychoanalytic Treatment of Homosexuality: Some Technical Considerations" (1981), we get stunning examples of practices that gave American ego psychology a bad name. Hartmann's notions of adaptation were perverted into analysts' blatant interference with their patients' lives and into an imposition of norms and goals that had nothing to do with analytic change and everything to do with social conventionality, social adaptation, and, in the case of homosexuality, even notions of sin and evil. Mitchell points out that, given (then) current practices and beliefs, no "knowledgeable homosexual person" (1978, p. 262) could seek the benefits of self-knowledge and open inquiry that psychoanalysis can bring because of the presumption of pathology in his sexual orientation. Rather, the genetic fallacy and betrayal of the principle of overdetermination mean that neither a person's sexual orientation nor other aspects of his life can be open to investigation. Moreover, psychoanalysts in general cannot engage in "open, unbiased research on the nature of the phenomenon" (p. 262).

As we read Mitchell's account of these horrendous descriptions of the directive-suggestive approach, which may also fit our prejudices about classical ego-psychological technique, it is important not only to remember Mitchell's (1981) initial caveat, that he is not talking about most psychoanalysts, but also that we remember the very different psychoanalytic atmosphere that has emerged more recently in the United States, in contrast to in Europe. By today, whatever their private anxieties or uncertainties, many or most American analysts have certainly revised their public views of the automatic pathology of homosexual object choice as well as their attitudes

[2] Such an observation is the takeoff point for Lewes (1988), who points out that all sexual formations, including normative heterosexuality, originate in the conflicts, traumas, and inhibitions of the Oedipus complex, castration, and the preoedipal period. Pathology cannot be automatically inferred from the outcome.

in clinical presentations and writings.[3] All American analytic institutes accept gay and lesbian candidates.

This American situation contrasts starkly with both Kleinian and French theory and practice. In theoretical and clinical writings and in public discussion, practitioners from these perspectives more often pathologize homosexuality, and American colleagues report discussions with European colleagues who cannot understand how we can accept gay or lesbian candidates. Based on psychoanalytic arguments about the centrality of the heterosexual oedipal couple, the difference between the sexes, and the law of the father, the French National Assembly has prohibited lesbians and gays from civil unions, as well as single women from adopting children (Butler, 2001).

Mitchell's astute intelligence does not allow him to restrict his criticism only to analysts. He shows how similar beliefs constitute "anti-intellectual and obscurantist positions" (1978, p. 261) on the other, pro-gay, side. These non-psychoanalysts, he notes, do not, as we would later do, attempt to find a broader story for the development of sexualities. Rather, they deny developmental origins entirely and agree with midcentury analysts that developmental and psychodynamic explanations by definition mean pathology. Thus, they prefer to see homosexuality as innate and inborn. Similarly, their alternative to the virulent parental blame found among psychoanalysts is not to defend parents or to claim that all sexualities emerge partially from relations with parents. Rather, it is to claim that parental behavior and relations to parents have nothing to do with the development of homosexual object choice. Mitchell, by contrast, suggests that warm, loving—positive—feelings between parents and children may help to create less-conflicted homosexual, as heterosexual, object choice.

In his later writings, Mitchell (e.g., 2000) was particularly able to fine-tune clinical examples to exactly the theory he was discussing or the point he was making, and these early papers are no exception. In 1978, Mitchell shows how the case of Ms. X demonstrates overdetermination and the case of Mr. Y, secondary autonomy. These cases, perhaps (we can only speculate) provided Mitchell his most surface reason, but certainly not enough of an explanation, for the critical and generative tour-de-force that constitutes his early paper.

Ms. X, a woman who began treatment with impoverished and thin relationships with men, developed during treatment a much richer relationship, with a woman. Mitchell describes both the dynamic contributions to her relationships with men and the regressive contributions to her homosexual relationship, but he argues that, on balance, the homosexual relationship had more adaptive and growth-enhancing qualities. Only by looking at all

[3] The public forum, "Homophobia: Analysis of a 'Permissible' Prejudice," at the American Psychoanalytic Association in 1998, drew an audience of over 700 (see Hoffman et al., 2000).

the meanings, motives, and developmental origins of Ms. X's object choices were he and she able to evaluate these.

Mitchell's case of Mr. Y (like his 1981 discussions of the pseudoheterosexuality that emerged from so many directive-suggestive treatments) may provide one of the first clinically based arguments in the psychoanalytic literature that we cannot infer pathology from sexual orientation. Mr. Y came to treatment not for his homosexuality, which he did not wish to alter, but for depression, work inhibitions, and, somewhat secondarily, problems in the quality of his relationships. Mitchell does what he says in his later paper ordinary analysts should do: He treats all the problems in an analytic fashion, such that work inhibitions and depression lifted. Along with this, the patient found himself (although he also dated a few women) in a new relationship with a man that had a different, much more rewarding quality than previously.

Mitchell claims that Mr. Y could have chosen a heterosexual route, but that for a number of psychological and social reasons he felt more desirous of being with men. He argues for the secondary autonomy of Mr. Y's outcome, as the *meanings* of his object choices changed and were less based in their conflictual developmental origins. With some irony, Mitchell says, "It would be possible, of course, to interpret the new homosexual relationship as a flight from emergent heterosexual feelings. This is a clinical judgment, and in the estimation of the analyst, the relationship did not constitute a defense or flight from anxiety" (1978, p. 258). Mitchell concludes: "In the cases of Ms. X and Mr. Y, neither the presence of a current psychodynamic motive for the behavior nor the historical origin of the behavior in psychodynamic conflict can be used as an exclusive basis for evaluating the health or pathology of the behavior" (p. 259).

When I was writing "Heterosexuality as a Compromise Formation" (1992), I did not find Mitchell's 1978 article because I was searching not for writings on homosexuality but for (virtually nonexistent) writings on heterosexuality. So, I did not know that Mitchell had made my basic point almost 15 years earlier. He says:

> It is also clear that there is much we do not know, both about homosexuality and about the development of heterosexuality. The presumption of the pathological nature of homosexuality has in psychoanalytic thinking, been complemented by the presumption of the "normality" of heterosexuality. The latter presumption has been just as much an obstacle to research as the former. ... Heterosexuality is not some sort of pure efflorescence of "Nature" but is powerfully influenced by and can originate in other motivational systems which can become "sexualized." (p. 262)

Mitchell is one of the first analysts since Freud, Reich, and Horney to assert how central social values and meanings are to one's sexual behavior and choices.

Where "Psychodynamics, Homosexuality, and the Question of Pathology" has often an ironic and drily clever tone—we are astounded at its erudition, its ironclad logic, its seriousness and respect for both patients and the analytic enterprise—"The Psychoanalytic Treatment of Homosexuality" (1981) is more militant, in spite of its modest subtitle: "Some Technical Considerations." Technical considerations indeed! Mitchell is very careful—I think rightly (certainly for strategic reasons and probably also for reasons of empirical accuracy)—to note at the beginning that he is not writing about most analysts:

> Most psychoanalysts approach homosexual material produced by their patients as they would any other experiences of their patients—simply as material to be inquired into and analyzed. Such analysts are not likely to write about psychoanalytic approaches to treating homosexuality, since they would tend to feel that homosexuality does not pose particularly distinctive or unique features in terms of analytic work. (p. 68)

After this disclaimer, however, we get the full force of Mitchell's critique, along with a reminder not only of what analysts did, but also of what they felt undefensive enough to describe in days not so long ago. Mitchell's method here is similar to that in his previous article. He takes directive-suggestive practices and treatments to their logical consequences. Most apparent, he argues, is the distinctly unpsychoanalytic focus, in the case of homosexuality, on behavior rather than on dynamics, the quality of internal experience, and object relationships. With characteristically wry humor, Mitchell notes, "These questions are not often raised, since the behavior, or more concretely, the type of genitals the patient is juxtaposing to his own, is seen as containing all the relevant information" (1981, p. 68).

Thus, in the case of directive-suggestive analysts, if exclusive heterosexuality is achieved, there is no further analytic interest in that sexuality—in, say, the quality of relatedness, defensiveness, or transference meanings. A truly analytic approach, however, should lead the analyst to focus equally (as Freud once suggested) on exclusive heterosexuality. Moreover, the assumption that change is desirable eliminates any possibility that a patient himself will develop and change as a result of genuine analytic inquiry.[4]

Most interestingly, Mitchell uses the then-current theory of the origins of homosexuality against the directive-suggestive approach itself. Since Freud, compliance, submissiveness, and passivity were thought to characterize homosexual character and pathology, yet directive-suggestive treatment

[4] There will be readers of these two pieces who find Mitchell, in spite of his radical challenge to psychoanalytic orthodoxy, still leaning toward a normative heterosexuality—toward implying that a homosexual might decide on his own, as a result of psychoanalysis, to change his sexual orientation, or that a genuine heterosexual orientation might well emerge.

relies, ironically, on just these characteristics. Change in this model involves transference compliance and a patient's adapting surface behavior to conform and submit to the analyst's values. Mitchell's concrete examples, from Ovesey, Hatterer, Bieber, and Socarides, provide us with some of the most horrendous misuses of psychoanalysis we can find in the literature, and it is a mark of the taken-for-grantedness of homophobia in their era than none of these self-respecting analysts hesitated to describe his techniques (by contrast, Freud's notorious busybody interference in his analysands' lives was not something that he put into professional print, though he certainly did not think he had to keep such practices from his correspondents). Ovesey gaslights a patient who confronts him about the patient's (completely accurate) feeling of being forced to relate to women or risk the analyst's displeasure, and Hatterer does the same in his response to a patient who notices his analyst's excited animation at hints that he is changing his sexual orientation. Hatterer actually turns his patient's observation into a further attack on the patient. Bieber enumerates all the behavioral indices of cure and then counts his cure rate.

Such clinical examples make the reader's hair stand on end, but if it were not at the cost of a real person's life, she would have to laugh as she read Mitchell on Socarides. Socarides describes drawing diagrams of heterosexual intercourse for his homosexual patients, and he claims that a patient's dream, just before his first experience of heterosexual intercourse, that Socarides was on top of him, was in fact a positive indication of the patient's growing heterosexuality. Socarides takes at surface value the patient's emphasis that both patient and analyst were clothed, and he interprets the dream as expressing the patient's coming to experience the analyst as a good father with whom he can identify.

Mitchell argues that heterosexual, like homosexual, behavior can be motivated by compliance and passivity, especially in the case of a homosexual patient more or less bullied into heterosexual behavior by his analyst. Somehow, these analysts all convinced themselves, as Mitchell puts it,

> that heterosexual behavior (no matter its origins) is invariably motivated by a genuine erotic responsiveness, arising spontaneously, and not influenced by other motivational processes, in contrast to homosexual behavior, which is assumed to be motivated either by non-erotic, pre-genital motivations, or else by a defensive retreat from a more basic heterosexual erotism. (p. 72)

Here, Mitchell advocates following Anna Freud, who "suggests that classification be made not in terms of the overt behavior, but in terms of the fantasy, active or passive, accompanying the act, consciously or unconsciously" (p. 72), and he advocates extending these criteria to all sexual behavior.

The analyst's focus should be "on the fantasies and internal relatedness to the major significant object, including the analyst" (p. 72).

Mitchell's case examples in his second paper again document his argument. He shows how a heterosexual "cure" from the first analysis of Mr. A was based on passive compliance toward the analyst and a repetition of problematic configurations in relation to the patient's mother. Pathology was retained and reproduced, but the "priest and policeman" analyst, interested in "establishing ethical norms and inducing people to act in conformity with these norms" (p. 77), neither noticed nor cared. The patient's homosexuality had indeed condensed and expressed a number of problematic object ties, but his heterosexual "cure" did not address these at all.

Mitchell returns to Freud, as he argues for the centrality of insight over (what was, in the case of the directive-suggestive analysts, unconscionable and not unintentional) influence and for the working through of the transference, in order to enable structural change. He concludes, sounding still like a traditional American early 1980s analyst rather than the postmodern relational analyst that he became, "If psychoanalysis is to remain the most radical form of human transformation, it must rest on value-free inquiry" (p. 79).

I barely knew Stephen Mitchell; we met only two or three times. My sense about several of his last writings—Mitchell's combining of relational and Kleinian thinking in *Hope and Dread in Psychoanalysis* (1993); his writings on Loewald, Fairbairn, and Bowlby in *Relationality* (2000)—was of uncanny recognition of a cognate mind, of papers I had on my computer, in press, or in my head. I do not know if this experience was widespread, as it may well have been, given this extraordinary thinker whose ideas everyone would want to share and claim. My experience rereading these early papers only increased my sense of identification and of sadness: Like me in my writings in the 1970s that challenged psychoanalytic orthodoxies in the case of femininity, Mitchell was a 30ish American who was a theoretical synthesizer, drawing from object-relations theory and ego psychology as necessary and interested in the social and cultural surround, who took on psychoanalytic orthodoxies of theory and practice in the case of homosexuality while remaining respectful of and committed to psychoanalysis. What a fine colleague we have lost!

Chapter 6

Gender on the modern/postmodern and classical/relational divide

Untangling history and epistemology

In March, 2004, I participated at the Division 39 meetings, along with Helen Gediman and Adrienne Harris, on a panel on the history and epistemology of psychoanalytic gender theory and the psychology of women and our own identities within these. One orienting framework was a proposed tripartite periodization—premodern, modern, and postmodern—of psychoanalytic gender theory and the psychology of women. *Premodern* encompassed theories, beginning with early Freud, that create false binaries and make masculinity and male development the norm. *Modern* gender theory gives a separate gender and genital identity and line of development to women. *Postmodern* theory disrupts the gender binary and claims that there is no innate gender. These tendencies overlap different periods in the histories of psychoanalysis and feminism, as well as differentiating classical and relational analysts.

The panel gave me an opportunity not only to locate myself—characteristically, in the middle, as modern/postmodern and classical/relational—but also to express a private passion, my chagrin at a tendency for psychoanalysts to be isolated from main currents of academic thought and to write and speak about such currents without knowing the literature. In the case at hand, defining as premodern any theory or approach within psychoanalysis seemed to ignore mainstream historical periodization and the literary, social scientific, and historical fields that substantively characterize and differentially compare the premodern and the modern. Passions are not fully rational. Thus, it is no surprise that my tone in parts of the chapter is emphatic and even intemperate.[1]

How do we conceptualize the history and character of psychoanalytic thinking about gender, and how does each of us who works in the field situate himself or herself within it? My reflections here address and reflect two divides, most explicitly that between modern and postmodern, but also

[1] An earlier version of this chapter appeared in *Journal of the American Psychoanalytic Association*, *53*(4), 2005, pp. 1097–1118. Reprinted with permission.

that between classical and relational.[2] In this chapter, I attempt, sometimes focusing on trends in my own work, to unpack and disentangle these two divides, which themselves seem to overlap in an easily observed though not universal tendency among practitioners, in which classical analysts seem to be more modernist, whereas relational analysts lean toward postmodernism. Our project, I suggest, requires distinguishing the different nature of each divide, even as they are in empirical observation intertwined. It also requires distinguishing periodization from epistemology.

Overlapping historically with feminism itself, psychoanalytic thinking about gender has two periods of efflorescence, the 1920s, 1930s, and early 1940s and the contemporary period beginning in the 1970s. Two divides have characterized our gender thinking, the modern/postmodern and the classical/relational. From the early theorizing of the 1920s and 1930s until around the early 1990s, most psychoanalytic thinking about gender should be considered modernist, as it draws on traditional views of scientific evidence and holds more universalistic and dichotomized conceptions of men and women. A few historical outliers of postmodernism can be found before the 1990s. In the contemporary period, although postmodernism tends to be associated with relational psychoanalysts and modernist thinking with classical analysis, the divisions overlap. To consider any psychoanalytic theory as "premodern" is misleading: From its inception, psychoanalysis formed part of modernism.

WHY EARLY PSYCHOANALYTIC GENDER THEORY IS NOT PREMODERN

I begin with some extended remarks about why I consider it inaccurate and confounding of an already complex reality to think, as have my colleagues, in terms of a tripartite premodern/modern/postmodern history to psychoanalytic thinking about gender.[3] Such remarks take us by necessity

[2] We are all much clearer about what we mean by relational than by classical, which can have, as I note in the discussion here, both historical and comparative meanings. In this chapter, except where noted, I use classical comparatively, to refer to analysts trained in the institutes of the American Psychoanalytic Association—broadly, ego psychologists—in contrast to relational approaches and relational analysts. The often-used term "mainstream" is unmoored from the specifics of theory and technique and simply reflects, from within the hegemonic center, the politics and history of American psychoanalysis (see Chodorow, 2004a). "Ego-psychological" seems too narrow to capture the contemporary identities of many "mainstream" analysts and institutes.

[3] Gediman (2001, 2005) originally proposed the periodization in 2001 and made it central to our subsequent exchange. Harris (2005b) borrows the periodization but does not make it critical to her account. The literary critic and feminist theorist Stimpson (2005) agrees with my critique. She says, "Harris adapts Gediman's reperiodization. Chodorow does not. Nor do I, believing that Gediman misuses the concepts of premodern and modern" (p. 1120).

to epistemology and the history of thought, which I hope to help illuminate for the specific case of psychoanalysis.

Psychoanalysis is from the outset a preeminently, perhaps exemplary, modern practice and theory, modern and modernist in both 18th- and late 19th-century forms.[4] It arose in the late 19th century, in a period sometimes considered to be the apogee of modernity and modernism, contemporaneously with modernism in the arts and literature.[5] It is rooted also in many elements of an 18th-century Enlightenment thinking and praxis that almost definitionally instituted philosophical and sociopolitical modernity historically and that separated modernity from the premodern. In its rejection of the premodern, Enlightenment thinking focused on the (bourgeois) individual creating himself instead of being inserted by God into a fixed place in the sociopolitical world. As exemplified in the French and American Revolutions, such thinking encompassed emancipatory goals in general and in particular the notion that freedom comes from reason and thought. Similarly, Freud centered the psychoanalytic project on individuals creating and re-creating themselves in analysis and freeing themselves from internal fetters through self-observation and self-understanding.

The premodern-to-modern transformation also encompasses the rise of a scientific, research-and-evidence-based weltanschauung, rather than one based on religion, and here again, psychoanalysis locates itself with the former.[6] In Lecture 35 of the *New Introductory Lectures*, "The Question of a *Weltanschauung*," Freud (1933) contrasts the religious, prescientific point of view with the scientific perspective of psychoanalysis. He makes clear that for him, psychoanalysis was certainly (or certainly aspired to be) a modern science. Of subsequent psychoanalytic debates also, it can safely be said that no historical or contemporary epistemological debate about psychoanalysis (here and now vs. there and then; construction and narrative vs. history and development; hermeneutics or art vs. science; medical science vs. social science; etc.) takes a stand with what we conventionally call premodern.

Finally, Freud's theory of the mind is consonant with, and part and parcel of, other late 19th- and early 20th-century definitionally modernist portrayals, especially that of Nietzsche, who described a psychological individual torn between Apollonian and Dionysian impulses, anguished, and prone

4 For help in thinking about modernism and modernity, I am indebted to Elizabeth Abel and Gabriel Chodorow-Reich.

5 The journal *Modernism/Modernity* claims to address artistic and literary currents and social and intellectual history from 1860 to the present.

6 To cite entire fields that discuss the rise of Enlightenment thinking and modern science, as well as the library of works that differentiate modernism from postmodernism, is well beyond the scope of this chapter. For books that focus specifically on the rise of a modern individuality and individualism that could be thought to set the stage for psychoanalysis, see Heller, Sosna, and Wellbery (1986) and Taylor (1989).

to resentment. Similarly, modernist pictorial arts, contemporaneous with Freud, rendered unconscious forces and psychic fragmentation, while composers disrupted the tonalities and chord structures of the 18th and early 19th century and in their operas, as we see forcefully in Wagner, portrayed their characters' internal drives and conflicts. All of these forms signal and reflect the "Freudian" internally divided, decentered, self-critical, and drive-impelled individual. Contemporaneously, in modern social theory, we find psychological conceptions like Durkheim's anomie and Weber's iron cage and routinization of charisma.

Even as it is the culmination of the Enlightenment focus on the reasoning, self-understanding individual and exemplifies a fin-de-siècle modernist understanding of mind, elements in this fin-de-siècle modernism, as in psychoanalysis, also implicitly point to and articulate what we now consider to be a postmodern critique of identity. In this context, Freud's is both the culminating modernist and the original, anticipatorily postmodern theory of the individual. The Freudian individual is modern, seeking self-understanding and individuality through self-observation and self-reflection, and postmodern, in being composed of conflicting parts and engaged in primary and secondary process thought and repression and splitting of the ego, all these going on at the same time, all incompatible or incommensurate one with the other.[7]

In the arena of gender and sexuality also, Freud is modern. He from the outset describes a radical male/female divide and fixed developmental trajectory. He is also anticipatorily postmodern, claiming that all people have homosexual and heterosexual components of identity and desire and masculine and feminine identities that all repress and express one another (see Chapter 2).[8] Freud thus founded the modern Enlightenment science of individuality, and he at the same time established, along with fin-de-siècle modernism, that the individual is divided, set upon internally by sexual and aggressive drives, and conflicted.[9]

There is only one cluster of ways, I believe, in which psychoanalysis could be said occasionally to participate in premodern thinking. Like practitioners in all fields, and against his officially stated views, Freud sometimes allows

---

[7] As I read the literature, these very elements, which for contemporary psychoanalysts may point toward a postmodern psyche, are for literary and cultural critics what defines the psyche of modernity.

[8] On gender, modernism, and modernity, see for example Felski (1994). Felski outlines a debate about the different relations of men and women to modernism and modernity, but it seems to me that either side of the debate as she describes it, as well as the periodization she puts forth, situates psychoanalytic approaches to women within modernity and modernism.

[9] Whether or not we want to call psychoanalytic views of the fragmented and affectively charged subject modernist or postmodern, there is no question that in terms of the perspectivalism and relativist views of truth that define postmodern epistemology, Freud, just as he was not premodern, was not postmodern. In his *Weltanschauung* lecture, Freud excoriates contemporary trends toward epistemological relativism and the critique of evidence-based science (1933, p. 176).

unsubstantiated pretheoretical assumptions to enter his theorizing. More explicitly, he takes a premodern, religious stance when he lays out criteria of belief—"shibboleths"—without which people cannot call themselves adherents of psychoanalysis. Finally, he has himself sometimes been treated, like premodern priests and rulers, as infallible. In spite of these exceptions, however, I suggest that conceptualizing psychoanalytic thinking about any subject in terms of a tripartite premodern/modern/postmodern history creates an idiosyncratic and inaccurate historical periodization divorced from conventional academic usage. Moreover, it conflates history with epistemology, and it ignores the basic premises and historical location of psychoanalysis itself.[10]

To apply this general observation of the modernist character of classical psychoanalysis to the problem of gender, we can look back on the modernist scientific epistemology of one of the most important early women writers on the subject. In her remarkable and original article, "The Evolution of the Oedipus Complex in Women" (1927), Jeanne Lampl-de Groot can be said to have discovered the psychic significance of the girl's preoedipal attachment to her mother and of the negative Oedipus complex. Her article formed the primary basis for Freud's radical reformulation of the theory of female sexuality (1931). Lampl-de Groot's theory, like that of all the early writers, exhibits one indisputable characteristic of modernism: respect for science and evidence. In a paragraph that begins, "This view confirms Freud's hypothesis," she puts forth a modest suggestion: "But, in contradistinction to Freud, we are assuming that the castration complex in female children is a secondary formation and that its precursor is the negative oedipal situation" (p. 12). Lampl-de Groot elaborates upon her observation and theory and gives two case vignettes as evidence in support of her claim.

We can find in Lampl-de Groot's article also a premodern tinge that exemplifies my earlier claim. Before putting forth her own ideas, Lampl-de Groot spends ten pages reviewing and approving of Freud's previous theory (Freud, needless to say, did not reciprocate when he later drew upon Lampl-de Groot's article). Here, in her submission to an almost religious authority and her implication that Freud is infallible, but not in the method or content of her theory itself, is a premodernism—a submission to him that Freud, in spite of his ostensible commitment to science, was not averse to in his followers. We find such submission and lack of questioning of authority in much of the early writing on women, especially in those writings by women who were analyzed by Freud (see, e.g., Bertin, 1982, on

[10]Levy (2004) warns against the "splendid isolation" that threatens psychoanalysis when it remains uninformed by relevant intellectual currents. In the present case, I worry that arbitrarily identifying particular substantive psychoanalytic points of view on gender as premodern, modern, and postmodern or identifying as premodern one substantive point of view within this late 19th- and early 20th-century field that is thought to have helped define modernism, succumbs to this very danger.

Bonaparte; Deutsch, 1973, Roazen, 1985, and N. L. Thompson, 1987, on Deutsch; and Young-Bruehl, 1988, on Anna Freud).

Except for her obeisance to Freud, then, Lampl-de Groot's account is emphatically modern. And just as it is not premodern, so it is not postmodern. Lampl-de Groot grounds her claims in evidence from her patients. She does not draw from personal, non-clinical experience. She assumes that there is a general developmental story that applies to "the girl," rather than making claims, as might a postmodernist, for many gender or sexual narratives, although she does (anticipating Freud, 1931) describe three possible outcomes of the girl's conflicts. She does not challenge the masculine-feminine binary, and she does not argue that there is nothing innate to gender, sexuality, or object choice. Nor is Lampl-de Groot interested in history, culture, language, or power. Although we do not know this from the text, Lampl-de Groot is typical of women of her psychoanalytic generation in that she did not hold the second-wave feminist belief that the theoretical is personal (let alone political). In an interview in the early 1980s, when I asked her explicitly if thinking about herself or her daughters had contributed to her radical reformulation, Lampl-de Groot said, "No, it was only in thinking about my patients."

Like Lampl-de Groot, all of the 1920s and 1930s gender and sexuality writers are basically modernist and not premodern, whether beginning from the presence or absence of the penis, or, as Horney, from a proto-primary femininity theory—though we can find a few postmodern elements here and there. Lampl-de Groot, for example, points toward a perspectival view of evidence when she notes that the patients she discusses were unable to progress with male analysts. Joan Riviere (1929) alone among early theorists could perhaps be said to be postmodern, as she shifts epistemological focus and tells her readers, disingenuously and playfully, that womanliness is both a masquerade and the real thing. It is only in the contemporary period, and then not from the beginning of second-wave feminist rethinking but from perhaps the late 1980s, that we can speak accurately of postmodern as distinct from modernist trends.[11]

[11]In Gediman's original division, as I note earlier, premodernity adhered to theories that took male development and sexuality as the norm, whereas primary femininity theory, beginning with Horney but found mainly in writings beginning in the 1970s, was modern. Gediman further linked "modern" primary femininity theory with the "women's liberation" movement of the 1970s, which she contrasted with "second-wave feminism," which undergirded postmodern gender theory. The problem here, again one of splendid isolation, is that second-wave feminism refers precisely to the women's movement that began in the 1970s—second wave in contrast to the 19th and early 20th century "first wave." Primary femininity theories, postmodern theories, and most of the critiques and developments of the last 40 years arose originally out of second-wave feminism (see Chapter 1).

Women analysts of the second and third generations who contributed to the literature of the 1920s and 1930s were affected, if at all, by first-wave suffragist or socialist feminism of the 19th and early 20th centuries, as well as by the greater sexual liberalism of the post-Victorian era (see, e.g., Deutsch, 1973, on her socialist roots, and Meisel & Kendrick, 1985, on the Bloomsbury cultural and sexual radicalism of the Stracheys).

As these mid-second-wave feminist developments occur, we can begin usefully to map the modern/postmodern onto the classical/relational divide. Before beginning, however, we need briefly to consider a second confusing entanglement. Like premodern/modern/postmodern, classical and relational have both historical and theoretical referents. In the United States, we are used to thinking of ego psychology, in all its contemporary derivatives, and the institutes of the American Psychoanalytic Association, as classical, which we contrast to relational psychoanalysis and the relational institutes (in much of the rest of the world our "classical," because it is ego-psychological, is distinctly anticlassical).

But we also contrast classical with contemporary. In this historical sense, all of the 1920s and 1930s European Freudians, as well as those founding cultural school and interpersonal analysts who wrote about women, Karen Horney and Clara Thompson, could be considered classical. We can thus contrast "classical" thinkers, whether Freudian or interpersonal, with contemporary thinkers who locate themselves in the current period as either classical or relational (we also provide a history for relational writing that can go missing when we assume that "classical" psychoanalysis has a history but that relational psychoanalysis emerged from nowhere).

Yet, although we might imagine that relational analysts would be more likely to incorporate the work of the historically classical interpersonalists, those like Horney, Thompson, and Mabel Blake Cohen who pointed to the cultural beliefs and social and interpersonal experiences that explain penis envy and women's devalued sense of self, whereas ego-psychologically trained analysts might have been more likely to have continued to emphasize, following Freud, Deutsch, and others, the drives and the sexual-reproductive body in gender formation and experience, none of these distinctions is firm. There is no contemporary classical thinker who ignores culture and no contemporary relational thinker who ignores the body (or the ego).[12]

In terms of historical periodization, then, instead of premodern, modern, and postmodern, it is more accurate to say that there is a classical period of psychoanalytic thinking about women, mainly in the 1920s and 1930s with a few outliers in the early 1940s, and a contemporary period. This classical period includes those who follow Freud in making the penis cen-

[12]In our original roundtable discussion, Harris suggested that I was the subject of a possible custody war between classical and relational analysts. Similarly, I would suggest that among historically classical analysts, Horney, especially, lends herself to such custody disputes. Horney from the outset intertwined in her thinking a psychic and physical primary femininity based on the reality of the primary female genitals, vagina and clitoris, with what she called a non-defensive primary penis envy, based on the reality of observability and exhibitionistic urination. She conceptualized a non-derivative feminine form of the Oedipus complex and castration fears. She insisted on the primary importance of motherhood, including suckling the infant. Finally, well before she joined the ranks of the neo-Freudians, she developed a critique of the patriarchally charged nature, cultural and personal, of Freud's own thinking (see Horney, 1967).

tral to everyone's psychological gender and sexuality and those like Klein, Jones, and Horney, who, wherever they stood on penis envy, also developed variations of what we might call a proto-primary femininity theory that acknowledged in different ways the female-generated psychic reality of the female body and the female Oedipus complex. Finally, there are those who, like Horney and Thompson, add consideration of the role of culture in shaping psychologies of femininity and masculinity. With the exception of Riviere, all of these classical theorists are modernist when it comes to how they reason, their attitudes toward evidence, how they conceptualize the psyche, and what they think.

To turn to post-1970s contemporary thinking, both phallic monism theories, which certainly inspired the eminently modernist scientific research of Roiphe and Galenson (1981) and whose contemporary vestiges can be found in Lacanian-inspired "sexual difference" thinking (see, e.g., Matthis, 2004; Mitchell & Rose, 1982), and primary femininity theory, which has classical roots in Horney, Jones, and Klein, although it was developed more fully in the contemporary period (see, e.g., Bernstein, 1990; Mayer, 1986), are, in terms of their epistemological bases and their forms of theorizing, modern. They are modernist in that they provide unitary theories of the girl and the boy and in their empirical reliance on evidence. Both positions—phallocentrism and primary femininity—argue from a position that postmodern perspectival feminism, borrowing from Nagel (1986), would claim to be the objectivized "view from nowhere" (see, e.g., Haraway, 1988). Freud's view, that there is only one genital for both boy and girl until puberty, that the psychology of women is driven by penis envy and of men by castration anxiety, that we define masculine as active and feminine as passive, these are all, from our contemporary perspective, incomplete or sexist, but they are not different in kind from the primary femininity theories that originate in the classical period with Horney, Jones, and Klein and that were elaborated even before second-wave feminism by Kestenberg and Stoller.

The phallic monism that begins with Freud, then, is no more premodern than primary femininity theories that make an empirical, clinical argument against Freud's original formulation. Although the latter are an advance in terms of clinical and developmental evidence, primary femininity theories retain Freud's anatomical and developmental determinism. Moreover, with the exception of Kestenberg (1956a, 1956b, 1968), they retain a focus on the external genital as defining of psychological femininity that seems to derive from an attempt to counter the emphasis on the penis (Balsam, 2003, describes the psychoanalytic scotoma toward the pregnant body). The contents of these theories differ, but both universalize about the boy and the girl, and both base their claims on a single element—anatomical construction and its sequelae. We can see a substantive shift, with phallic monism more dominant in the 1920s and 1930s and primary femininity theory in ascendance in the contemporary era, but the epistemology of these theories does not differ.

Some primary femininity and some phallic monism (the term is originally Chasseguet-Smirgel's, 1976) writings from both eras, particularly concerning the question of universalism and unitary gender, anticipate postmodernism. I have mentioned Riviere's sense that womanliness is both real and created. On the side of the phallic determinists, Freud, following Lampl-de Groot, does in fact give us three developmental stories, three non-predictable, individualized integrations or non-integrations of body configuration, identification, and desire regarding the sequelae of penis envy, even if only one constitutes normal femininity, just as he has earlier, in 1905, given us a radically gender-and-sexuality-bending account of the individualized integrations of homosexual and heterosexual desire and masculinity and femininity in everyone.

Primary femininity theory may do better than phallic monism on unitary gender and multiplicity, perhaps because of the actual on-the-ground empirical multiplicity of the female anatomy.[13] This theory, although it holds, like phallic monism, that anatomy is destiny and thus centers itself on the importance of female bodily configuration, nonetheless is drawn to being non-monolithic, perhaps of necessity drawn somewhat toward postmodern. The reader of primary femininity theories finds, alternately, an emphasis on outer genitals—the girl's vaginal opening, vulva, labia, or clitoris—or on inner genitals and inner space. She finds attention to the potential for pregnancy or to the developing breasts. She finds givens at birth and bioanatomical experiences, like breast development, menstruation, pregnancy, and lactation, that are anticipated and represented by the little girl but will only come to fruition in adolescence or adulthood. Primary femininity theories describe many elements in female bodily experience, each of which will have its own trajectory and its own combination with other elements, and they emphasize, in contrast to the monolithic phallocentrism of penis envy, different kinds of experience—diffuseness of genital representation, anxiety and fear of penetration or of being closed over, fantasies about pregnancy or the uterus, and so forth (see, e.g., Balsam, 1996, 2003; Bernstein, 1990; Elise, 1997; Holtzman & Kulish, 1996; Mayer, 1986, 1995; Notman, 2003; Pines, 1993; Richards, 1996).

[13]Of course, in our assumption that female sexual and reproductive anatomy is more complex, physically and psychically, than male sexual and reproductive anatomy, we may again be in the realm of premodern authority, still in thrall to Freud's ignoring of other aspects of male genital anatomy than the penis itself, instead of engaging in our own observations of psychic fantasy (for some challenge to Freud's position, see Fogel, 1998; Limentani, 1984).

FROM THE SECOND GENERATION TO THE SECOND WAVE: THE DEVELOPMENT OF MODERN AND POSTMODERN THOUGHT

American feminism in the early 1970s bequeathed us a dual attitude toward psychoanalysis. On the one hand, it introduced into politics, as previous social movements had not done, the idea that feelings are important. It argued that much of what women suffered was not in the sphere of the workplace or the public realm, but rather in women's feeling objectified, devalued, ignored, and confused about their sexuality and desires. It addressed personal relations in the family and between women and men as worthy of political attention and redress. On the other hand, even as the "personal" was "political," all of these feelings were seen as externally caused by the social relations of male dominance, and Freud was the enemy.

Yet a few of us thought things were more complicated and that we had better find a theory that helped us understand them. My own first foray into understanding the psyche, "Being and Doing" (1971), drew from psychological anthropology and sociology, both rooted in psychoanalysis, though I did not know at the outset how much. By the time that paper was published, I had read all of the classical writings on women, as well as a lot of Freud. During the same period, the leading British New Left feminist theorist, Juliet Mitchell, turned to psychoanalysis to understand male dominance and family relations (Mitchell, 1974). Our trajectory was mirrored by a few other outsider-newcomers. Gayle Rubin's still-remarkable article "The Traffic in Women" (1975) drew feminist attention to the preoedipal girl's prohibited lesbian love for her mother and the unnamed invisibility of the same-sex incest taboo, and Dorothy Dinnerstein's apocalyptic *The Mermaid and the Minotaur* appeared in 1976.

Meanwhile, the 1920s–1930s writings on women began to resurface, though not because of attention from "mainstream" analysts. The Sullivanian analyst J. B. Miller published the anthology *Psychoanalysis and Women* in 1973, which was followed by *Women and Analysis* (Strouse, 1974), an anthology of classic papers with new introductions, almost half by clinicians. My own 1971 paperback copy of Clara Thompson's collected papers, *On Women*, opens to a page asking, in large boldface type, "**IS WOMAN A CASTRATED MAN?**" Miller's cultural psychoanalytic *Toward a New Psychology of Women* appeared in 1976. In most of these writings, by clinicians and non-clinicians alike, there is a sense that the theorist is generating theory through internal conviction, seeing connections among different levels of empirical reality (the psyche, the sociocultural, the historical), and rereading, with a feminist eye, psychoanalytic accounts of "gender-y" issues (the psychologies of men and women, sexuality, the Oedipus complex, observations of mothers and fathers) in novel ways.

I describe this early history in the context of considering the relations between psychoanalytic theories of gender, the intellectual and political époques and settings in which these develop, and the personal biographies of those who create these theories. Second-wave feminism in general, and the specific contributions of the 1970s in particular, instigated reconsideration both at the margins and at the center of psychoanalysis. With the exception of Miller, all of the second-wave interventions arrived from outside clinical psychoanalysis (and Miller herself was certainly outside the mainstream of American psychoanalysis—and perhaps, I do not know, outside the Sullivanian mainstream as well). The non-clinician Strouse had solicited contributions from Person and Stoller, two "mainstream" (though not mainstream in their focus on gender) analysts, as well as from Erik Erikson.

All of these interventions occurred in the midst of a discontinuous historical trajectory that, with the rise of renewed psychoanalytic attention to women in the 1970s, mirrors the two waves of feminism itself. This trajectory began with the foundational, though contested, 1920s and 1930s papers of Freud, Lampl-de Groot, Brunswick, Deutsch, Riviere, Horney, Klein, and others. The two waves of feminism and psychoanalytic interest in women were separated by Fliegel's (1986) "quiescent interval" (p. 17), broken only by those I have come to call the "lone voices" of Kestenberg (1956a, 1956b, 1968), Chasseguet-Smirgel (1964) and her colleagues, and Stoller (1965, 1968). Of the second generation, Benedek and Bibring also stand out during this quiescent period as having continued their interest in the psychosexuality, especially the reproductivity, of women (Benedek, 1952, 1973; Bibring, 1959; Bibring, Dwyer, Huntington, & Valenstein, 1961).

All of this changed in the 1970s. The upsurge of theorizing and feminist politics from the margin generated a strong response from the center. We are not, here, in the realm of modernist "normal science," with theories revised mainly on the basis of new evidence, but in the realm of the sociology and politics of knowledge. A first response included, most notably, the 1976 supplement on women of the *Journal of the American Psychoanalytic Association*, Chasseguet-Smirgel's ground-breaking naming of and challenge to phallic monism (1976), and Notman and Nadelson's multivolume *The Woman Patient* (1978, 1982; Nadelson & Notman, 1982). As we consider the sociology and politics of knowledge, we notice that with the exception of Kestenberg, those within American psychoanalysis who seem earliest and most consistently to be considering gender in new ways—Stoller, Nadelson and Notman, Person (whose extensive reconsiderations begin in the early 1970s and continue throughout the 1980s and later; see Person, 1999)—all come from psychoanalytic communities closely tied to universities, presumably closer to the challenge and ferment of feminism. Contemporaneously with this beginning psychoanalytic rethinking, several second-wave feminists, including Juliet Mitchell, Jessica Benjamin, Jane Flax, Muriel Dimen, Adrienne Harris, and myself, all went into psychoanalytic training.[14]

This historical/theoretical trajectory of feminist psychoanalytic thinking and the contemporaneous training of theorists maps onto the history of psychoanalysis, depending on whether training was classical or relational. It also divides generational cohorts. In terms of periodization, I take these 1970s/early 1980s interventions to have initiated the contemporary period of psychoanalytic thinking. They followed chronologically from, and in some cases drew upon, the lone voices, but we were not, I believe, aware of the importance of these voices as opening revisionist salvos.[15] Along with the rest of the psychoanalytic world, we saw the debates as shaped by the 1920s–1930s contributions, all basically modern in their approach, and either classically drive/body based or, in the cases of Horney and Thompson, also drawing on culture.

In the contemporary period, the divisions classical/relational and modern/postmodern begin to have substantial salience. But before we parse these distinctions, a necessary word on culture. Classical psychoanalysis is supposedly more intrapsychic and innatist than relational psychoanalysis, and it is certainly the case that classical rethinking has focused, inter alia, on the body, whereas relational thinking, initiated by political feminists who became analysts, has made more central the internalized psychopolitics of male dominance, as well as the intrapsychically constitutive and continuously reemerging and shifting role of family-child and analyst-patient interaction and relation. Yet, like Freud, all contemporary classical (i.e., "mainstream") theorists think that culture helps to shape sexuality and gender and has had as well an impact on psychoanalysis.[16] When we contrast *relational* and *classical* in the current period, then, differentiation does not inhere mainly in the view of culture, but in more subtle distinctions about focus, primacy of interest or emphasis, and clinical modalities.

As you begin to have classical, in the sense of "mainstream" ego-psychological, in contrast to "relational" psychoanalysis and theories

[14]Virginia Goldner is obviously missing from this group of contributors. Goldner had from the outset trained as a clinician.

[15]My personal contact with owners of these lone voices has given me more awareness of their role. In conversation and in her writings, Janine Chasseguet-Smirgel described her sense of having taken up, after decades of complete European silence, the question of femininity. After my two first books, she sought me out as a sympathetic and understanding colleague, as did Robert Stoller. In my interview with her, Judith Kestenberg took great care to explain what her project had been and why it was important. I think as you read Kestenberg—perseverative, long, and emphatic—you also read her sense of isolation and of mission.

[16]I have suggested (Chodorow, 2004a) that psychoanalytic thinkers on women who come from classical training and institutes (writers like Balsam, Bernstein, Holtzman, Kulish, Mayer, Nadelson, Notman, Person, Tyson, and others like them) might be considered, when it comes to gender, "cultural ego psychologists."

of gender, you can also begin to distinguish an overlapping but not congruent development of modern and postmodern strands. An overview of trends in my own thinking can help us see the ways that modern and postmodern elements have played out in our literature.

First, characteristic of my second-wave feminist generation (including the postmodern relational feminists), my early forays were extremely leery and suspicious of any acknowledgment of the sexed body. Here we see, I think, a distinct contrast with the medically trained early second-wave feminist psychoanalytic thinkers like Nadelson, Notman, and Person, later Balsam, who were able to distinguish sexist and inaccurate understandings of the body from the importance of the body itself. For those who were not medical, Freud's "essentializing and universalizing," his "anatomy is destiny," had turned most second-wave feminists against him. Even those of us who were fervently psychoanalytic believed that such biologically determinist assumptions had harmed women both inside and outside the field. We argued that cross-cultural and historical empirical investigation documented extensive variation in women's roles and psyches, and that clinical evidence showed created psychological meaning, not biological cause. For Lacanians like Mitchell, language rather than body created the psyche. You could say that we folded our emotions into modernist evidential claims.

Second, for 1970s feminists the personal was not only political. It was also theoretical and epistemological. We measured theories, and developed our own, against personal experience and a critique of power, writing about mothers and daughters, competition among women, intrapsychic lesbian taboos, power and sexuality. This epistemological skepticism and reference to the self constitutes the first "postmodern" input into the psychoanalytic rethinking of femininity. Following the sociology of knowledge, postmodernism claims that knowledge is perspectival, that there is no "view from nowhere" (except, of course, the view that there is no view from nowhere). Contemporaneously, we also borrowed from poststructuralism (often fused with postmodernism, but with its own theoretical roots) and followed Foucault and the early Marx in arguing that power inhered in knowledge. For us, psychoanalytic theory presented not only a masculine perspective but also a masculine perspective that was hegemonic—based in political and sociocultural male dominance. As the postmodern zeitgeist enters psychoanalysis, we can trace a decline in tentativeness in primary femininity and mother-daughter theories (Horney, anything but tentative and dutiful, is the obvious early exception here), from the many qualifications and bracketings with which Lampl-de Groot introduced her radical but carefully clinically grounded observations, to forthright contemporary arguments about phallocentric (or phallologocentric) theory and language.

Calling upon the realm of female *experience*, experience read through clinical observation but drawing explicitly or implicitly on personal affect, outrage, self-observation and observation of non-clinical others, which began with primary femininity theory, came to distinguish all contemporary critiques of historical theories and to some extent all new theories.[17] In this limited sense, all second-wave psychoanalytic thinking is postmodern. It was only second-wave feminism that gave women psychoanalysts permission to begin from their own subjective intuitions in challenging and rethinking established theory, at least without, like Horney, finally being excommunicated. I stress this contrast, in terms of the attempt to sort out modern and postmodern in the present context, without wanting to minimize the gatekeeping that went on. In the 1980s, classically trained women who were taking feminist stances or bringing in culture, like Notman, Nadelson, Zilbach, and Person, were often criticized and dismissed by reviewers in the leading classical journals (personal communications).

Such thinking differentiates the second wave from the second generation. Lampl-de Groot, as she told me, listened to her patients. Margaret Mahler talked extensively about her personal sense of femininity in relation to her mother, but when I asked if she had thought about the theory of femininity in relation to herself, she said, "It didn't go through my brain." They did not—Horney's (1926, p. 60) famous self-reference, "I, as a woman, ask in amazement, and what about motherhood?" is the exception here—use themselves, except clandestinely, to think about the psychology of women. When they did, as we now know was the case for Anna Freud, Deutsch, Riviere, Klein, Bonaparte, and others, they disguised themselves in modernist garb, as "cases." Like other early writers, Lampl-de Groot may have turned herself into "an acquaintance, the mother of two girls" (1927, p. 6).

Reflexivity and a perspectival epistemology, then, exemplify the first postmodern input into the rethinking of femininity. Experience and perspective in turn led to a second postmodern step. Even while epistemologically critical of the masculinist perspective, most psychoanalytic writings of the 1970s and 1980s retained a gender binary and a unitary conception of each gender, describing men and women, the boy and the girl, the mother and the father. By contrast, recent classical as well as relational writings suggest that there are many masculinities, femininities, and sexualities and that each person's psychic gender and sexuality are clinically unique and individual (even the *Revue Française de Psychanalyse* used the plural in titling a 2003 issue, "The Homosexualities").

This challenge, requiring a focus on individual differences, multiplicity, and shifting partial identifications, came from both feminism and postmodernism. Academic and political feminism demanded: How can you generalize about women when there are women of different colors, sexual orientations, ethnicities, and cultures? Postmodernism asked: How can you

[17]Notice, for example, Mayer's (1986) title "'Everybody Must Be Just Like Me,'" and her opening vignette of a little girl, not a patient.

talk about "femininity" when identities are partial, fragmented, situated, and overlapping? Such challenges influenced classical and relational thinkers differently, but there is no easy divide.

Thus, we can locate the classical/relational divide, defined by training, identity, and institute affiliation, more easily than the modern/postmodern divide, which is appropriated differently by different contemporary writers (and sometimes differently by the same writer). Benjamin, a prominent relational analyst, has developed a complex but more binary and generalizing theory, in which there is "identification with difference" and postoedipal gender, but in which the meanings of masculine and feminine, the roles of mother and father, and an emphasis on sexual difference remain (see, e.g., Benjamin, 1995). The relationally trained Elise (1997) is a leading contemporary primary femininity thinker who argues for the psychic sequelae of bodily configuration. By contrast, the relational analysts Dimen (2003), Goldner (1991, 2003), and Harris (2005a) locate partial identities, uneasy compromises, and combinations at the heart of multiple genders and sexualities, while the independent hybrid political philosopher and clinician Flax (1990) explicitly addresses the intersections of psychoanalysis, postmodernism, and feminism.

Among classically trained analysts, we find similar variation. The classically trained analysts Schuker (1996) and Tyson (1996) claim that there are many paths toward female development. By contrast, the classical Kulish and Holtzman portray a more unitary developmental reformulation (Holtzman & Kulish, 2000; Kulish & Holtzman, 1998, 2008).

There is a further distinction among those who draw on postmodern assumptions. Some in the postmodern camp favor performative gender-bending theory and use playful alliterative language. Others who draw on postmodernism are without skepticism toward straightforwardly presented evidence and do not challenge modernist language, but they nonetheless make empirical arguments for epistemological perspectivalism, as well as for clinically observed, multiple, partial, overlapping facets of identity and psyche. Classical analysts, it seems to me, find themselves closer to the body and focus on its innately propelled fantasies and desires. For them, the intrapsychic forms primary clinical reality. Relational analysts are, by contrast, more likely to conceptualize the body and psychic life as interactionally co-constructed. So also, those who begin from a classical identity and training tend more toward a traditional, modern use of language and evidence, whereas those who have a more relational identity also find themselves drawn to postmodern epistemology and language.[18]

[18]These stylistic differences can easily be found by comparing the tables of contents of the *Journal of the American Psychoanalytic Association* and the *Psychoanalytic Quarterly* with *Psychoanalytic Dialogues* and *Studies in Gender and Sexuality*.

My own self-location in the modern epistemological and linguistic camp, even as I agree with what I have defined as foundational postmodern claims for perspective and multiplicity, arises from several sources. My clinical work with patients, probably sustained by classical ego psychological training, has led to a rethinking that accords more recognition to the actual body and its determinative importance in psychic life. I worry less than formerly about anatomy being destiny, and here I am very much in the classical tradition. I now think that bodies, especially our sexual and reproductive bodies—primary and secondary sex characteristics from birth and throughout the developments of adolescence; reproductivity; the erotogenic zones that Freud described; libido and drive—that all of these experiences intrinsically demand psychic and fantasy elaboration and representation and are likely to get embroiled in conflict.

I am substantively both modernist and postmodern in this anatomical determinism. I go with an empirically discovered clinical individuality and hold that the conflicts, fantasies, psychic elaborations, and representations that constitute this will not be the same for everyone. I claim, rather, that elaborations of sexed and gendered body intertwine with all aspects of psyche, and that identity is shaped through contradiction, conflict, and compromise formation (compromise formation is perhaps a preeminently postmodern, if also a preeminently ego psychological, concept). Sexed and gendered bodies are shaped from birth and even before by the maternal surround. Much as Loewald (1951, 1978) argues about language, or, as we might say with Laplanche (1997), psychosexuality develops and is bathed in the mother's flow of words, fantasy, and body.

But our biological makeup makes a difference. Genitals, breasts, arousal, menstruation, erection, ejaculation, these will all be psychically (and culturally) elaborated in a way that shoulders or feet will not. These elaborations receive a push from our innate psychobiological makeup, however much they are also shaped by the mother's, the father's, and the culture's choices of organs and bodily experiences in which to invest. In contrast to Harris, who claims that primary femininity modernists[19] see a body that is raw and a mind that is cooked, I suggest that contemporary classical and contemporary relational analysts both see body and mind as, in Harris's phrase, "cooking each other" (2005b, p. 1087), and that both agree that part of the seasoning of the soup comes from culture. But we may have different views of the order in which ingredients get added.

The psychoanalytically influenced feminist philosopher of science Evelyn Fox Keller (1987) nicely elaborates this middle ground. She argues against postmodern critiques of empiricism that claim that there is no reality that is out there being studied. Bodily and other physical realities exist

[19]She is following Gediman's formulation here, in which primary femininity theory is construed as "modern."

in the natural world. They are not wholly created or constructed and do not gain meaning only through the discourse that invokes and describes them. However, traditional Enlightenment empiricist assumptions are also inadequate, since naming and discursive practices, including those in the natural sciences—and for our purposes in the family, in the culture, and in psychoanalysis—do help to shape how we conceptualize (and therefore what we think of as) the physical world. There is not just one correct way to observe and understand nature, but nature does constrain and influence our ways of observing and understanding accurately, such that some ways are more adequate than others.

My own perhaps overly driven modernism and unease with postmodernism arises also from my dual historical location in the consulting room and the university. Postmodernism has grown from and is intertwined with the academic humanities, where a related deconstructionism has made an innovative and playful use of language central and in which the favored psychoanalytic theory is Lacanian. In the university, there is a wide split between these postmodern humanities, which are often skeptical, dismissive of, or hostile toward traditional research, and the empirical social and human sciences, among which I locate myself and psychoanalysis. To be pushed toward a strong clinical and theoretical modernism, you have only, as a psychoanalyst, to listen to cultural studies scholars, who have not worked with or witnessed actual patients who suffer, dissociate, or encrypt frozen memories. These scholars draw on psychoanalysis to describe, in richly elaborated reflexive language, "embodiment," torture as a "discursive trope," "traumatic gender aporias," and the ways that "we" appropriate the Holocaust or "figure" suffering. They see "melancholy" as a romanticized Werther-esque 19th-century romantic anguish or sadness about social configurations, rather than referring to the actual pain and terrors of clinical depression.

How to sort out modern/postmodern and classical/relational? In the contemporary period, both classical and relational gender theorists are postmodern: They begin from experience, a freedom to challenge, a view that knowledge is perspectival and embedded in power, and an awareness of the multiple constituents of individual genders and sexualities. They are also modern, relying on clinical evidence and rooting for the individual. My contribution here hopes to help all of us to unpack these overlapping and crosscutting divides—classical/relational and modern/postmodern—these subtle epistemological, theoretical, and methodological distinctions that interact with the contents of theory and the biographical location of theorists, and that have enriched and challenged our attempts to think clinically and theoretically about gender and sexuality.

Part II

Gender and sexuality in consulting room and culture

Chapter 7

Glass ceilings, sticky floors, and concrete walls

Internal and external barriers to women's work and achievement

> For a 2000 conference in Atlanta of the Committee on Women and Psychoanalysis of the International Psychoanalytic Association, "Constructing and Deconstructing Women's Power," I was asked to present on a panel, "The Glass Ceiling: Is It Internal or External?" As I note in the chapter itself, I was a bit cranky about this invitation: Why, after being an analyst, or an analyst-in-training, for 15 years, and having never written on or taught the sociology of work, was I asked to write about an exclusively sociological concept? Nonetheless, as is always the case when you are asked to notice just about anything, I began to notice the various ways that my patients expressed conflicts about themselves in relation to work and to think about how these various forms of expression could help us to make more complex the initially simple concept of the glass ceiling.
>
> Through this lens of the internal and external glass ceiling, I could also think back upon the history of women in psychoanalysis and the second- and third-generation women psychoanalysts whom I had interviewed in the early 1980s. Thus, my work with patients, my research on the history of women in psychoanalysis, and my inadvertently imbibed sociological knowledge enabled me to craft an informal, conversational chapter that could contribute to our understanding of different kinds of conflictual self-limitation and undermining by others particular to women in the workplace.[1]

How is the personal political, or at least economic? How is the economic personal? We begin from the glass ceiling—is it internal or external?—and thereby immediately run into trouble. We tread a fine line, as the very concept under discussion, the glass ceiling, was created precisely to draw attention to external causes. Those who coined the phrase *glass ceiling* meant

[1] An earlier version of this chapter appeared in B. J. Seelig, R. A. Paul, & C. B. Levy (Eds.), *Constructing and Deconstructing Woman's Power* (pp. 18–28). London: Karnac, 2002. Reprinted with permission.

precisely to describe structural and behavioral barriers to women's promotion. The phrase was designed to correct a popular belief, and common corporate defense, that women's lack of upward mobility was caused by fear of success, by noncompetitive values and goals, or by other psychological, internally generated restraints and beliefs.[2]

Of course, the glass ceiling is indeed internal as well as external. To the extent that sociologists and economists have repeatedly and in detail documented its externality, it would seem that we, as psychoanalysts, can really only contribute to an understanding of the ways that glass ceilings are still—though in more complex ways than "fear of success"—also internal. Yet in so doing, we need to be careful. Psychodynamic explanations of being subordinate, or of letting oneself be mistreated, always pose a danger. A focus on internal factors shifts the blame, relieving those with power and authority from the burden of instituting change or acknowledging responsibility.

The term *glass ceiling* began to appear in the mid-1980s. By 1991, the federal government had established a "Glass Ceiling Commission" and instituted the "Glass Ceiling Act," an act designed to punish corporations that discriminated against women in the upper tiers. *Glass ceiling* is an appealing metaphor, carrying with it the sense that what is immediately above—an upper floor, the sky, even—may look reachable but, when a woman tries to reach it, a previously invisible glass barrier turns out to be in the way. In the 1990s, scholars suggested that we also needed to consider glass *walls*—barriers to horizontal mobility across jobs and professions—and other commentators argued that metaphors like *sticky floors* and *concrete walls* better describe the rigidity and tenacity of glass ceilings. In this chapter, I consider a variety of external and internal barriers to achievement in women, beginning with the most blatant forms of discrimination and exclusion from without and moving to examples found in the consulting room of the great variety of gender-inflected personal expressions of self-limitation.

In order to deepen our inquiry, it is perhaps worth extending the concept of glass ceiling to refer to *unnoticed* or *indirect* assumptions and practices in addition to intentional discrimination. Here, I think, psychoanalysis can especially contribute to our understanding of how and why these unnoticed, indirect assumptions and practices operate. Moving from external to internal, on the most blatant level, we can look at those

[2] I am indebted to Christine Williams (personal communication, 2000) for all of the information in this essay on the history of the concept of the glass ceiling and for the alternate metaphors of limitation and self-limitation that I consider here. A psychoanalytic sociologist, Williams has written several books on gender and work (1989, 1995), looking especially at men and women in cross-gender jobs. Williams (1992) coined the term *glass escalator* to describe how quickly men rise to the top in female-dominated professions.

well-documented concrete walls and glass ceilings through which men have, traditionally, simply kept women out: power organizations like male-only clubs or the proverbial locker rooms and golf courses where men conduct business. In explaining the male-bonding dynamics of these venues, and men's need to exclude and belittle women that these venues facilitate, we cannot improve upon Karen Horney's still-powerful psychoanalytic classic, "The Dread of Woman" (1932), or upon the more recent psychoanalytic feminist classic, Dorothy Dinnerstein's *The Mermaid and the Minotaur* (1976).

To move to a slightly less overt dimension of discrimination, I turn to a *New York Times* article written by Natalie Angier (2000), who spoke with women astronomers about the "glass ceiling in the sky." Adding to our cache of metaphors—glass ceiling, glass or concrete walls, sticky floors—the article describes women "leaking out of the pipeline." Of PhDs in astronomy, a larger percentage of men than women receive postdocs; of postdocs, a larger percentage of men than women become assistant professors. According to Angier, the same thing happens in medical schools, as more men than women move from residency to fellowship and then from fellowship to academic track. As Angier describes it, the woman astronomer investigating the glass ceiling in the sky collected testimonies from her colleagues about being ignored in collegial conversations, being asked to do housewife errands for visiting scientists, and being stereotyped as cute little women who could not possibly be interested in scientific puzzles. Angier notes that these are small slights and benign neglect, but that at the same time they are "molehills that gradually accrete into mountains."

Angier (2000) describes a set of conservative responses, rebuttals that return from the external glass ceiling to two "internal" accounts, which she calls the "free choice" and "wilting lily" explanations. First, according to a male scientist informant, women do not succeed in scientific fields because they do not like them, and therefore they do not excel. This is the "free choice" argument. Second, women are "less prone to the intense, cut-throat aggressiveness that usually marks the successful research scientist or engineer." They are, that is, "wilting lilies." Whereas both of these explanations generalize and stereotype, one can see that neither involves straight-out discrimination.

When we turn to our own profession of psychoanalysis, we may be further from outright discrimination and further in the direction of implicit stereotyping and taken-for-granted assumptions. We can note that only two women have run for (and lost) the presidency of the International Psychoanalytical Association (IPA). The IPA has elected only three women as secretary. The American Psychoanalytic Association has elected only three women presidents and appointed only two women as chair of the

Board of Professional Standards (and neither of these latter served in the last 35 years).[3]

We certainly cannot assume that either losses or wins in these psychoanalytic elections were a direct result of a particular candidate's being a woman, and we have also to notice a historically softer glass ceiling in psychoanalysis compared to other professions, one that allowed these few women to run for office in the first place. My own research on the role and impact of second- and third-generation women psychoanalysts elicited an interestingly textured glass ceiling, porous in some places and firm in others (see Chodorow, 1986a, 1986c, 1987, 1989b, 1991b, 1999b). I found that in both Europe and the United States (there is national variation here, including the important British Society-saving compromise presidency of Sylvia Payne, which is beyond the scope of the present inquiry), women were historically overrepresented as training analysts, while they were underrepresented in official leadership positions—presidents of societies, chairs of training committees, and so forth. Fortuitously, in this one role of training analyst, classically the arena of highest prestige in the field, stereotypes about women, and women's own self-identities—as clinicians, people who communicate well orally, teachers and trainers, and nurturers of the next generation—all enabled women to reach the top. In another arena—that of elected or appointed position of power or authority—psychoanalysis had a glass ceiling or, more likely perhaps, a sticky floor. Noting the paucity of women in psychoanalytic politics, some of my women interviewees pointed to two factors: first, that women were uninterested in the arcane and internecine psychoanalytic in-fighting that characterized the profession, and second, that the men did not want women leaders.

Various characterizations spoke to this barely below-the-surface fear of strong women. One American interviewee described the "little patriarchy" at the Anna Freud Centre. An eminent second-generation British Middle Group man, alongside his profession of great respect for the many women who had been leaders in the history of the British Society, described the Kleinians as a "phalanx of women, and they all wore black." A woman Kleinian concurred: Klein and her colleagues, she claimed, were treated as "an awful regiment of women." This interviewee reported her relief when some men joined the Kleinian ranks. A man trained at the Boston Psychoanalytic Institute in the 1950s described at one point in his interview the terrifying "Boston matriarchy" of Helene Deutsch, Grete Bibring, Beata

[3] 2011 note: This chapter was presented in 2000 and published in 2002. My data on women's participation in psychoanalytic politics have not been updated, and I believe that they still make their point. Paraphrasing the sociologist Rose Laub Coser's paper (1981) on women and work, "Where Have All the Women Gone? Like the Sediment of a Good Wine They Have Sunk to the Bottom," I titled a paper for a Coser festschrift, "Where Have All the Eminent Women Psychoanalysts Gone? Like the Bubbles in Champagne, They Rose to the Top and Disappeared" (Chodorow, 1991b).

Rank, Eleanor Pavenstedt, Helen Tartakoff, and others, and at another point described the same women analysts as a "group of *bubbes*."

A kindly and well-meaning third-generation interviewee, formerly president of the American Psychoanalytic Association and chair of the Board of Professional Standards, claimed that all the women powerhouses with whom he had worked were first and foremost "lovely women." In response to some challenge on my part[4]—chairing the Board of Professional Standards is, after all, the apogee of power in the field—this interviewee insisted that the woman chair of the Board of Professional Standards with whom he had worked closely when he was president "didn't have an ounce of politics in her body."

We cannot know in specific cases if women are "too lovely" to be president of the International or American Psychoanalytic Associations or chair of the Board of Professional Standards, if potential women candidates see themselves as part of an "awful regiment of women," or even if such considerations have had any substantive impact. But we can see in a general way how such attitudes, many of which are not in the first instance directed toward exclusion or channeling, could have contributed to a porous and uneven glass ceiling in the history of psychoanalysis, a glass ceiling fostered internally by women themselves and externally created collaboratively by both women and men.

I found myself, in writing the present chapter, mulling over a personal example, which I bring forth because it comes with an emotional resonance and a potentially unnoticed subtlety that I think is part of the complexity of the glass ceiling as both internal and external. This example—we could call it clinical or countertransferential—shows how unnoticed assumptions, or individually varying assumptions, can subtly perpetuate external glass ceilings or glass walls—in this case, professional, rather than gendered, glass walls.

As I perused the brochure for the "Women and Power" conference for which I had written this chapter, a conference sponsored by several international, national, and local psychoanalytic associations, I noticed that I was listed exclusively as professor of sociology, not as an analyst or as a faculty member at a psychoanalytic institute. I reflected further upon my assignment to a panel on the glass ceiling, a sociological concept, when virtually all of my professional writing, including my several books, has been psychoanalytic—about female psychology and development, maternality, femininities and masculinities, sexualities. With the best of intentions, the conference organizers were clearly picturing me as a sociologist, assuming that I had in addition to, or in spite of, my nearly exclusive track record as a thinker about psychoanalysis and women, some expertise on women

[4] As I describe (Chodorow, 1989b), my interviews were rather overly driven by my feminism. I was not a neutral investigator who listened as openly as I might have done.

and work, and also that being a professor at the University of California at Berkeley was a position of pride and eminence.

We can see here how even the most well-meaning "external" others—and each of us is an external other to some other person's "internal" identity and desires—can, because of preconscious assumptions, contribute to the perpetuation of felt glass ceilings or concrete walls. My own (we could call it) overdetermined professional/personal countertransference reaction was to feel that I could not, finally, ever be accepted as a psychoanalyst.

Thus far, I have suggested that the externality of the glass ceiling moves from blatant, overt exclusion and discrimination to, as in the case of me as a professor of sociology or the "lovely women," subtly stereotyping assumptions by well-meaning others. When we move to internal glass ceilings and walls, sticky floors, or even to concrete ceilings and walls, it is much too simple, I think, to speak of one form of "internal" glass ceiling, as if all women have internalized the same assumptions about legitimate aspirations and ambitions. Rather, we are in the well-investigated realm of conflict, fantasy, and inhibition—internal glass ceilings engaged in by men as well as by women—as well as in the psychoanalytic realm that says that any choice or behavior is a complexly created compromise formation that attempts to manage anxiety or other threatening affects. Internal glass ceilings are produced by many factors—oedipal guilt; anxiety about separation, loss, or castration; or conflicts and self-sabotaging in those wrecked by success. They are produced by the spoiling and self-spoiling powers of envy; by grandiose, narcissistic fantasies that lead to fears of humiliation; by conflict about aggression; by punitive superegos and survivor guilt; and by many other unconscious and conscious fantasies—all of these put together differently by different individuals.

Few psychoanalytic papers address the glass ceiling phenomenon. A classic theoretical and clinical treatment of internal glass ceilings can be found in Joan Riviere's 1929 paper, "Womanliness as a Masquerade." In this paper, Riviere discusses professionally successful women who present themselves in overly feminine ways in their appearance and in their roles as wives and mothers, and she describes women who work to appear incompetent. Women engage in these patterns of conflict and behavior in order to deny and avoid punishment for the fantasy of having achieved success through stealing the father's penis. These successful women want to masquerade, Riviere says, "as guiltless and innocent." In "Some Observations on Work Inhibitions in Women," Adrienne Applegarth (1976) also describes several motivations for an internal glass ceiling, as does Ruth Moulton in "Professional Success: A Conflict for Women" (1986). Recently, Adrienne Harris's "Aggression, Envy, and Ambition: Circulating Tensions in Women's Psychic Life" (1997) describes how internally charged these three affects and desires—aggression, envy, and ambition—are in many women, in relation to issues of separation or of feeling as though one's aggression and envy can displace and kill, and how all of these make achievement with pleasure and without self-punishment difficult.

Thus, any woman's internal glass ceiling is a product of her own subjective gender and sexuality—her conscious and unconscious fantasies about being female, as well as whatever else goes into her internal, affectively charged world and her characteristic fears, conflicts, and defenses. As I reflected on my own practice, I could not think of one person, male or female, in whom the senses of gender or sexuality did not contribute in some way to an internal glass ceiling. I remembered women who felt that to do math well was to be masculine or to invite male aggression; men who could not play sports to the best of their ability or could play only defense well but not offense, for fear of oedipal victory; women who thought that assertion was the same thing as destruction and killing; and so forth. For this chapter, I chose three women, one with an internal glass ceiling, another with an internal sticky floor, and a third with an internal glass wall.

Glass Ceilings. For N, a young woman whom I describe in *The Power of Feelings*, an *internal glass ceiling* was a product of guilt, specifically, guilt at being able to have pleasures and achievements that her mother could not have. N had emigrated as a child with her parents. In their country of origin, both parents had had professions. After emigration, N's father continued his professional participation and development, but her mother became a subservient housewife, coping with her husband's patriarchal demandingness and difficulties in reestablishing himself and with her children's integration into a new culture. N's father worked hard and was critical of his wife, who, as she became depressed, let the household and cooking go and did not pay attention to her own well-being and appearance. In college, N herself did the minimal work necessary to stay in school, but she kept herself from competing for good summer jobs and from shining as a student. After college, she could not take pleasure in her work.

Like other women from patriarchal societies, N "wept for her mother" (see Chodorow, 1999b). She described how she could not make herself food, keep her apartment clean, or pay her bills because she felt guilty for living on her own and having a career. She felt that she should not do these things if her mother couldn't. She reported that almost every time that she found herself enjoying something—partying late, wearing a sleeveless dress, driving alone, even enjoying the beauty of the Bay area—her next thought was "My mother couldn't do this." Then she would feel guilty and sad: She could not take pleasure or be happy in her achievements if her mother was not happy.

Sticky Floors. Finding a clinical example of a *sticky floor* is difficult because the concept itself is sticky. I remembered K, whom I had recently described (1999b) who experienced a tangled stickiness in which so many factors intertwined in her attempts to manage gender, sexuality, and success that unproblematic work and advancement were difficult. K wanted to be successful, but she thought of success as totally masculine. Reflecting back on her childhood, she said: "Images of what it meant to be an admirable person were all male. Or there was the single, lonely, pioneering path to something women don't do, the few successful women, like Jo, in *Little Women*. She's the most interesting character in the book—she's a tomboy; she strides everywhere. There are no men in the book. Her father is away. Then, she's transformed through love into a 'real woman' who's married and has children!"

When I asked about Jo's transformation, K replied, "Defeat! The end of the line! Maturing for women is being transformed in a way that puts a damper on her activity, turns her into a wife and mother. That's all there is: Accept your fate, your limitations. 'Accepting fate' is part of maturity! Being tamed into a wife and mother, giving up fantasies of being powerful, important, and active. The other side is getting a man, of your *very* own! Giving up *being* a man, or the hope of being a man, for *getting* a man. Where are the heroic images of women *as women?* I'm stuck in a desire for heroism, for recognition, acclaim, being admired."

As we looked at her dilemma—that if she finally became an acclaimed and admired hero she would become a man—K said, "I guess it's the only way to get there," and she cried, saying "but then, there's the fear of retaliation. If you're assertive or aggressive—that's me, competitive!—it's also associated with men. In the books, you're a prince. You don't *have* to compete if you're a prince—your position is already assured. In our society, there's competition, and it's frightening."

K once described a meeting made up exclusively of women, and she noted how impressed she was with these women's competence. She said, "it wasn't a kill-or-be-killed model of interaction, but I'm not committed to it. I'm stuck in the kill-or-be-killed model. I didn't know how to behave in that setting. I'm more comfortable in the other—what I gloss as men, but it's not only men. I know how to handle myself in situations with lots of direct challenges to ideas. It doesn't make me happy, but it's involving. I feel prevented from fitting into a more flattened landscape, one without hierarchy. If it's not up or down, on the way up, or on the way down, struggling against being put down, I'll disappear."

K did not have an emotional or intellectual space for competent yet nonhierarchical women, and she felt that her own aspirations and ways of thinking and preferring to interact were masculine. But these aspirations themselves created conflicts. She liked and didn't like the kill-or-be-killed model, and she was always worried that she would be brought down as a woman if she used it. "If you're feminine and passive," she claimed, "you're too weak, not tough enough to be in the world. Dependent." At work, K wanted to be "top man on the totem pole" and "one of the boys," and she wanted acknowledgment and recognition of her position from male coworkers. But the problem was that wanting recognition was itself dependent, putting her right back in the feminine, weak place from which she was trying to escape. It was a lose-lose proposition: a reminder that she was female if she wasn't top man on the totem pole, but a requirement of dependence on men to acknowledge her top-manness, which in turn reminded her of her femininity.

On another occasion, K got herself into a tangle by e-mailing a complaint to her work unit about a sexist remark made by one of her colleagues, because she thought her response was clever and sophisticated. Instantly upon pushing "send," she felt extremely vulnerable and open to humiliation. Feeling that her prose was flashy and sexy had collapsed too readily into feeling that she was displaying herself sexually. K's oscillation between fantasies of intellectual power and flashiness and potentially humiliating sexuality left her continually upset and brought her professional life to a near standstill.

Glass Walls. A session with S portrays an internal glass wall—S's inhibitions about moving from one field to another. S had a full-time job and professional success in the field for which she was originally trained, but she had, for a time, left another secure job in this field to go to graduate school in music. Music was her first love, and she hoped to become a musician and composer, but now, she had stopped playing or writing music. In the session, S was describing how she would let down her boss if she quit her job or went part-time, but that another friend from graduate school had recently told her how much she and her friends had loved S's work, how they wanted to hear more of it. With S, we see someone who has two career identities, and we see a very complicated glass wall—a glass wall that can be seen in even one session's work—that keeps her from the career that she consciously most wishes to pursue.

I asked S if she could just think about music, composing, performing—what images, memories, or fantasies came to mind. Her first association was in Spanish, though she is not a native speaker, to the word *ociosa.* After some reflection, she was able to find the meaning in English, "idle rich." Music, indeed, all the visual and musical arts, were for the idle rich. Her thoughts went from there to a Latino boyfriend, a Marxist who said that only the rich could study the arts, and thence to a Mexican protest song she remembered about an *ociosa* housewife with servants and a landlord husband, who was contrasted in the song with a Jesus-like man who worked to save the poor.

Just as her professional school friends and her current boss represented either side of her music/job dilemma, so S's husband, from a culture in which women don't display themselves, is seen to be the one who keeps her from another expressive form—from singing. S has told me that she has a good voice, and that she used to love to sing in public, but that she doesn't do so anymore. Back to music school, conflict, and being *ociosa*, S said that when she was in graduate school, several students had once remarked that only she and one other student had not gone to conservatories as undergraduates: She and this one other student had not been rich enough to do so. But then she reversed herself, associating to starving artists in garrets in Paris, to *La Bohème*, and to Gauguin, giving up being a banker in order to become an artist in Tahiti.

Another conflictual image surfaced. S had wanted to live a bohemian lifestyle as a musician, but she remembered once seeing a very famous artist in an elevator in Manhattan on the way to this woman's art opening. The artist wore designer clothes. Art openings led to further conflict: S imagined going as a musician to parties and salons with other artists, musicians, and poets and then, in an arena that is very charged for her, having to be brilliant and witty.

I reflected back to S all the different meanings of her musical identity, and she replied, as she became very teary, that she had an image, right then, of being, every day, in a studio at the piano, with other instruments nearby, how that would be such an amazing, wonderful life. She remembered the same bursting into tears when she had told a coworker years ago that she was leaving her job to go to music school. I said that it seemed to me that it was unbearable, in some way, for S to think about playing and hearing music, daily, and she replied, still crying, that it was the ultimate risk.

Clinical vignettes never make an argument, but they enlarge and enrich our ability to see and understand. I have suggested that when once you get down to individuals, what it means to consider "the" glass ceiling as being internal is in no way self-evident. Achievement, success, wearing a sleeveless dress, playing the piano, singing, being a productive professional, rising to the top, being unproblematically competent and non-hierarchical, all these can be conflictual goals. They are tied to images of femininity and sexuality, to images of mothers and fathers, to fears about risk, to selfhood and identity, and to culture of origin. These internally created glass ceilings, glass walls, and sticky floors meet those generated by layers of externally created structural and professional barriers, constraints, exclusions, and expectations, and they meet explicit and implicit cultural and personalized cultural assumptions about women in general and about particular women in particular times and places.

Chapter 8

Too late

The reproduction and non-reproduction of mothering

"Too Late" was first presented in Nice at the 2001 meetings of the International Psychoanalytic Association, where I was invited by Janine Chasseguet-Smirgel to speak at a panel on the contemporary family. The paper was published in 2003. I wrote it shortly after my new foreword to *The Reproduction of Mothering*, in which I had re-evaluated the importance of psychobiological maternality. The two patients who are its focus were the patients most puzzling me at the time, and it was through considering the focus of each on her own central issues that I was able to see their commonalities and the common crisis, linking non-fertility and time—too lateness—that they each faced. The chapter's original subtitle was "Ambivalence About Motherhood, Choice, and Time."

Because "Too Late" addresses a topic that continues to have resonance and relevance, I have been asked to present it on many occasions, most recently at the 2009 conference in Berlin of the Committee on Women and Psychoanalysis, called, after Judith Kestenberg (who would have been so pleased, after her years of hard work and feelings of marginality), "The Female Body—Inside and Outside." The present chapter includes some of the addenda I have written for such presentations, including reflections about how the paper itself informed my own subsequent clinical work.[1]

In this chapter, I consider a particular constellation of fantasies and defenses that lead some women to delay childbearing. I explore how destructive wishes toward and fantasies about a woman's own womb and her mother's lead to behaviors that sabotage fertility and pregnancy. These fantasies and behaviors meet up with an unconscious belief in and commitment to time standing still and with cultural tropes and trends that obscure intrapsychic conflict and denial about motherhood, aging, and time. Like childbearing, analysis is constrained by the reality of time. The complex clinical untangling

[1] 1 An earlier version of this chapter appeared in *Journal of the American Psychoanalytic Association*, *51*(4), 2003, pp. 1181–1198. Reprinted with permission.

and connecting of these not obviously related threads—biological fertility, fantasies about internal destruction and destructiveness, culture, and time—may not occur until it is, for the woman who now wants a child, too late.

"Too late," then, constitutes a particular expression of the non-reproduction of mothering. *The Reproduction of Mothering* recast female development, and especially the development of women's maternality, in terms of an internal mother-daughter world. I argue there that women's maternal orientation—choice to become a mother, sense of self as mother, and differential relation to daughters and sons—reflects preoedipal and oedipal mother-daughter constellations that are revisited and consolidated first in adolescence and then, with maternity, in adulthood. As the book's last chapter concludes:

> Women's mothering capacities and commitments ... are built developmentally into feminine personality. Because women are themselves mothered by women, they grow up with the relational capacities and needs, and psychological definition of self-in-relationship, which commits them to mothering. ... Women mother daughters who, when they become women, mother. (1978, p. 209)

These words capture the essence of the book's main argument, and my clinical experience, garnered well after I wrote it, confirms their psychological truth. Whether she has children or not, each of my women patients, in her own individual way, brings her conscious and unconscious relation to her mother into her psychological and psychophysical maternal identity.

At the same time, clinical experience has led to a rethinking. In the tradition of most psychoanalytic developmental theorizing, *The Reproduction of Mothering* puts forth a generalized developmental account. For each woman, however, the particularities of her internal mother-daughter world, her sense of self as maternal, and her actions that express these, must be studied in the individual clinical case. Moreover, as I also write later (see Chodorow, 1999b; Chapters 10 and 11, this volume), individuals create their psychological gender through a variety of constitutive components, including projective and introjective filterings and experiences of culture and of biology. Although we can separate out the intrapsychic from the cultural and the biological as theoretical categories, we cannot do so in individual, lived clinical reality.

In these later writings, I also claim that affective constellations and fantasies that do not seem directly related to subjective gender enter into individualized animations of gender. In this chapter, I describe a specific way that the internal mother-daughter world filters both culture and the body, and I document how a particular, non-ostensibly gender-related psychological phenomenon—the experience of time—affects directly gendered experiences like motherhood or its absence. Having myself discovered this relationship only quite late in (or after) the treatments that I describe, I suggest that it behooves us to pay particular attention clinically to the ways that seemingly non-gender-related phenomena affect gender.

In particular, I address here a difficulty found in early feminist psychoanalytic work like *The Reproduction of Mothering.* Both in the 1970s and today, feminism challenged psychoanalytically and culturally normative views of femininity, including motherhood, that were rooted in generalizations and universalizations about the necessary sequelae of living in a female body. But it did so by denying the centrality of bodily and biopsychological experience to lived and invested gender. As I came to recognize, certain bodily, genital, and reproductive configurations and potentialities universally demand psychological (and often cultural) elaboration, even as this psychological elaboration will be clinically individual (and culturally variant). The present investigations of too-lateness document my claim, as I revisited *The Reproduction of Mothering*, that "biological mothering is itself specifically cast intrapsychically partially in terms of this internal, bodily imaged mother-daughter world. ... Pregnancy, childbirth, the felt reproductive drive [are] filtered through the prism of the intrapsychic and intersubjective reproduction of mothering" (ch. 4, this vol., p. 59).

With the patients who initiated my concerns here, they and I have had to recognize that although they now very much want to bear children, they will never do so. We have had also to recognize that this not having children was due to their own psychic realities and the behaviors that these realities generated. Our role as analysts is to mitigate psychological suffering and to promote self-understanding and self-acceptance, yet we are drawn to case reports with fairy-tale endings: "When we terminated, Mrs. A was enjoying her work, sexually responsive to her husband, and pregnant."

As we recognize the biological clock and the ending of possibility, such an external fairy-tale ending cannot happen for the women I am discussing. My experience has been, moreover, that it is particularly difficult for these women to mitigate their guilt and self-blame. The challenge, then, is to help someone in this situation to get beyond feeling that her lack of motherhood is her fault, and that she has damaged not only herself but also others in the process. For the analyst, perhaps particularly if she is a woman (like myself) whose maternal identity is powerful, one who does feel, deeply and profoundly, that there is no substitute for motherhood, there are also strong countertransference feelings to confront: It is hard not to agree with the patient that on some level, there is something absolute and irretrievable in her situation.

Specifically, I describe here how a constellation of unconscious mother-daughter-sibling fantasies, anchored by an imploded aggression against both self and object, can destabilize and undermine fertility and maternality. Partly because, as I discovered somewhat after the fact, these fantasies may coexist in the same person with not-obviously related experiences of time standing still, women with this particular fantasy constellation may put off thinking about motherhood or not notice their own age.

In our era, these women's internal conflicts and fantasies, about having children and about time standing still, meet up with external, cultural and social, changes that have occurred in gender roles and family patterns; in our beliefs about biology, aging, and time; and in the actual biological constraints of age. When internal and external rationales to postpone meet, the clinician sees painful crises, in which the wish to have children gets psychologically disentangled when it is simply too late. For the women whom I consider here, there is an intrapsychic conflation of attacks on the maternal womb and on their own womb and reproductive possibilities. Looking at their internal, object-relational experience of maternality and its difficulties, as I put it, "allows us to see bodily experience in psychologically more accurate ways" (ch. 4, this vol., p. 58).

I am concerned here, then, not only with women who have used various feminist or career-derived reasons for delaying motherhood and who then find themselves up against the fertility clock. I have in mind also women who have, perhaps hidden under these normative practices, more actively sabotaged their fertility. I am considering, further, women for whom time plays a particularly potent role in their psychology and the progress of their treatment: hence, too late. Among all factors that go into mothering, I am not in this context making a sharp distinction between the experience and treatment of the reproductive body—more directly bodily-centered wishes and conflicts about being pregnant or fertile—and fantasies about maternality—the maternal sense of self or the relation to the child.

MOTHERING IN PSYCHOANALYTIC THOUGHT

Pregnancy and motherhood are central from the beginning to women's psychosexual, self, and object-relational development, but classical psychoanalysis made these experiences lesser features of women's development than external genital experience and difference.[2] They also constitute adult developmental phases and psychosocial crises (see Balsam, 1996; Bassin, Honey, & Kaplan, 1994; Benedek, 1956, 1959, 1960; Bibring, 1959; Bibring et al., 1961; Chodorow, 1978; de Marneffe, 2004; Kestenberg, 1956a, 1976; Langer, 1992; Notman & Lester, 1988; Pines, 1993; Raphael-Leff, 1993).[3]

[2] In my view, the sexual difference perspective, including many primary femininity formulations, often continues this limiting and limited focus on the external genitals (see Chapter 10).

[3] 2011 note: Throughout this volume, I have not updated bibliographic references, which would be a writing and research project in itself, but I want here to acknowledge two major recent psychoanalytic contributions to our understanding of mothering: Balsam, *Women's Bodies in Psychoanalysis* (2011), and Almond, *The Monster Within* (2010).

As *The Reproduction of Mothering* suggests, motherhood begins internally in the conflictual, intense cauldron of childhood sexuality and object relations, especially in the mother-daughter relationship and its internal symbolic and fantasy transformation in the developing girl. Maternal identities and desires are overdetermined, filled with fantasy, and complex. Whether expressed in youth, fulfilled belatedly, or never fulfilled, the desire for children contains layers of affect and meaning. Having children, just as not having children, can be freely chosen or pathologically driven, mired in conflict or relatively conflict free. Each of these choices can have multiple meanings, and with either, we hope for a certain amount of secondary autonomy—a predominance of elements that have come to be independent of originary conflicts. If motherhood were not filled with so many different meanings and motives, we would not expect a mother to have a maternal identity and the special sense of herself in relation to her children that allows her to mother.

In considering the non-reproduction of mothering, I am not suggesting that it is all women's destiny to bear or raise children, or that it is pathological to choose not to be a mother.[4] Just as with all developmental theories (for example, we now distinguish a consolidation of erotism and object choice as developmental desiratum from normative heterosexuality), we need to be careful to distinguish the inevitable internal working with and through of the developmental challenge of bodily reproductivity and generativity and any assumption of a normative psychological or behavioral outcome. Moreover, although all women (and men) give fantasy and dynamic meaning to their reproductive selves, bodies, and object relations, and although there are prevalent developmental patterns within this, the universality of such features of psychic life does not vitiate clinical individuality or preclude potentially infinite individual variation in their meanings and patterns of organization.

Here, specifically, I consider *particular* patterns of relationship to fertility and maternality and *particular* women, not fertility and maternality in general. The dynamic and relational constellation that I describe as leading to "too-lateness," for example, differs from that described by Bergmann (1985), who also found in a number of patients a culturally and psychologically-generated delay of motherhood (one that I recognize in other patients) originating in a precociously sexualized dyadic relationship to the father and symbiotic relation to the mother. Finally, we need to remind ourselves that although motherhood is usually one central meaning of generativity for women, generativity for both sexes means more than parenting one's

[4] From the beginning, and at each subsequent presentation of this paper, listeners have asked whether I am prescribing, once again, anatomy as destiny. In this paragraph and the following one, both found in the original essay, I work hard (although, it turns out, not with complete success) to allay such fears.

own biological children. It can involve many kinds of creative and caring activities or activities that foster the next generation or the environment (Erikson, 1950). Such activities may directly express the parental components of generativity even as they sublimate the biological reproductive components and felt drives.

Further caveats: Just as I have emphasized that I am not beginning from the position that motherhood is the natural destiny of all women, or that the choice not to have children is by definition pathological or problematic, I also note that the too-lateness I consider here is regretted delaying, which may or may not result in infertility. I do not suggest that infertility in these older women who find that it is too late is a sign of continued internal conflict about pregnancy. Psychoanalysts have been more likely to investigate infertility than delay (Bergmann, 1985, is an exception here), and although we can still fruitfully explore and treat cases of psychogenic sterility and infertility (see, e.g., Leuzinger-Bohleber, 2001; Pines, 1993), I agree with Apfel and Keylor that "it is time to retire the term 'psychogenic infertility' as simplistic and anachronistic" (2002, p. 100).[5] That is, I am taking my patients' current wishes to have, or to have had, children at face value and their current infertility to be a likely product of biological age or, as they do also, of former sexual and reproductive behavior.

CULTURAL CONTEXTS AND PSYCHOLOGICAL DEFENSES

In the last half century, we have seen remarkable changes in the family and work lives of more privileged women. Numbers of women and men choose not to have children, and women are typically older at the time of first birth. Professional women especially, often including our patients and colleagues, do not have children until their mid-30s, their 40s, and even, occasionally, their early 50s. For many individuals, and even for "society," "the family" seems to have moved from a necessity to an option. In the United States, work is for the most part organized without regard for parenthood, yet one reads articles and op-ed columns in which writers argue that workplaces actually discriminate against non-parents when they give pregnancy leave, allow part-time work, or enable mothers to leave work on time. The implicit attitude seems to be not that all of us need (or "society" needs) to have children be born and well cared for, but rather, that having children is a personal preference of some self-indulgent individuals who should not be coddled. And although "the family" is not an option from the child's point of view, in the United States, at least, policies from welfare

[5] Apfel and Keylor also point out that "assisted reproductive technologies offer a more direct route to parenthood" (p. 851) than analysis.

regulations to pregnancy-leave benefits and workplace requirements seem to assume that children do not need mothering—that somehow a caretaker or caretakers will be found.

Most of us favor those changes that have enabled women to engage in fulfilling and remunerative work (many of us *are* those women), and, as the question of "choice"—family life as an option—also arises around women's right to abortion, most of us are firmly in favor of this right. Because of such beliefs, it may be hard for us to recognize some of the potential psychic concomitants and costs of the general growth of "choice"—not just the choice to keep or not to keep a pregnancy, but of our current cultural belief (one that I certainly share) that, for the individual woman, having children should be a choice rather than an assumed destiny. These concomitants and costs are more likely to arise today than formerly, when it was simply assumed that most women would marry and have children, so that it required as much passive role acceptance as active psychological capabilities to achieve these ends.

For contemporary women, including the patients I am considering, a variety of culturally supported beliefs have provided conscious rationalizations for attitudes to motherhood. First, they may agree with a widespread notion (a notion which, in the United States at least, has much external reality to support it) that motherhood and professional life are incompatible for women, that the demands of modern professions for total commitment and a 60- or 80-hour work week assume a wife/mother in the home or a high-powered professional without children. For many women, supported by some strands of feminist ideology, the cost-benefit analysis goes one way: What are the costs to a high-powered career of motherhood, rather than the costs to motherhood of a career?

Thus, we find many professionally successful women in our practices who find themselves, in their late 30s or mid-40s, surprised not to have children. Psychobiological self-sabotage and toxic internal mother-daughter relationships may not figure so much, but culture has kicked in: These women have not noticed motherhood, as they were on an academic calendar, fast-tracking at a law firm, or climbing the corporate ladder. They may have been sexually and relationally adventurous, feeling more like traditional men in the freedom not to settle down, and thinking, vaguely, that you could have children into your 50s.

In a more personally felt appropriation of cultural and feminist critique, patients report observing their mothers' entrapment, passivity, suffering, and subservience to their fathers, as well as their mothers' inability—from the daughter's point of view "because of the children"—to assert themselves or leave their marriage. Generated from this observation of trapped mothers and from feminist ideology among women who have themselves not yet reached the too-late stage but who might, unless they pay attention to their personal uses of cultural defenses, is an insistence (for which, I ruefully find, my own early advocacy of shared parenting sometimes explicitly provides fuel) that a woman will not have children unless her partner promises to do exactly half the caretaking.

This appropriation of cultural tropes as defenses obscures both conflicts about work and conflicts about motherhood. Work threatens too much involvement or fear of failure. On the other, it threatens success.[6] Motherhood threatens, on the one side, a pull toward total envelopment in a relation to a child, fantasies of triumph over one's mother, or fantasies of maternal-sexual voluptuousness and bountiful wombs and breasts. On the other, just as potent, lie fears of triumph over or regressive merger with one's internal mother, fears of losing oneself and one's identity, graphic fantasies about the ravages of pregnancy, bodily depletion and deformity, or imagining being too regressed to think. Divergent conscious and unconscious conflicts about work on the one hand and motherhood on the other thus converge into a single conscious conflict, career versus motherhood, obscuring the anxieties and conflicts within each realm.[7]

Other cultural-psychological confluences are also notable. Anorexic themes extend into the childbearing years. Women express a wish for a tight, non-maternal body, often going along with hyperexercise and work drivenness—which itself in turn may connect, unconsciously, with still wanting to be the prepubertal, sharp, intelligent, latency-aged girl whom father loved and who found welcome separation from being too attached to mother. They express a horror at the softness of pregnancy or terrors imagining the rupture of childbirth. There is a fine psychological (as well as physiological) line between "fitness" and getting rid of the feminine body.

When it is true that you have to get on with your career, when it is good to be fit and slim, when it is a woman's right to choose and to control her own body, when it is unfair that men find it easy to be both a parent and a professional, then powerful internal conflicts about pregnancy and motherhood themselves can go unnoticed.[8] For the clinician who supports a woman's right to choose and to control her own body, exploring the decision to have an abortion or past abortions, separating out political beliefs from guilt or a sense of having been self-destructive, attempting to address acting rather than analyzing, all these become a delicate matter.

Our current cultural climate, then, and perhaps feminism itself, provide a cover for internal conflicts and fears. These enable women to mask conflicts and ambivalence about motherhood by turning them into conflicts between motherhood and career or motherhood and lifestyle. Sometimes, we see

[6] Much more, of course, but this is not my topic here. For some discussion, see Chapter 8.

[7] The formulation, divergent and convergent conflicts, comes from Kris (1984, 1985).

[8] The reader may notice an almost associative, primary-process quality in my articulation here and in the previous paragraphs about women's fears of pregnancy and motherhood. I seem unintentionally to have reflected the rapid-fire conflation of thoughts and feelings that arise in women as they try to cover in their own thinking all the aspects of this fraught topic.

women early enough so that they can examine the function of such beliefs in keeping deeper fears of motherhood and pregnancy from surfacing. That way a real choice can be made. But in women for whom it is too late, this is not possible. Culturally infused defenses thin out as psychological fears and conflicts are seen directly to have affected reproductive potentialities.

TOO LATE, OBSERVED AND ANALYZED

A variety of behaviors express the undermining of fertility. Women may have multiple abortions or take sexual risks, having multiple partners and not protecting themselves or not attending to vaginal infections or endometriosis. One patient's early 20s menopause must certainly have been an unfortunate biological anomaly, but this woman herself attributed it to rage at her mother and at herself, to wanting to destroy her own uterus. Women who undermine fertility may also more generally avoid or inhibit generativity. They choose jobs that masochistically punish and traumatize rather than fulfill them, sometimes extremely demoralizing jobs, or jobs that involve working with ravaged and destroyed people, but without a professional support infrastructure. They may describe creative blocks.

J was in her early 40s when she came to treatment. She had been living with the same man for 4 years and had hoped, she said, to have children with him, but she had not gotten pregnant. J was the oldest of five children, three spaced less than 2 years apart, followed by a gap of 5 years, then another closely spaced two. She reported memories from earliest childhood of total adoration and protectiveness of her two immediately younger siblings and tremendous guilt that their lives had been harder than hers. She spoke of her siblings in a way that bespoke frantic keeping of her jealousy of them at bay. Her parents had been off-and-on separated for 4 years when an accidental pregnancy returned her father to the home. Shortly after the last child was born, her mother, again pregnant, had a miscarriage with severe hemorrhaging and was rushed off to the hospital for a hysterectomy, leaving J to take care of all her younger siblings. J, terrified that her mother would die, was also relieved that there would be no more babies and confirmed in her perception of her father's brutal maltreatment of her mother and the family. To her ostensible relief, her parents shortly afterward divorced.

When I met her, J reported that she desperately wanted a family. She also described six abortions between the ages of 20 and 30 (six representing the number of children that her mother would have had but for the hemorrhaging and hysterectomy).[9] As we reconstructed things, there had been a

[9] Pines (1993, pp. 103–113) describes a similar patient whose "planned abortions" (p. 107) and inability to stay pregnant were symptoms of a deeper need to remain empty, dead, and entangled in a destructively fused relationship with her mother.

drivenness to these pregnancies, acquired either through brief one-night stands or with boyfriends whose even slight hesitation was used as a reason not to keep the pregnancy. J had gotten pregnant, it seemed, almost in order to have an abortion.

When J decided in her mid-30s that she wanted to have children, and with this intention became involved with a man, J chose a divorced man with a checkered paternal history, one who never saw his children. They began immediately trying to get pregnant, but with no success. As J turned 40, she began to look into fertility treatments. *Began*: Her search was done with only surface acknowledgment of her biological clock. J took her time finding doctors, and she had trouble getting her boyfriend to join her for appointments. She did not want to tell either her boyfriend or her doctors about her abortion history.

In treatment, J's several abortions were a constant source of self-punishment, a constant reminder that she had only herself to blame for ruining her chances to become a mother as well as for destroying her potential babies. J was quite sure that through her abortions, she had destroyed her capacity to get pregnant, and given her age and reproductive history, her belief seemed realistic.

Uncovering the self-attacking, in addition to the sibling-attacking, reasons for J's abortions was the work of long treatment. Before J began treatment with me, she had been for many years in analysis in another city. She aborted that progressing treatment by deliberately finding a job that required her to move. During our work together, J often came late or had to leave early. Sometimes, she was supposed to be in three places at once—her hour and two different meetings. We noticed J's conscious and unconscious denial of time and became aware of her need that time not exist, because to recognize that time moves forward would be to acknowledge the reality of being too late. She also occupied her hours with trivia from work, as she began to see, to keep feelings at bay.

As she reached her mid-40s, J had given up, recognizing that she would never be a biological mother. She had neither the resources, the stable relationship, nor, it seemed, the biological capacity to become pregnant. We came to understand that for J, fertility, getting pregnant, meant not only, or even mainly, becoming a mother, but also making reparation and undoing the damage she had done to herself, her siblings, and her mother. As J reached the "too-late" time, she felt that she could never undo this damage, never get over her sadness, guilt, and anger at the destructiveness in which she had engaged. She had not protected but had destroyed her younger siblings, had wanted to destroy them, had destroyed her own potential children and her own reproductive capacities. At some point, J announced that she had begun looking into adopting. This effort accorded with her tendency to act to get away from feelings, but it nonetheless promised at first to resolve, in some fashion at least, the actual childless outcome of her painful conflicts and self-destructive behavior. This search itself, however, took on a timeless quality and did not seem to progress.

J drifted out of treatment. Over the course of time, she had become less persistently self-critical about her abortions, but she could not, it seemed, attain a successful mourning of her lost fertility and her past. When we discussed what it would mean to terminate rather than to end—to see her life as the life she had lived; to come to feel compassion for herself—J said that if that was what termination would take, she could not finish treatment. She will always feel regret, will never accept what she has done with her life. Also, to try to accept herself would take time, and then she would be even older.

S, for whom it was also too late, was able to resolve her internal feelings differently. Like J, S came from a large family—six, of whom she was the youngest. S always felt that there was not enough to go around: Her siblings had taken everything from her mother already, so that by the time S was born, her mother was tired, depleted, and unable to give. Several of her siblings were successful, but, like J, S felt that her own destructive envy had been the cause of incapacity in those who were not. S expressed indirectly and directly an imploded anger at her mother for being unavailable, along with an unyielding, self-punitive belief that her mother's exhaustion was S's fault: S's own birth and feeding, specifically, had been responsible. S had exposed herself to sexually transmitted diseases through risky and unprotected sex, and since she had never gotten pregnant, she speculated that she must have ruined her fertility.

As I was reflecting upon too-lateness, writing about J and S, and thinking about their putting off of motherhood and bodily self-sabotage, I noticed more sharply, though we had talked about it piecemeal many times, how, over our many years of work, S had, with conscious and unconscious elaboration, kept her analysis and life timeless. In her mid-40s, she thought of herself as a young woman or girl. Unlike J, for whom each friend's pregnancy was another painful blow, S simply did not notice that her friends were marrying and getting pregnant, or she noticed but at the same time thought that she herself was not old enough to have children. She talked about "keeping things timeless," "rolling back the clock," and "running in place."

As it entered the consulting room, this sense of time standing still proved a formidable resistance, not allowing our relationship to shift and develop. For some time, it was a quiet and unnoticeable narcissistic cocoon, a tacit assumption that manifested only indirectly, as S's treatment did not progress, and S did not improve. S described herself as Scheherazade, telling the same story over and over for 1,001 analytic hours. But eventually, investigation of S's cocoon, in which time stood still and in which S needed time to stand still in order to keep her destructiveness from having happened, allowed S to accept that, among other things, her non-fertility might be a result. In her late 40s, S met a widower with two children of appropriate age for her to have been their biological mother.

S was thus able to achieve both a sublimation of her generativity and a successful mourning. As she finished her analysis she was able to accept, without self-punitiveness, the life she had lived as hers, and she found herself engaging in generative nesting—remodeling a house, taking great pleasure in creating a beautiful flower garden, and learning how to relate to her new stepchildren. As she put it, "I have regret, but I can't change the choices I made. I'll never have children, and I have to go on with things. I can't redo my childhood. I can't undo my age, or my choices to be single for so long. There's no going back."

TIME AND TIMELESSNESS

J and S illustrate the psychological filtering of biological fertility and maternality especially through the internal mother-daughter psyche and through fantasies of time and timelessness. J treated daily time as if it did not exist, and S knew that she kept things timeless.

Freud tells us that the pathological illuminates the normal. An attitude toward time, I came to see, is intertwined with maternality and often a wider index of conflict about generativity. I noticed how a woman in her early 50s found it entrapping to keep a datebook and to write down changes of appointment. She had always consciously not wanted children, but she wrestled with a writing block, and she described the sibling envy, rage at her mother, and multiple abortions that I had found in other women who have sabotaged their fertility. In the treatment of women for whom it is too late, we often discover that, quite apart from their current recognition of this too-lateness, time has in unconscious fantasy stood still. Analyzing the unconscious attitude toward time then becomes a primary route into understanding the psychology of the too-late non-reproduction of mothering.

Motherhood is in conscious and unconscious fantasy first and foremost a gendered, bodily, object-relational, and cultural experience for women. But gender, here as elsewhere, also gains personal meaning and is constructed from phenomena that are not ostensibly gendered. In the women I am considering, this non-gendered phenomenon often involves a relation to time that itself has implicit cultural as well as psychological underpinnings. Many cultural commentators have noticed the contemporary cult of youthfulness and the flight from aging. Indeed, these trends have been supported by astounding changes in longevity and health. As people change careers in their 50s, as men remarry in their 60s and father children, as fertility treatments allow women to get pregnant in their 40s and 50s, we can come to be fooled by time. For women, such biocultural changes can contribute to the fantasy that there is no biological clock.

The relation of time, change, and gender is intrapsychic as well as cultural. Building on Nietzsche, the psychoanalytic cultural critic N. O.

Brown (1959) theorized that the denial of death and fantasies of immortality generate morbid neurotic transformations, a deadened culture, and a constant striving for change, inhibiting the capacity to live life fully in the present. In a more clinical vein, several analysts (e.g., Buechler, 1999; Cooper, 2000; Hoffman, 1998) have explored the contradiction between the necessarily slow unfolding of an analysis—taking the analytic dyad out of ordinary time and recognizing the timelessness of the unconscious—on the one hand, and, on the other, the requirement that we acknowledge that time is in fact passing as an analysis progresses—that aging, life lived in the present, and mortality are really before us as we work.

In a particularly beautiful clinical paper germane to my considerations here, Arlow (1984) describes how variations in the senses of time and timelessness can in some instances access moments of eternity and in others lead to a paralyzing inability to make any life choices, from writing down an appointment on a calendar to applying to college or planning a family, that imply a future to be planned for or years to be counted. Arlow describes a young woman musician who feels penetrated by light and transformed during a Christmas Eve performance, briefly sensing herself as being outside of time and part of eternity, as she merges momentarily with her music, her mother, her father, and an imagined virgin/Madonna pregnancy.

Time links with generation, which is intrinsically, as Chasseguet-Smirgel (1984) and McDougall (1986) argue, part of gender, and perhaps time has a characteristic resonance for women. Kristeva (1979) claims that "women's time"—time from the unconscious point of view of motherhood and reproduction—is cyclical and eternal. She is referring to the cyclicity of the menstrual cycle and to women's place in the cycle of generations, on the one hand, and to the monumental, out-of-ordinary-time-and-space, tied to nature rather than culture, sense of pregnancy and involvement with a baby, on the other. This cyclical-eternal sense is to the time dimension what the oceanic feeling or primary oneness is to fusion in the dimension of space.

Women's time helps to create part of the earliest experience and sedimenting of being for the child and for the mother, who in relation to her child draws from her own experience of being mothered. It is part of what many women bring to their maternality. Kristeva contrasts women's time with the linear and teleological time of history, society, and politics. Time thus links gender with generation.[10]

A distortion, or perversion, of woman's time seems to figure into the timelessness or time standing still psychic phenomenon of women who have

[10] 2011 note: I do not know how, in this discussion of time and timelessness, I could have missed Orgel's (1965) extraordinary "On Time and Timelessness," which centers particularly on mother-daughter clinical examples and how these, as the denial of time, enter the consulting room.

put off pregnancy and maternity.[11] Because of the rooting of the internal mother-child relation in early unconscious fantasies of destruction rather than generativity, the timelessness of the early mother-child bond that a woman takes with her into her own reproduction of mothering has acquired a stagnant and imploded quality, rather than that of an emerging chrysalis. Cyclical time, rather than being active and in movement, becomes stopped or repetitively circular, and monumental, eternal time freezes. The psychological clock stops, as age and time stand still, time becomes repetitive or circular, and the biological clock is eliminated. To return to culture, my speculation is that this unconscious sense of time standing still is potential in any time and place, but that it may be more likely in a culture like ours, with its emphasis on youth, no aging, longer lives, later fertility, and a family life cycle that seems to have no fixed routine and to be voluntary rather than taken for granted.

TOO LATE: REFLECTIONS AND CONCLUSIONS

Too-late women begin from the feeling there was not enough of mother, often especially because there were several siblings. Mother seemed depressed, downtrodden, submissive, and tired, especially from taking care of so many children. Patients come to recognize a belief that they themselves destroyed their mother, quite bodily, with greed or envy, but they also discover and elaborate upon an implacable envy of siblings and memories of wishing to destroy them, sometimes defended against by exaggerated adoration. In another internal logic, the brother or sister's need for protection and adoration was because of the threat of destruction posed by the patient herself. There is thus ongoing anger at the mother, and a fear of having destroyed as well as a desire to destroy her, and siblings loom especially large.

We are in classical Klein territory here, specifically Klein's description of early hatred of the mother and the wish to destroy the mother's insides. Klein reminds us—but we often forget, in both our general descriptions and our case accounts—that these fantasies of the maternal womb include siblings. Yet these daughters do not, as Klein might also predict, fear maternal retaliation for their destructive wishes and fantasies. They have already deadened both self and object, including their own, and in fantasy their mothers', uterus, and their mothers, already tired and weakened by motherhood, perhaps especially by the patient's own demands and her fantasied attacks on her mother's being and uterus, do not have the energy to retaliate.

[11] Chasseguet-Smirgel (1984) describes the relations among creativity, perversion, and the acceptance or non-acceptance of reality—in the present context, real time and the realistic possibilities of fertility.

The mother herself needs protection, and accordingly, the patient has to take her own deserved destruction upon herself. Accordingly, an imploded anger becomes central in the psyche, not a volatile or active rage, but rather a leaden, quiet self-destructiveness that covers both self and mother. In fantasy, this disruption of bodily and relational generativity goes to the earliest mother-child relation, to a core of strong but numbing anger that has been turned both outward and against the self and the reproductive and sexual body. In virulent too-lateness, destructive wishes against the mother and against the self become conflated.

These developmental outcomes, set in early childhood, run up against, or alongside, a lack of recognition of the reality of time and a denial of time passing. In unconscious fantasy, time has stood still. Both treatment and life are more or less maintenance operations rather than progressions. The patient may for some time believe that she does not deserve to improve, but only to hold things steady and not be totally miserable. She may be surprised at or deny her own age, and time may form a psychic retreat, manifested in talk (as with S) about rolling back the clock or doing things over. Photos capturing particular childhood moments that resonate with conflicts with siblings and mother are fixed in the imagination as screen memories.

As I note earlier, this sense of time standing still, progressing cyclically rather than linearly, proves a powerful resistance. It may be a quiet and not immediately noticeable resistance, a tacit assumption that manifests only indirectly in that the treatment does not progress. But whether analyzed or not, the denial of time is inexorable and relentless since one of its functions is, by rolling back the clock to before siblings became damaged or mothers died or became depressed and hopeless, to deny the harm the patient believes she has done. For S, the analysis of time standing still as a psychic retreat was endlessly discussed and analyzed and finally enabled termination. As I also note, however, it was only as I was writing this chapter and considering J, whose sabotage of her fertility was virulent but whose attitude toward time was in the background, that I recognized the close connection between keeping things timeless, denying age, and not acknowledging the biological clock.

Like all aspects of the gendered psyche, the non-reproduction of mothering is both patterned and clinically individual. I am describing a pattern, a continuum of family resemblances and constitutive ingredients, in different women's psychological and bodily maternality—their reproduction or non-reproduction of mothering. Not being a biological mother was for S an arena of sadness, mourning, and anger at herself, but her presenting concerns were not so centrally around the question of motherhood and fertility. A relentless stasis, repetition, and denial of time passing, which had frozen her life, were central. J's presenting concern was her horror and guilt about her abortions and her stuck incapacity to get pregnant or have a child. Her actual body, the actual fact of infertility and abortions, and of her mother's miscarriage and hemorrhaging, loomed large. Until after I had written this paper, our analysis of the denial of time had been more tied to the immediate transferential present of not getting to sessions.

We might wonder if particular family experiences underlie differences in unconscious feelings about motherhood and a woman's reproductive body. Pregnancy, getting pregnant, having or not having abortions, and an immediate reaction to the maternal uterus might be more prevalent in older daughters of large families, like J, who have watched their mothers' subsequent pregnancies, than in youngest daughters like S. It may be that such more conscious differences in emphasis help to explain what looks, after the fact of discovery, to have been a blindness on my part, especially in the case of S, to the close connections between, on the one hand, time standing still or repetitively cycling nowhere as a psychic retreat (even in the context of understanding the relation of the denial of time to endless unresolved mourning and self-blame), and on the other the virulence of her attacks on her internal mother-self and her putting off of pregnancy and motherhood.

In our time, these internal constellations that lead to not having children meet a shifting culture in which conflicts in relation to motherhood are obscured by many cultural tropes and social trends. These include a view of motherhood as an active choice for women, a statistical rise in maternal age, and medical advances that enable prolonged fertility, fetal monitoring, and increased longevity. Such tropes and trends can be further potentiated by feminist claims for women's careers and demands for male involvement in child care. Finally, less visibly but perhaps more insidiously, they include a conflating of women's time with a culture that denies biological aging and implies that all things are possible.

As our literature describes, it can be extremely painful and sad, for both patient and analyst, when a woman has trouble conceiving. This is especially the case when a woman feels consciously and unconsciously that she herself is at fault, not just for reasons of hormonal happenstance or having put off getting pregnant, but as she discovers virulent antifertility forces within. Here, I have examined internal constellations of fantasy and feeling that lead to ambivalence about motherhood and the reproductive body or to more active sabotaging of bodily internal mother, siblings, self, and a woman's own potential babies. "Women mother daughters who, when they become women, mother." Except, as I describe here, when they do not.

Just as, when we work with physically ill patients or patients dealing with bereavement, we can only work within the absolute reality of death but cannot make death disappear, so, I think, we may need to accept that there may be a sense in which, for women who very much want, but cannot have, children, there is no possible substitute. Recognition of this reality, perhaps particularly with women who have denied the reality of time and for whom it is too late, may help us to help them to mitigate the virulent self-punishment and blocking of all creativity and generativity that can result—to accept their lives with integrity rather than despair. And if we can recognize the signs of potential too-lateness—the ways in which almost embodied, but not ostensibly gender-related, unconscious fantasies of frozen time underpin and obscure the putting off of motherhood and the progress of treatment—perhaps, then, we will be able to analyze these before it is too late.

CLINICAL POSTSCRIPT

After I had published "Too Late," I began to notice the denial of time passing in other patients, in men who are stuck in unfulfilling relationships or in work, in patients who, like J, have appointments to be in two or three places at once or who never leave enough time to get from one place to another. I noticed patients who were always late for appointments, others who kept the clocks in their homes set at different times or always 10 minutes ahead, or who used snooze alarms, hoping thereby to stop time. Time, a patient told me, is the enemy: How could I possibly not think so?

Especially, denying or playing with time is now a marker that I notice in women who have put off childbearing. Several years ago, a high-powered 40-year-old professional woman, M, came into my office wanting to figure out why she did not have and was ambivalent about having children. She came from a family of five, and all of her siblings had children. She came late for her second session and told me that she thought she should find someone closer to home: She's always late for everything. Alerted by the time marker, I suggested that her lateness might be related to what she had come in about. She decided to stay in treatment.

As she began, M described how important it was to keep herself busy, how even our 50-minute hours were interruptions. I was not surprised to find along with this feeling a devaluation of M's mother and of motherhood. M's mother, in her view, had spent all of her time driving the children to hockey practice and music lessons and nagging them about leaving sports equipment in the entryway. Meanwhile, her brilliantly successful father raced in late to dinner. At dinner, each family member went around and said what they had done that day, but M's mother was not asked. M was action oriented, and her commitment to treatment was choppy. If I took a break or changed a session, she was ready to quit, to "shed" me.

M did not have the punitive history toward her own body that I had found in other patients. She had used contraception responsibly and not had abortions. She treated her body in a generic young professional—perhaps male—way. She ran, did triathlons, and was very thin. A female variant upon Freud's "a special type of choice of object made by men," M talked dizzyingly about several men whom she could not decide among, none of whom seemed likely candidates for marriage or fatherhood. After a while, M seemed to settle in with one boyfriend, but she mainly talked dismissively about him and his sentimentality. She occasionally noted his taking her face in his hands and commenting lovingly on each feature.

At some point, M announced that she was pregnant, supposedly without intention. My reaction was without warmth, a caricature of analytic neutrality that is not at all my usual mode. A few days later, I could recognize a counteridentification, as M's mother's first reaction to the pregnancy was to comment about her boyfriend's divorce not being final. We could then work further on M's judgmental internal and external mother and look at her fears of maternal identification: She had always been loved more than loving, was not the one who takes a face into her hands and focuses on every feature. We could look at her hope that I could, along with her fear that I wouldn't, help her to develop the capacity to love more than you are loved, as she intuited was important to being a mother. M kept her sessions until just before her due date. She called me the day her baby was born, her active, achieving self now internally completed, and I never heard from her again.

Chapter 9

Hate, humiliation, and masculinity

In the late 1990s and the early years of the current millennium, I was asked to write papers addressing contemporary political issues like ethnocide and terrorism from the point of view of gender, specifically of men and masculinity. These were, inevitably, speculative and synthetic papers. Worldwide, we faced a kind of ethnic warfare, genocide, and terrorism that we had not thought much about except in relation to the specific historicity of Nazism. I myself was certainly not an expert on such matters. Masculinity was an understudied field, within psychoanalysis and without. "Hate, Humiliation and Masculinity" appeared in 2003, in a volume of papers, *Violence or Dialogue? Psychoanalytic Insights on Terror and Terrorism*, edited by the psychoanalysts Vamik Volkan and Sverre Varvin and published by the International Psychoanalytic Association in response, specifically, to 9/11.

What is striking about my thinking here, as I look back from the vantage point of 2011, is that I had very little to go on. The psychology of masculinity was just beginning to flourish, and the nearest to a psychoanalytic consideration of male violence was the psychiatrist James Gilligan's book, *Violence: Reflections on a National Epidemic*, published in 1996. Stoller (1965) had written about the sense of maleness; Fogel, Lane, and Liebert's groundbreaking volume, *The Psychology of Men*, appeared in 1986; Fogel's work on inner genital space in men appeared in 1998; Person published on male sexuality in the 1980s; Corbett had only begun to publish, and his key article on male humiliation, "Faggot = Loser," did not appear until 2001. It was a challenge to write about men, and in particular, what few psychoanalytic writings there were focused more on male sexuality, whether gay or straight, on identification and identity, on fathers, and so forth. Even violence against women was not much noticed. Subsequent to writing "Hate, Humiliation, and Masculinity," I also tried to address the relative lack of attention to men through convening a panel, "The Riddle of Masculinity," at the 2005 winter meetings of the American Psychoanalytic Association (Brady, 2006).

"Hate, Humiliation, and Masculinity" has a quality of invention. I am trying, from what I know about the psychology of men, male development, and men in society and culture, to tie such knowledge to a consideration of what was, and in its impact still is, a shocking, world-shattering event, the bombing of the Twin Towers. The paper is speculative, doing the best I can, but read back from a consideration of what we now know about men, masculinity, homophobia, and homosexual-homosocial desire, preliminary. Especially, Ruth Stein's first considerations on the fusions of love for god, son-father love, and homoerotic bonding in fundamentalist terrorism appeared in 2002, just as I was editing page proofs for "Hate, Humiliation, and Masculinity," and psychoanalyst and Veterans Administration psychiatrist Theodore Nadelson's *Trained to Kill: Soldiers at War*, did not appear until 2005.[1]

> Michael Gerson ... asked Kissinger why he had supported the Iraq war: "Because Afghanistan wasn't enough," Kissinger answered. In the conflict with radical Islam, he said, they want to humiliate us. "And we need to humiliate them."
>
> Mark Danner, "Iraq: The War of the Imagination," *New York Review of Books*

> It is to moments of humiliation such as these that we owe men like Robespierre.
>
> Stendhal, *The Red and the Black*

In its lead editorial of Wednesday, September 12, 2001, the *New York Times* noted that the September 11 attacks required enormous coordination but that, finally, you needed to understand hatred: "Commentators throughout the day yesterday dwelled on the scale of the planning this terrorist mission must have required. ... But," the editorial continued, "it is just as important to consider the intensity of the hatred it took to bring it off" (p. A26).[2] Several months later, also in the *Times*, columnist Nicholas Kristof described a conference on terrorism. Discussants there, he noted, claimed that poverty and illiteracy are themselves undesirable, but that they are not root causes of terrorism. Most terrorists are of middle-class or privileged origin and well educated, and those who support them are likely to be more

1 1 An earlier version of this chapter appeared in S. Varvin & V. D. Volkan (Eds.), *Violence or Dialogue? Psychoanalytic Insights on Terror and Terrorism* (pp. 94–107). London: International Psychoanalytic Press, 2003. Reprinted with permission.

2 2011 note: As I remind readers in my introduction, this chapter was written, specifically, for a psychoanalytic volume responding to 9/11. Its historical and cultural examples date to this period.

educated than their fellow citizens. Among the three factors most responsible, he suggests, the first is humiliation. To back up his point, he quotes Harvard scholar Jessica Stern: "This word [i.e., humiliation] is extremely important in explaining why terrorists are so successful in recruiting large numbers of young men" (Kristof, 2002, p. A31).

While the world, puzzled, continued to try to understand and address the horrors of terrorist violence, a private episode of violence had taken place in the United States in July 2000, when one angry father of a young hockey player pummeled and killed another father. After the (light) sentencing of the father, the *New York Times Magazine* in January 2002 published an article about youth sports and the problem of parental overinvestment. A "father of a peewee goalie" responded the following month:

> Hockey is a passionate game that requires commitment and character. It requires toughness, both mental and physical. McGrath asks why, in an age of parental effort to reduce risks, we would let our kids play such a rough and aggressive game. I would remind him of the men of Delta Force, on the ground in Somalia and now in Afghanistan, who routinely wear tricked-out hockey helmets. I would remind him of the citizen-athletes in Pennsylvania who prevented even more casualties on Sept. 11. ... I would remind him that life is a risk. (Castro, 2002, p. E4)

Small boys, this father argues, need to play "rough and aggressive" games in order to develop the toughness, character, and commitment of the men of the Delta Force.

Traditional economic, political, and social explanations for terrorism and violence, then, are not enough. Emotions like hatred and humiliation are also central. Sociopolitical conditions certainly affect motivation, feelings, and action, and we can look, as many social scientists might, at motivation as if it is directly caused by abstract and generally described political or material conditions. We can label such behavior as anti-imperialist, nationalist, or borne of religious fervor.

Such an approach, however, frees us from keeping at the forefront of our minds that *particular* individuals engage in suicide missions, mass murder, torture, ethnic cleansing, or genocide. These individuals have conscious and unconscious wishes and fantasies, have, indeed, conscious reasons and rationalizations that make such behaviors feel acceptable and even laudable. We are looking at *individuals* who hate, commit violence, and polarize the world into good us and evil them.

All people individualize cultural and political belief systems according to their particular psychology and their particular developmental and interpersonal history. They infuse religious and political ideologies with the affects that justify and lead to their behavior, whether violent or pacifist, and they get personal gratification or a sense of coherence from participating in causes, connecting with certain people, and disconnecting from others. The question becomes, then, how and why these conditions and causes affect different people differently. Within a particular population of perpetrators, whether among contemporary Islamic fundamentalists or even in Germany during the Second World War, it is never the case that all members engage in extreme violence or even support it.

Yet, as Stendahl, Stern, Kristof, and the father of the peewee goalie imply, but as none notices explicitly, most of the people who engage in extreme violence are men. After September 11, as I was riveted to the *Times,* and as I continued thereafter to read about religious–political and national–ethnic violence in the Middle East, the Indian subcontinent, Serbia, Bosnia, Kosovo, and elsewhere, I began to notice the taken-for-grantedness of this fact. In the public media, men stood without comment for humanity, as American newspapers displayed photo upon photo picturing "Serbians," "Taliban," "rioters in Kashmir," "Palestinian demonstrators," "Saudis," or "Jewish settlers," without noting that these purported ethnically generic and universalizing photos were entirely of men. Gender dynamics in many cultures, including in many of those that are engaged in religious or ethnic wars and genocides (as well as in those that portray them in the media), rendered women invisible.

Terrorism, suicide bombing, the violence of nationalism and ethnic cleansing, all, it would seem, involve a desire to humiliate a male enemy. This masculine desire to humiliate defeated men and to shore up male identity intersects further with misogyny, such that cases of ethnic cleansing often include the mass rape of women and girls, and that political torture usually includes, specifically, the sexual torture of both men and women, as if the perpetrators are enacting male dominance as well as political or ethnic dominance.

We need to ask, then, not only about the psychodynamics arising from hate and humiliation in general of extreme violence like terrorism, mass murder, suicide bombing, rape, or torture, but why it is largely *men* who engage in the vast majority of such violence, whether on an individual or a mass scale.[3] As ordinary soldiers, men make war, and as politicians and generals, they send younger men to war and lead the fighting. Historically and cross-culturally, the military in all societies has been, by definition, masculine (Israel may be an exception here), and military training often involves the invocation of ideologies of aggressive masculinity and explicit, often

[3] 2011 note: When I wrote this chapter, in 2001, I noted that there had been a very few Palestinian suicide bombers who were young women, that these young women were often seen to be motivated by personal crises, and that their families seemed more likely to express sorrow than pride. In the last 10 years, there have certainly been more women terrorists and suicide bombers, and we know that at Abu Ghraib, women as well as men soldiers were involved in the humiliating torture and taunting. Nonetheless, I think it is still fair to say that the vast majority of terrorists and torturers are men.

sexualized, deprecation of women (and, more recently, of gays) (Williams, 1989).[4] Women, by contrast, tend not to be fighters, and historically women may have a special relationship to peace and pacifism (Ruddick, 1989).

Men also engage in extreme violence. They are, mainly, the concentration camp guards, the SS, those who perpetrate genocide, mass ethnic rape, torture, and the wartime murder of children and old people. They find themselves and organize themselves into groups the goal of which is extreme violence, and perhaps—if we read, for example, some of the September 11 and Palestinian suicide bombers' letters and notes (Stein, 2002)—these men get pleasure from envisioning this violence.

Yet, we cannot contrast men's universal aggression with women's universal non-aggression. Aggression is found and develops in pathological and non-pathological ways in both sexes, and some women are violent. Even if we take for granted typical hormonal differences between women and men, hormones can take us only so far since most men are, in fact, not violent. Moreover, while there is certainly typical hormonal variation between the sexes, it is hard to imagine that Serbian men, for example, have higher levels of testosterone than do their more peaceable Slovenian neighbors, or that the Israeli settlers and Orthodox Talmudic scholars who attack fellow Jews who violate the Sabbath, or who attack and destroy Palestinian villages, have higher levels of testosterone than do their Peace Now brothers.

Nor can we minimize the social and political organization of gender that has its own historicity and sociocultural level of functioning. Even if we are mindful of great cultural and historical variation, many cultural constructions of masculinity clearly foster or enable male violence. In the current period, as our attention is drawn to 9/11, to Israel–Palestine, to India–Pakistan, to Taliban and warlord Afghanistan, we might be tempted to link extreme male violence to Islam. Therefore, it is important to remind ourselves that 5 years ago our image of vicious male violence was provided by Serbian ethnic nationalists, who were European Christians, and 50 years before that by Nazis, also European and Christian.

THE PSYCHODYNAMICS OF VIOLENCE

Freud argued that pathology illuminates normality. Accordingly, because, in the psychoanalytic literature, as elsewhere in our culture, gender is figured as female, the disorders and dynamics found predominantly in women are usually seen as female. But when Freud and others study a behavior found predominantly in men—as, for example, in *Civilization and Its Discontents*

[4] 2011: My (admittedly not systematic) impression is that the increasing presence of women (and gays, closeted or not) in the military has not radically changed this.

(Freud, 1930), violence and aggression—this behavior is seen not as a masculine but as a *human* problem (see Chodorow, 1998). However, although not all men are violent, just as not all women are bulimic, we do need to acknowledge that gender is *also* male, and that violence seems predominantly a pathology of masculinity. Our question, then, becomes: What, in the psychic organization of ordinary masculinity, leads a not-negligible number of men to develop hatred and to react to humiliation with violence and aggression in a way that most women do not? As many have pointed out (for early statements, see Horney, 1932; Mead, 1935), men in most modern societies and throughout history have been powerful and dominant, but their power and dominion seem a fragile and vulnerable business, constantly threatened, and consequently, constantly threatening. What can psychoanalysis contribute to our understanding of these phenomena?

In order to investigate this question, I begin by outlining the psychodynamics that seem to go into forms of extreme violence like terrorism. I then investigate the psychic fault lines of masculinity in order to inquire how these seemingly gender-free dynamics of violence and the dynamics of masculinity become linked. My inquiry into political and religious terrorist violence, perpetrated by men against regimes seen as dominated by men, gives us further insight into the pathologies of masculinity beyond that gained by a focus on violence against women. We know that approximately one third of women killed in the United States are killed by current or estranged male partners, and we are now aware that tribal Pakistani courts routinely punish male sexual infringers by ordering the gang rape of these men's female relatives. We are horrified as we learn of the restrictions and punishments of women under the Taliban and those reported from Saudi Arabia.

As I elaborate elsewhere (Chodorow, 1998), two clinical complexes seem to me especially useful in thinking about terrorism and other extreme violence: first, paranoid-schizoid splitting and projective identification and, second, narcissism and humiliation. In the paranoid-schizoid position, as elaborated by Klein (1946), hatred and aggression/badness are thought to reside in the other, or the object, and the self retains all the good, leading to anxieties about persecutory retaliation and thereby to further splitting. As splitting increases, the self is threatened also by fragmentation and disintegration. If it can, the self manages the bad object in fantasy by reintegrating it so that it can be controlled. Eventually, it is hoped, it sees that bad and good are found in both self and other, and splitting decreases.

By contrast, in violent fantasy and action the solution to persecutory or paranoid fears seems to be to destroy whatever or whoever has received the bad-object projection. Violence based on paranoid-schizoid splitting projects badness into the object, leading to persecutory anxiety and to seeing the self both as all-good and as threatened. As Mitchell reformulates this (1993), aggression becomes a reaction to threats to psychological selfhood, which, through projective processes, are experienced as coming from another and intended by another. If someone's internal world becomes centrally organized around these feelings of threat and danger, so that their unconscious fantasy life revolves around aggression and attack, they are likely to experience the world as attacking and threatening and to respond accordingly.

Just as analysts would locate hate-filled violence on the paranoid-schizoid level, focusing on splitting, the projection of hatred and aggression, and basic threats to psychological selfhood, so, similarly, terrorist and other nationalist, religious, and ethnic violence is ideologically justified in split, projective terms. The group that is being attacked or eliminated is objectively evil, destructive, and bad; it may threaten basic existence and may not even be seen as human. Thus, for example, the existence of the United States threatens *our* Islamic existence as ethnicity, tribe, or nation, and we are thereby justified in our (from the point of view of the United States, terrorist) attacks.

Ideological legitimation of national-religious-ethnic violence often seems to use the language of splitting: *we* are all good, *they* are all bad; *they* should be killed, exterminated, or tortured. It is as if ethnic commonality is identity on a social scale, the social equivalent of psychic selfhood, with the same deep roots and same centrality to a sense of being recognized and being whole. Such dynamics characterize the language and behavior of much extremist Islamic anti-Western hatred and Islamic fundamentalism in several nations, the horrific ethnic cleansing and mass rape in the former Yugoslavia, the continuing violent Indo-Pakistani conflict in Kashmir, and the endlessly escalating back-and-forth Israeli and Palestinian not backing down, needing to retaliate, meeting attack with attack.

It was frightening to many Americans when, after having suffered the shock, and often the personal losses, that resulted from September 11, and having begun to learn about Islamic fundamentalism, we were reminded by our own government leaders of an American tradition of similar rhetoric. "America" (*not* the United States) was involved in a crusade against Evil, with God on the side of the Good, who is we. We thus reciprocated ideologically with the same psychological splitting and demonization of the other that had justified the original attacks—a splitting and demonization that continued to characterize Bush administration rhetoric, both domestically and internationally.

In contrast to splitting and projective polarization, a related psychic complex, primary fragmentation and disintegration, seems less relevant to recent Islamic terrorism (except indirectly, as many terrorists are themselves willing to be blown up, thus somehow linking their hatred with the fragmentation of self and other).[5] In fact, Islam in some manifestations has

[5] 2011 note: And see Stein, who suggested in 2002 (see also 2009) that part of the psychic underpinning of September 11 was a regressive pull to fusion and explosive merger with the preoedipal father/God.

a long, organized history of polarizing self and other (in other manifestations, of course, Islam has a history of great tolerance for difference).

Psychosocial images of fragmentation, as opposed to splitting and polarization, are central to other racial–ethnic violence. In these other cases, polarization and splitting seem often a way to defend *against* fragmentation, to hold psychosocial group identity together when it has threatened to disintegrate. Thus, historically, when polities break apart that previously did not provide for adequate mentalization, illusion, and psychosocial depressive-level integration, or that previously did not enable subjects and communities to see themselves as whole, related peoples—for example, the former Soviet Union and Yugoslavia or colonial regimes like the British Raj—we witness a collective disintegration that is defended against by splitting, projection, and violent enactment of projective fantasies.

In addition to paranoid-schizoid splitting, a second dynamic arena that helps us to understand recent hate-filled violence is the complex of shame, humiliation, and narcissism. This complex is addressed by many psychoanalysts but in relation to terrorism perhaps most aptly by Rothstein (1984), who writes of "identification with the humiliator" and the "sado-narcissism" (p. 98) that results. Just as we find clinically that individuals who feel humiliated and shamed are likely to react with rage and grandiosity, the language justifying collective violence and terrorism often explains expansionism, ethnocide, and terrorism in terms of past humiliations and defeats.

Thus, in addition to the language of oppression and humiliation justifying the terrorist attacks of September 11 and the Palestinian suicide bombings in Israel, we are reminded, for example, of the German response to the humiliation at Versailles that helped to support the rise of Nazism, and of the rhetoric of humiliation and necessary self-defense invoked by Serbia and brought explicitly to our attention by Milosevic in the Hague. This rhetoric, justifying ethnocide and murder in Bosnia and Kosovo, relied on events that go back as far as a 13th-century Serbian defeat in Kosovo (Volkan, 1997). We notice the language of the Israeli right wing, justifying aggressive expansionism in terms of centuries of anti-Semitism and a need to go it alone. As Kissinger indicates ("we need to humiliate them"), American rhetoric explaining our post-9/11 actions in Afghanistan often implied that it was humiliation and national pride, rather than safety or national security, that required these.

I am describing two forms of reaction to challenges to the collective self. These in turn mirror individual reactions to such challenges.[6] First, on a more organized and articulated level of unconscious fantasy, one that finds

[6] I cannot address this in the present chapter, but it is important to remind ourselves that there is no simple one-to-one correspondence here. *Individuals* bring a huge variety of personalized fantasies, identifications, conflicts, and transference templates to their participation in movements (on this, see Chodorow, 1998; Smelser, 1998).

expression and reflection in *conscious* collective fantasies and ideologies, humiliation and shame are called upon to justify extreme violence. Defeat and the inability to achieve goals take different forms, depending on how these feelings of shame and humiliation are put into collective fantasy. A sense of humiliation or impotence linked to defeat leads to more narcissistic retaliatory rage, "defeat with honor," to less. Second, on a less ideologically articulated level, social disintegration seems to generate fantasies that are similar to those we find in psychic disintegration. Here, we find a desperate, unarticulated sense that life itself is psychically at stake, for instance, when Tito, controlling, but at least providing some overall containment, dies; when the British pull out of India–Pakistan or Israel–Palestine; when the Palestinians feel abandoned by the United States, or Israel by the rest of the world.

Polities and movements differentiate among enemies (or victims), and this differentiation, based on whether victims are more or less dehumanized, may bear some relation to whether humiliation or splitting fantasies are more prominent. To what extent, on the one side, are enemies thought to feel and suffer, so that there is identificatory joy in the bombing, killing, torture, or rape that constitute sadistic retaliatory violence for humiliation? On the other, to what extent are enemies, in contrast to the collective self, which has a monopoly on personhood, thought not to have thoughts or feelings but to be, rather, non-human bad objects who should be expelled and destroyed?

THE FRAGILITIES AND FAULT LINES OF MASCULINITY

I have been describing the dynamics of paranoid-schizoid splitting that result from felt threats to the self, and humiliation that reacts to narcissistic injury, as if these are experienced by humanity in general—which they are. But, as I have also pointed out, when we are talking about terrorism and other extreme political violence, we are talking about the expression of these dynamics almost entirely by men. We need to ask, then, what, at the psychodynamic level, might make men particularly reactive to such experiences.

We begin with a mediating contradiction. On the one side, men are the perpetrators and enactors of extreme violence, so that it would seem that such behavior, and the psychodynamics that underlie it, must be related to masculinity. On the other, the identity involved in much of this violence is ideologically ethnic-religious-national. The sense of gender in this context comes in only secondarily, as the language of ethnic or religious hatred is often cast in gendered and sexualized terms. Moreover, as I suggest in the previous discussion, national and religious ethnicity or peoplehood are experienced psychodynamically not directly as gendered but as cultural selfhood, and threats to such identities are experienced directly as threats to the cultural-national self.

Thus, in order to understand the psychodynamics of extreme social and political violence, even when this violence is framed in national, religious, and ethnic terms, we need to understand something about splitting, humiliation, and selfhood in men. What, specifically, would link men or masculinity to these dynamics? We begin, I suggest, by considering the fault lines of masculinity.

A first psychic fault line of masculinity involves gender and selfhood in relation to women and femininity. Men's relationships to women, forged originally in the relationship to the mother, bring up a range of threats to masculinity and the male sense of self—especially fears of dependency, abandonment, and loss of self, as well as an intolerance and fear of women's sexuality. This negotiation of maleness in relation to the mother—masculinity as developmentally not-female and not subordinate to women—is one component of masculinity. Masculinity, here, has to do, fundamentally, with not being a woman or dependent upon a woman. Freud, Horney, Stoller, and many psychoanalytic feminists have shown how the repudiation of women and fears of feminization, beginning with the threat of humiliating inadequacy vis-à-vis the powerful mother, are developmentally fundamental to masculinity and tied to the male sense of self.

Because of this developmental context, issues of *selfhood* as well as of *gender* tend to differentiate men from women, such that the male's sense of self may typically be more defensive and in need of protecting its boundaries than the female's typical sense of self. Masculinity thus defines itself not only as not-femininity and not-mother, in a way that femininity is not cast primarily as not-masculinity or not-father. In addition, seeing the self as *not* the other, defining the self in opposition to the other, does not seem generally as important to women as to men, nor does merging seem as threatening (see Chodorow, 1978, 1979).

A virulent example of the need to maintain the gender boundary and gender domination would be the Taliban treatment of women and, more generally, the treatment of women in much of the fundamentalist Islamic world. Closer to home, we might wonder whether the threat of maternal power and female sexuality help fuel extreme antiabortion rhetoric and behavior. Women are, of course, also leading antichoice activists, but as far as I know they do not blow up clinics or shoot doctors who perform abortions. That humiliation seems in some way to affect men and women in different ways can be expected from the classical Freudian account of challenges to phallic narcissism and from feminist descriptions, as I note, beginning with Horney, of the humiliation of being a little boy in relation to grown women.

If the male's basic sense of self—thus, not only his sense of masculinity—is more defensive, then insofar as a cultural politics of identity is involved, it makes psychological sense that women would not feel as psychologically endangered as would men by threats to political or religious selfhood. Of course, the unconscious and conscious ideological infusion of nationhood, religion, ethnicity, and otherness with ideologies and psychologies of gender and sexuality would further reinforce the felt danger to men, whose sense of masculinity is also generally more fragile than women's sense of femininity. Hence, we find that male sexual terrorism enters into much recent ethnic fighting, as in the mass rapes in the former Yugoslavia and other locations of ethnocide and genocide.

The male's need to maintain his masculinity against the threat of feminization and developmentally related anxieties of identity and selfhood have been well theorized, but we need to consider a second fault line. As I turned my attention from the intrapsychic and interpersonal dynamics of masculinities, femininities, and sexualities to public masculine behavior—to religious-national-ethnic violence and virulent homophobia (see Chodorow, 1998)—I came to expand my understanding of masculinity and male selfhood. I came to think that, for men, individual and cultural narcissism and humiliation derive also, and perhaps more prominently, from male-male relationships than from the relationships of men to women.[7]

Thus, complementing my previous writings, I suggest here that an equally fundamental component of male selfhood and identity to the dynamic of male as not-female—a fundamental dynamic that perhaps particularly underpins terrorism and other male political and ethnic violence—is masculinity as being an adult man and not a little boy. Humiliation, specifically, is especially a male-male—originally father-son—affair. In the normal developmental course of events, much hinges on how a boy relates to his father and turns into a man—the delicate negotiation of this transformation, of identification, of how to replace or join without bringing on retaliation, castration, or humiliation. All of these, in turn, depend partly on a father's own sense of confident masculinity and selfhood.

As much as it is being not-female, then, masculinity is not being a boy/child in relation to an adult/father, and it is signaled psychically by not being subordinate to, shamed by, or humiliated by other men. Gay male psychoanalytic writing has been particularly clear about how a becoming-gay, not-masculine-enough little boy (thinking back to the father of the peewee goalie, we might extend this in some cases to any son who displays softness) can feel rejected and turned away from by his father.

In unconscious fantasy, the theme of masculinity as subordination or non-subordination to another man usually hinges on being not a little boy in relation to an adult father or more powerful men, although sometimes it can result, as Freud noted (1914, 1921) in a drive to submit to and identify with

---

[7] I have made such observations clinically, but I would expect that they are more prominently and immediately experienced, as a general rule, in a male-male clinical dyad.

a seemingly powerful and invulnerable male leader. This male-male world seems to figure in "ordinary" warfare as well as in childhood fistfights, in both of which the threat is of being defeated or humiliated by other males. In more virulent and pathological form, it seems primary in underpinning psychodynamically the kinds of religious, ethnic, and nationalist violence that have been so much at the forefront of our lives in recent years.

I am suggesting, then, that Freud was right in "Analysis Terminable and Interminable" (1937), when he suggested that men's conflicts about passivity with regard to another man are psychological bedrock. He was wrong, however, to call this a fear of feminization (Corbett, 2001, also makes this point). The superordinate-subordinate, male-to-male relationship is not reducible to that of male-to-female.

We can find a mythic developmental representation of this dilemma of humiliation and subordination to another man, but it is not Oedipus. In "Freud on Women" (Chodorow, 1991a), I suggested that Freud's account of "female sexuality" might be better rendered through Persephone and Demeter than through Oedipus. If we are interested in myths that capture the inevitable challenges, anxieties, and conflicts of two generations, two genders, power and powerlessness, and desire and its limits, then the story of Persephone is, for girls, a typically more accurate mythic specification.[8]

In the same vein, I would in the context of an investigation of hate, humiliation, and masculinity—and perhaps of male development more generally—suggest that if the actual Oedipus myth may help to describe typical male conflicts around the mother and women, it does not do justice to their conflicts around men. Oedipus's father, Laius, is a shadowy background figure. His attempt to kill Oedipus begins the story (and sets male development in a narrative of senior male aggression), but he figures in Oedipus's own narrative only as a troublesome man met on the road. He is killed almost before the story of Oedipus as agent begins.[9]

In order to capture the intense and driven power in male psychology of male-male/superordinate-subordinate conflict, I would suggest that men are vulnerable to an *Achilles complex*, that a core developmental and psychodynamic narrative comes not from Sophocles but from Homer.[10] Who

[8] *The Reproduction of Mothering* (1978) focused specifically on the development of maternality in women, but, in my several chapters on the female "Oedipus complex," and especially in my description of "oedipal asymmetries and heterosexual knots," I elaborate the bisexual triangle that constitutes normal female heterosexuality: the constant pull back to the mother from the father, to women from men, and the attempt to keep both attachments at once, in both the internal and the external world. Kulish and Holtzman (1998, 2008) later provided extensive clinical grounding along with an elaboration of this developmental account.

[9] Bakan (1968) emphasizes Laius's many fantasies and fears about his own son, and his attempted filicide, but filicidal wishes are generally not much marked in "oedipal" narratives.

[10] My considerations on Achilles were not in the original text of this chapter.

can forget the opening lines of the *Iliad*, when Homer calls on the goddess to sing of Achilles' rage at Agamemnon and in a few short lines summarizes for us how this rage will almost destroy the Greeks? Achilles is a junior man, powerless, humiliated, and taunted by Agamemnon, a senior man who already has a wife and children. On a whim, to feed his own narcissism and to humiliate and taunt this challenging young warrior, Agamemnon takes away Achilles' prize, Briseis, a women of Achilles', not of Agamemnon's, generation. In his sulking retreat bred of humiliation, Achilles does not care if the entire war is lost. There is a woman involved here, certainly—Briseis (and earlier in the narrative, Agamemnon has sacrificed his daughter Iphigenia, who had been promised to Achilles)—but the attachment to her seems minor compared to Achilles' passion about his treatment by Agamemnon.[11]

As my invocation of Achilles would imply, the superordinate-subordinate male-male relationship may particularly underpin terrorism and other male political and ethnic violence. Another way to formulate this mythic developmental story is to suggest that the Achilles heel of men and boys—that is, of both the father's and the son's generation—is the fear of narcissistic humiliation by another man, or by other men, and that the currency of this humiliation is often capricious and arbitrary control through war and conquest, or the monopolization, not of the mother, but of younger women who should rightfully belong to the younger man.[12]

Yet, the worst male violence may occur when fantasies of humiliation by men—the man-boy dichotomy of the Achilles complex—become linked with fears of feminization—the male-female dichotomy—especially as this intertwines with threats to selfhood, that is, when the fantasy and developmental relation to men and to women are combined. In the present context, this occurs when challenges to ethnicity and nation threaten individual or collective selfhood, and the close developmental and experiential

[11] Freud revisits the senior-junior man narrative in *Totem and Taboo* (1913), where the women monopolized by the senior man also play a very secondary role in the psychic focus of the junior men.

[12] Actually, as Slater (1967) showed long ago, you find male vulnerability to narcissistic humiliation throughout Greek mythology, in almost every myth or legend *except* Oedipus. This theme, of an older man's hostility toward (and humiliation as a result of) a younger man's potency, military prowess, and sexuality, and his use of his power to humiliate and deny the younger man, can be found across the operatic canon, perhaps most overtly in Verdi's *Don Carlo*, in which King Philip steals his son Carlo's betrothed, shames him, prohibits his political participation, and eventually has him killed. Meanwhile, Carlo himself remains in a humiliated rage at his father (and Philip, in turn, lives in the shadow of his own powerful father and is humiliated by the Grand Inquisitor). Weaker variants of senior male humiliation-fueled aggression toward, or humiliation and deprivation of, sons or fictive sons are found throughout Wagner's *Ring* and in *The Marriage of Figaro, Tristan and Isolde, La Traviata*, and many other works in the operatic canon and in literature (I am grateful to Larry Hartmann, personal communication, for suggestion of these and many other operas to supplement my own observations on this point).

interlinking of selfhood and gender mean that masculinity is also threatened. An image of humiliation by men—defeat in war, subordination to a leader, occupation by another country, watching father's (personal or political–religious father's) humiliation and being powerless to help—become ideologically and in unconscious collective fantasy intertwined with threats to selfhood and gender, as challenges to social order or the individual psyche may be figured as softening, weakening of boundaries, and feminization. To extend the gender theme in "Group Psychology and the Analysis of the Ego" (Freud, 1921), links between men who see themselves as equals or who identify with a powerful male leader also stave off male-male humiliation and further enforce the repudiation of femininity and sexuality.

I have suggested that in order to understand the psychodynamics of extreme social and political violence, even when this violence is framed in national, religious, and ethnic terms, we need to understand something about masculinity. The psychic fault lines of masculinity and male selfhood—the structure revealed when the crystal shatters—include two developmental and defensive fantasy components: first, masculinity as not-female, and the male self as defensively separate from and warding off the female other, and second, maleness as adult man rather than boy-child, not humiliated, shamed, or defeated by another man. These structural fault lines in masculinity in turn give psychic meaning, respectively, to the splitting dynamics and the dynamics of humiliation that are found in the extreme nationalisms and ethnocentrisms that underpin terrorism and national–ethnic violence.

On the ground, my own historical reading is that both components of masculinity fuse in the Holocaust and in other genocides, where ethnic cleansing often includes the mass rape of women and the murder of helpless old men and boys, in the sexual humiliation and torture of men as well as women by right-wing dictatorships, and in those Islamic countries that restrict and terrorize women and punish severely those who violate sexual codes. Male sexual terrorism against women and men expresses ethnic, religious, and state power in reaction to national and ethnic humiliation through gendered and sexual psychic lenses.

We find similar dynamics in homophobia, which is often latent in terrorist ideology and direct in the torture and murder of gays, both in the United States and as we find homosexuality proscribed and brutally punished in other countries. In this context, homosexuality is figured both as submissiveness to other men and as challenging the male-female divide, making some men feminine. The particular dynamics that lead to homophobic violence are, of course, complex and varied, but I think it is worth stressing the regressive pull toward and fear of old libidinal and identificatory positions—in the case of men, schematically, to attachment to father and to a terrifying identification or fusion with mother.

Attraction to men from a boy identification, attraction to passivity and receptivity, feminine identifications vis-à-vis men, can all be deeply threatening to masculinity, threatening the hard-won achievement of active, aggressive, heterosexual masculinity. Characteristically, femininity and submissiveness to men have to be split off and projected outward, where these, in turn, become extremely persecutory possibilities. Those—like homosexual men—who represent these split-off projections threaten not only persecutory return but also disintegrative flooding: melding and fusion with the self. Accordingly, in the West, attacks on gays are often instituted by those who first "pretend" interest and then turn on the victim who has (or has not) responded. In Afghanistan, we learned that the Taliban punishment for homosexuality was to be crushed under a wall of stones, but we also learned that alongside this was a still-active—and, we must presume, attractive and therefore threatening—tradition in which grown men pick up, seduce, and support just-pubescent boys throughout their teenage years.

CONCLUSIONS

Since the Frankfurt Institute's work on the authoritarian personality and the mass psychology of fascism (Reich's term, 1946; see Adorno, Frenkel-Brunswik, Levinson, & Sanford, 1950; Horkheimer, 1936; Horkheimer & Adorno, 1947); Fanon's on the mentalities of colonizers and the colonized (1963, 1967); and Davis's and Dollard's investigations of American racial prejudice (Davis, 1937; Davis & Dollard, 1940; Dollard, 1941), some of the most insightful, if insufficiently influential, work in the social sciences has used a psychoanalytic frame to understand the human agency and desire found in racism, totalitarianism, militant nationalism, and, increasingly, religious and national–ethnic fundamentalism.

The present chapter contributes to that effort. Here, I have argued that the psychic fault lines of masculinity and male selfhood express two developmental and fantasy components: first, maleness as not-female, the male self as defensively separate from and warding off the other, defensively needing to split self from other if hatred takes over; second, maleness as adult man rather than boy-child, not humiliated, shamed, or defeated by another man. When these components are challenged, individually or in cultural or political experience, men react with violence. We cannot explain terrorism, religious or ethnic hatred, extreme violence, expressions of misogyny, or the creating of enemies by assuming that external factors—history, politics, or society—simply cause these individual and social processes.

Psychoanalysis helps to explain what underlies and motivates the most frightening and desperate of human actions and beliefs, helping us to learn about the dark side of human motivation and behavior, which is always a product of unconscious fantasies and conflicts—even as it also theorizes and models forms of subjectivity and intersubjectivity that provide images of meaningful well-being. It addresses internal senses of self and feelings about others, humiliation, hatred and self-hatred, envy, terror of disintegration, attacks against the self or attacks by the other, and the incapacity to see the other, or even the self, as a self, all of these expressed behaviorally in violence and rage and ideologically in justification of such behavior.

Importantly, clinical psychoanalysis also constitutes a form of intersubjective relatedness in which individuals work together to see the point of view of the other and to recognize that people's actions, however seemingly irrational, unacceptable, self-destructive, or destructive in the world, have motives and reasons that need to be understood. The psychoanalyst models for the patient an openness to understanding the self and the other and a form of listening to the other's subjectivity and many-layered meanings. Such intersubjectivity, based on the recognition of the other as a subject—even if this other engages in heinous acts and holds terrifying or alien beliefs—seems to me crucial to our understanding of terrorism.

Chapter 10

Beyond sexual difference

Same-sex/cross-generation and clinical individuality in the creation of feminine and masculine

"Beyond Sexual Difference" was written for the conference volume of the 2002 Stockholm conference, "Sexuality and Gender," of the Committee on Women and Psychoanalysis. Although the conference title does not reflect this, most presenters and participants at the Stockholm conference, with few exceptions, British, French, and northern European analysts, assumed and articulated a sexual difference perspective on gender. I presented the chapter also as the opening address at the 2003 conference, "Psychoanalysis, Gender and Race," organized by the Psychoanalysis Unit of the University of London. Characteristically, I begin from taken-for-granted theoretical or pretheoretical assumptions, here, sexual difference, and unpack the implications, contradictions, and limitations inherent within these.

"Beyond Sexual Difference" locates me within classical North American psychoanalysis, as I contrast my developmental and clinical approach, founded on multiple classical theories, with the "sexual difference" tradition, originally Freudian and Lacanian, but also characteristic of much European and British psychoanalytic thinking about gender. At the same time, my account implies that classical North American psychoanalysts need to examine an implicit reliance on a difference perspective, in contrast to a more emergent, constructionist view, and in this I join my relational colleagues. By extension, the chapter reflects a critique of poststructuralist and Lacanian approaches to gender that are hegemonic in the academy, and of the isolation of these academic psychoanalytic feminists from contemporary North American psychoanalysis.

In the context of the international volume to which this chapter was a contribution, it is, finally, worth noting that my starting from clinical experience, from a pragmatic rather than theory-driven view, and from iconoclasm toward Freud, may mark me as North American. Although some continental European, British, and Latin American analysts begin from an inductive view of theory, there is within these analytic cultures a tendency toward greater textual fidelity toward theory and theorists than in North America, and clinical work, though extensively presented, is often brought in to instantiate or exemplify theory.

"Beyond Sexual Difference" extends my thinking about the clinical individuality of gender and sexuality, revisiting themes in earlier writing. I theorize sexuality and gender as compromise creations/formations and describe the multiple constitutive components of gender. I remind us that our tendency to universalize psychosexual developmental claims is based partly in reluctance to move beyond Freud and partly in our reactions to the "anxieties of uncertainty" (Chodorow, 1999b) that confront us in clinical work.

As I describe how the multiple bodily, object-relational, cultural, and affective meanings of gender develop, range, and change, in childhood and throughout life, the reader can see my theoretical rootedness in developmental Loewald. Although Loewald did not write about gender and sexuality, his general thinking, as I first acknowledge in 1989, has long informed my work on these topics. In a Loewaldian vein, my account here suggests that gendered ego, gendered reality, and gendered drives all develop out of an individual and initially undifferentiated parent-child relationship, where language and body gain individual, internal meaning through this emotionally and interactionally particular matrix.[1]

Sexual difference has been one hegemonic lens through which writers in both psychoanalysis and the academy have conceptualized gender. This formulation is determined, indeed has been overdetermined, by the way Freud initially posed the problem. It was then selected especially by Lacan as *the* Freudian view, and it has been taken up in the second-wave rethinking of female psychology and femininity especially by British, European, and Latin American psychoanalysts, as well as by American, British, and other academic psychoanalytic feminists. Whether or not they consider themselves Lacanian, then, psychoanalysts who follow the sexual difference approach accept many of the Lacanian assumptions, as do those academic writers, whether psychoanalytic or poststructuralist, who refer intuitively to and elaborate upon "the feminine" and "the masculine."

This chapter argues that our theoretical thinking about the psychology of the sexes—whether we call this maleness and femaleness, masculinity and femininity, the problem of gender, or the problem of sex—has been limited by viewing the problem through the sexual difference lens. I claim that the perspective ignores the multiple components that go into gender

[1] An earlier version of this chapter appeared in I. Matthis (Ed.), *Dialogues on Gender, Sexuality, and Psychoanalysis* (pp. 181–203). London: Karnac, 2004.

and sexuality as compromise creations, as well as gender as an actively engaged psychological product rather than a fixed internal template. It does not allow for individualizing gender and sexuality, in theory and in the individual herself.

The specific observations that I bring to bear in what follows are not always new. Rather, I use clinical, theoretical, and ethnographic observations of our field to locate a problem and frame a position. My reflections begin specifically from my previous writings on Freud (see especially Chodorow, 1991a; Chapter 2, this volume), in which I suggest, in contrast to the sexual difference perspective, that Freud had many approaches to the psychology of women and complex, nonpolarized understandings of the sexualities and their emergent character (see also Chapter 11). The sexual difference perspective ignores this variety, multiplicity, and emergent character, whose contours have been described and theorized in recent years, sometimes drawing directly on Freud, by many colleagues.[2]

The sexual difference position takes as given that the sexes can only be and also are psychologically defined one in relation to the other, that male only gains meaning in relation to female, masculine in relation to feminine. It has both psychoanalytic and non-psychoanalytic roots. From Freud, it locates femininity and masculinity in relation to the external genitals and to genital-oedipal levels of development, deriving specifically from Freud's focus on genital difference—the presence or absence of the penis—as the criterial experience in the boy's and the girl's development. The observation of genital difference, Freud suggests, leads to castration anxiety/penis envy as determinative and central to the psychology of the sexes and sexuality throughout life and to presence/absence of the penis (castration fear or castration already accomplished) as generative of the boy's versus the girl's entrance into and resolution of the Oedipus complex, differential superego development, and so forth. Both Lacan and poststructuralism presuppose this Freudian psychoanalytic basis even as they move it from the realm of anatomy into the realm of fantasy. This familiar territory does not need elaborating.

This way of seeing sex/gender comes not only from Freud but also, equally, from a common rooting in Saussurean structural linguistics and, closely related, Lévi-Straussian structuralist anthropology. In these theories, which underlie or have been interlocutors for Lacan and poststructuralism,

[2] 2011 note: For such a claim, a revision and update from 2002 to 2011 expands the required list of citations to an entire manuscript. I point here to those writings of the last 15 or so years that have particularly expanded my own thinking on these matters. These include, at a minimum, Balsam (2011), Benjamin (e.g., 1995), Corbett (2009), Dimen (2003), Flax (1990), Fogel (2006), Fogel et al. (1986), Goldner (e.g., 1991, 2003), Harris (2005a), Lewes (1998), Notman (2003), Person (1999, 2006), and Yanof (2000, 2007). I am sure that I have omitted many, many others. Even classical American psychoanalysts (e.g., Tyson, 1996) are more likely these days to recognize the multiple paths and patterns of gender and sexuality.

meaning never inheres in a term itself but only in the relation it has to other terms.[3] Thus, by fiat masculine can only gain fantasy meaning in relation to feminine and male in relation to female. This linguistic-cultural theory is read back into a linguistically inflected psychoanalysis.

Following its proponents, I am calling the perspective under consideration the sexual difference perspective, though for me, it could equally be called the gender difference perspective.[4] For my purposes here, what is at issue is not whether we use the term *sex* or *gender*, or whether *sex* refers to the biological, unconscious fantasy, or sexuality, while *gender* refers to the preconscious or the sociocultural. What is at issue, rather, is whether psychologically, in clinical and developmental lived experience—in the realms of unconscious fantasy, transference, the internal world, and affect—masculine and feminine, or maleness and femaleness, must always be paired terms in which the dominant or exclusive meaning of the one is in relation to the other. I myself find the term *gender* useful. It helps us to distinguish, for heuristic purposes, two obviously related but distinct psychological complexes. These are, on the one hand, *sexuality*, that is, sexual object choice and other features of desire and fantasy, and on the other *sexed or gendered self*, that is, the senses of femaleness and maleness, or femininity and masculinity (I am using these to mean not just core gender identity but all of the unconscious and conscious fantasies and constructions that go into a person's subjective gender) and in problematizing what is sometimes seen as a necessary linkage between them. Freud distinguishes these by differentiating "the choice of object on the one hand, and ... the sexual characteristics and sexual attitude of the subject on the other," adding, "as though the answer to the former necessarily involved the answers to the latter" (1920, p. 170). My inquiry takes us to our clinical consulting rooms and thereby also to a reconsideration of how Freud posed the problem of difference in the first place.

In what follows, I suggest some consequences for the theory of beginning from our clinical experience and observation, instead of from theoretical fiat or from an a priori, unquestioned reliance on Freud. When we try to understand how individuals experience and construct their subjective gender and sexuality from such a beginning, we find that sexual difference (the contrastive set male/female, or masculine/feminine) may be for some people

[3] Butler (e.g., 1990) is the leading poststructuralist feminist who also draws upon psychoanalysis, but non-psychoanalytic poststructuralists (e.g., Scott, 1988) also argue, from a historical-culturalist poststructural perspective, explicitly for the exclusively relational meanings of male and female or masculinity and femininity.

[4] Scott would be an example of someone who uses the term *gender* more or less exclusively, except when she is specifically discussing sexuality, but who at the same time always thinks in terms of gender difference. Mitchell (2004), by contrast, is sharply critical of the term *gender* and dismissive and disdainful of those who employ it, and she has consistently written of the *sexual* difference.

a central part of the picture. However, for others it is not more basic or universally organizing than other sex/gender configurations.

I begin from my own previous critique of the sexual difference perspective. I suggest that the sexual difference perspective in particular ignores clinical individuality—the unique ways that individuals create gender and sexuality, which we can know, I would claim, only in the individual case. I then describe what I have come to call the constitutive components, or multiple ingredients, of femininity and masculinity, that we learn about in the consulting room. These include an affectively charged psychophysical body; an internal world; an individualized appropriation of culture; affective tonalities, and sometimes, seemingly non-gendered themes. Finally, each individual puts together a personal animation of gender that gives these components an overall character. Learning how a particular person combines the ingredients that together compose and express his or her gender takes us well beyond sexual difference.

Finally, within this account of clinical individuality and the constitutive components of sex/gender, I extract out and elaborate upon my observation that *same-sex*, *cross-generation* relations and comparison are often as central or, depending on the individual, more central, to the creation, definition, and experience of psychological sex than sexual difference, feminine/masculine, or presence-absence of the penis. Insofar as we theorize difference, I claim that femininity defines itself as much through woman/girl, and that masculinity defines itself as much through man/boy, as does either through male/female.

THE CRITIQUE OF SEXUAL DIFFERENCE: THEORETICAL ORIGINS

It is not surprising that I am skeptical of the sexual difference perspective since my thinking has from the beginning implied an alternative stance. I began my study of the psychology of women (and the contrastive psychology of men) from object-relations theory—a theory that attends to the internal object-relational world. As a result, I examined especially the generational, mother-daughter (or mother-son), constellation within that world, rather than beginning from Freud's focus on the genital distinction and its sequelae. I was led, via a rereading of classical writings by Lampl-de Groot, Freud, Mack Brunswick, Deutsch, and others, to an analysis of the development of maternality and mothering as fundamental to femininity, to a focus on preoedipal object-relational components within this femininity, and to an emphasis on the female oedipal constellation as equally a mother-daughter as father-daughter affair. In this reading, heterosexual father-daughter attachments play a role that alternates with mother-daughter attachments, but they are by no means exclusive.[5] My thinking, of course, was partly reactive. I could take for granted, as already sufficiently demonstrated, male-female, father-daughter elements in female development and psychology.

As others pointed out over the years, and as I myself acknowledged (see Chapter 4), psychoanalytic feminist thinking in the early and mid-1970s was overly leery and critical of any acknowledgment of the psychic role of biology and anatomy, which partially accounts for so many feminists' attraction to Lacanian psychoanalysis in the first place (in addition to Lacan's overlap, via text and language, with the feminist humanities).[6] In this early writing, I acknowledge the potential role of penis envy in female development (see especially Chodorow, 1978, Chapter 7), but I am critical of the view that penis envy is either universal or the driving force in female psychology and development, including, as Freud would have this, in girls' and women's desires for babies. The perspective of psychosexual mother-daughter dynamics, beginning as they do in the preoedipal, leads to a focus on "pregenital" as well as "genital" components of femininity, as well as to an elaboration of reproductive female sexuality and drives. My account would thus have led me more in the direction of primary femininity theorists, to Horney and Kestenberg, rather than toward sexual difference, a perspective growing from an (over)emphasis on genital presence/absence, in the mind as in the body.

In "Gender, Relation, and Difference in Psychoanalytic Perspective" (Chodorow, 1979), I take a more explicit stance against sexual difference theory. I was at the time only beginning to be familiar with Lacanian feminism and its French feminist detractors, those like Irigaray, Kristeva, and Cixous who emphasized a female bodily-linguistic perspective on difference, and I was not yet a clinician. In that essay, I argue that the sexual difference approach derives from a more typically masculine than feminine consciousness, one that needs to separate male from female and to see the two as radically non-overlapping. I claim that a strong developmental or theoretical emphasis on difference, whether it be the self/other or the male/female distinction, is a defensive emphasis borne of psychological conflict. Such conflicts are characteristically male more than female. This is true of separation-individuation theories that stress differentiation and difference over continuing but changing connection, and in views that see gender

5 As I suggest in 1991: Persephone and Demeter. In subsequent thinking (see Chapter 9), I have come to think that we have underestimated the same-sex cross-generational components of masculinity: Achilles and Agamemnon, powerful to the end, rather than Oedipus and Laius, weakly in the background and summarily killed off before the psychological story begins.

6 Within psychoanalysis itself at this point, there was little rethinking of the psychology of women, with the very important exceptions of Kestenberg (1956a, 1956b, 1968) and Chasseguet-Smirgel (1964).

mainly in terms of sexual difference, masculine as not-feminine or the reverse. In this early work, I suggest that even in primary femininity and women's voice and body/language theories, the sexual difference perspective itself already has a psychologically masculine, rather than a gender-neutral, cast.

CLINICAL INDIVIDUALITY AND THE CONSTITUTIVE COMPONENTS OF GENDER

My difficulty with the sexual difference perspective came through my reading and interpretation of psychoanalytic texts, as I tried to understand and theorize femininity and masculinity. Clinical experience expanded and grounded my views. Over the last number of years, I have come to suggest that we can best see lived intrapsychic gender and sexuality as composed of a number of ingredients, or constitutive components. These are on one level of abstraction universals. Each person, developmentally and in her psychic experience and organization throughout life, brings a clinically individual rendition of these components to her gender and sexuality. However, they are only lived in clinically specific combinations. In any individual, they are inextricably intertwined one with the other in a way that gives that individual his or her own particular experience.

Through the concepts of clinical individuality and constitutive components, I am trying theoretically to render what I have discovered clinically and to avoid what I think is a problematic overgeneralizing and universalizing, on an inappropriate level of concreteness, in much of our theorizing about gender and sexual difference.[7] For example, we are taught that *the* Oedipus complex is universal, and that all children pass through the stages of psychosexual development that Freud first described. But although, for example, we can find many boys (or former boys, now our adult patients) with the "fateful" combination of love for the mother and hatred for the father as a rival, we do not know much about any of these boys or men unless we know the particularity of their *particular* love and their *particular* rivalry, how these intermesh with their opposite, love for the father and hatred for the mother, and, finally, how these change, and changed, day to day, in particular manifestations. We learn about these particularities, not the generality Oedipus, from transferences and reconstructions, and we no longer read (or we are skeptical when we do read) in any case report that

[7] 2011 note: I developed this perspective over many years, first in Chodorow, 1994 and 1999a. Read back from Harris's account (2005a) of "gender as soft assembly" especially, but in general from our much greater contemporary reliance, often in metaphoric ways, on nonlinear dynamic systems theories, my individualizing and multifaceted account nonetheless remains more substantively stable, rather than clinically and developmentally emergent, and discovered as such, than I would now propose.

"the patient's oedipal fantasies were analyzed and resolved." And we find that for one man, "oedipal" fantasies are a driving force in his psychology, whether in the area of work or love, and that they are major themes in the transference, whereas for another such fantasies come up now and again. We also know that boys who are becoming gay typically (though within this, also individual uniqueness) bring a set of desires and fantasies to their oedipal love and rivalry that are typically different from those of boys who are on the way to heterosexuality (Corbett, 1993; Isay, 1989).

Similarly, to say that each child goes through an oral phase, or an early Oedipus conflict, or has unconscious fantasies about the mother's breast or her insides, does not tell us about the particularity of an individual's oral phase or early fantasies about the mother's breasts or insides, or the particular constructions of self and object that these produce through projective and introjective identifications. To take my own work, *The Reproduction of Mothering* suggests that mother-daughter dynamics are central to feminine psychology and the reproduction of mothering—an observation that for many has entered the taken-for-granted theoretical, developmental, and clinical lexicon. Yet this knowledge only alerts us, in a way in which we might not have been alerted by classical theory, to notice a woman who does not bring maternal transferences or fantasies into her treatment. It does not tell us what *particular* fantasies about the mother's or the self's uterus or reproductivity, or what *particular* intrapsychic mother-daughter fantasies and transferences, will emerge in a particular treatment and individual psychology. Psychoanalytic theory has conflated the universality of some problems that demand psychic representation or solution with the almost-infinite variety of unconscious fantasies and compromise creations that represent or attempt to address these.

A clinical individual draws from a number of components in creating her personal gender and sexuality.[8] We begin from the psychic creation of bodily experience. This includes observation, arousal, comparison with others, changes in bodily configuration. Freud stressed the observation of genital difference in the just preoedipal child, but the emotional tonalities brought to bodily experience and bodily fantasies begin the minute the child is born, if not before. From the moment of birth, there are subtle, unconscious transmissions of affect, feeling, and fantasy from mother to child that help to shape the child's earliest senses of body, including the sexed, genital, and reproductive body. These transmissions certainly include sexed, genital, and reproductive body—the particular mother's complex of

[8] I use the term *clinical individual* (see Chodorow, 1999d) to emphasize the distinction between the universals that our theory has tended to claim and the unique individuals whom we treat, whose particular instantiations of a theory will have been developmentally particular and, over the course of treatment, will be created in historically particular ways in the transference-countertransference and in other expressions and indications of unconscious fantasy.

feeling and fantasy about her child's sex. Importantly, this sex is itself not a generic sex. Rather, the mother creates its particularity out of her own feelings and history—the other representations of the child in her inner world in relation to her own family of origin, the unconscious and conscious early communications she received from her own parents, her own cultural location, her own conflicts and fantasies, and so forth.

Body and body experience in general, and because of their special physical intensity or startling absolutism, genital and other sexual-erotic experiences (a first period, breast development, excitement and orgasm, pregnancy, childbirth, etc.), particularly call forth affective fantasy representation. Body gets embroiled in sexuality—desire, practices, sexual fantasies, erotization, all of which are specific to the individual—which in turn gives further substance to the fantasy meaning of the sexed body. In theoretical shorthand, we might consider "Freudian" our recognition of the almost-raw, self-evident demands of sexual-bodily-genital experience and observation. The ingredients that go into bodily gender and sexuality will include some representation of sexual difference, but this may or may not be central for a particular individual.

A second element that goes into femininity and masculinity can be called, in shorthand, object-relational. Here, I mean that each person has a uniquely created internal world of unconscious fantasies, both whole object and part object, about self and other, mother, father, and siblings, created through a history of projective and introjective fantasies. Freud's originally theorized inner world that relates to gender and sex is the oedipal world, but it is from Klein especially that we learn about the inner world's complexity and its infantile origins, about how every step in its creation will be imbued with particular fantasy meanings about self and object. The mother's breast, for example, is unconsciously created as beneficent, aggressive, devouring, withheld, toxic, and the relation to it is one of manic control, omnipotent destruction, depressed longing, and so on. As with body experience, the internal world that helps to create gender begins at birth, well before the observation of or capacity to label the sexes or genital difference.

Third, we cannot think about the psychological experience of sex and gender apart from the cultural and linguistic, since these categories are both driven by ordinary anatomy and named and created within culture. From the point of view of the psyche, actual linguistic and cultural labeling is a latecomer. We learn from the research of de Marneffe (1997) that children recognize which genitals belong to them before they know that they are a girl or a boy, and we also know of the primacy of parental filtering. Any term that a child learns is learned in the context of the parent's unconscious and her or his own particularized femininity or masculinity, which is itself emotionally cast, shaped by fantasy, and includes many elements of affective tonality and context that that parent has built into gender. Loewald (1978) conveys this melding clearly: "Language is typically first conveyed to the child by the parental voice and in an all-pervasive way by the mother in the feeding situation and in all her other ministrations to the infant ... her speech and voice are part and parcel of the global mother-child interaction" (p. 180). Thus, he continues later, "The emotional relationship to the person from whom the word is learned plays a significant, in fact crucial, part in how alive the link between thing and word turns out to be" (p. 197).

On the other side, all linguistic and cultural labels, as they are received and produced, are themselves animated and tinted by unconscious fantasy and affect, which have to do with myriad experiences of body, self, and other that may or may not have direct gender content. Thus, the role of bodily-sexual masculine and feminine in the psyche, although having some basis in anatomic and parental reality, goes through what Klein (1940) calls "doubling"—a filtering through fantasy and transference such that external reality is taken into account but only as it is internally reshaped and created (see Chapter 3).

Fourth, affective tonalities, with or without associated explicit connection to gendered or sexed fantasy content, as well as non-ostensibly gender-related fantasies, help to shape masculinity, femininity, and sexuality (see Yanof, 2000).[9] One woman may imbue her sense of femaleness or femininity with a depressive casting, another with anxiety. Envy, narcissistic humiliation, reparative fantasies, or self-destructiveness and self-attack may shape the dominant affective fantasies connected to another's sense of gender. I have noticed that mournful guilt, "weeping for the mother," affectively tints the sense of gender in some patients from more patriarchal cultures (Chodorow, 1999b), and I have suggested (see Chapter 8) that a fantasy of timelessness or defensive denial of time passing, which has a separate existence from gender-inflected fantasies and identity, nonetheless becomes in some women constitutive of the sense of maternality.

These components—body, internal world, the transferential creation of language and culture, and affective tonality—all come together in each individual's personal animation of gender, a conscious and unconscious fantasy constellation that puts these different components together, with a characteristic emotional tonality and an organization designed to manage and contain particular anxieties and defenses.[10] Anyone's personal animation of gender—an organization in which, out of many complex components of different sorts (body, internal world, language, affect, dominant fantasies of self and other), certain are selected, for reasons of fantasy and defense, to have overarching valence—could be thought of as a compromise

[9] Yanof (2000) wonderfully elaborates the changing multiplicity of gender formations, the links between gender and self, and the defenses and conflicts that go into both, and she shows how these change in both patient and analyst over the course of treatment.

[10] Formerly, I called this a "prevalent animation" of gender (see Chodorow 1996b, 1999a), wanting to emphasize that it involves particular dominant themes or aspects that, in some sense, give anyone's gender creation some overall emphases or characteristics.

creation or formation. Personal animations of gender may bring to the fore particularly charged affects or particular representations of or relations to one parent alone. They may be so overwhelmingly driven by bodily experience—because someone has been born with particularly strong genital, oral, skin, or other sensitivities or because of a combination of innate sensitivities and parental handling and the unconscious parental communications and responses that have gone along with this handling—that from the point of view of the unconscious there is only one sex, that sex which brings with it all these myriad bodily experiences. For some, gender is a non-central part of identity and sexuality and the sexual divide uncharged and relatively unnoticed. Others may be obsessed, conflicted, and defined by sexual difference, the absolute of me as feminine in contrast to me as not-masculine, me with a female and not a male genital.

Although anyone's gender always includes some recognition of the difference between feminine and masculine, a particular individual's personal animation of gender may or may not be organized around the masculine-feminine difference. Even in those cases when it is, moreover, genital awareness or feelings about the genital difference between the sexes may or may not form its center. Masculine/feminine is not in any universal sense more basic than many other organizations of gender, and even when it is basic in a particular case, the components of difference do not necessarily privilege the actually observed genital difference or its fantasy-symbolic representation.

In those for whom the sexual difference dominates both the personal animation of gender and also the sense of self (that is, where femininity or masculinity are highly salient in psychic life compared to other elements that might differentiate or relate self and other), non-ostensibly gendered elements may or may not be projectively organized into the feminine/masculine divide. The whole world may or may not be divided along gender lines. Here, culture, both as it is prelinguistically filtered and as it is learned, can help or hinder such projective fantasies, as cultures themselves differ in the extent to which they make the sexual divide and difference absolute, salient, and central. As many feminists have noted, Western culture projectively maps the binaries of emotion/reason, soft/hard, passive/active, and so forth onto sexual difference in what we might call in the individual paranoid-schizoid fashion. In such a case, the divide is absolute, with one side representing all that is good and desirable and the other all that is bad and to be devalued.

I have described the creation of gender as a developmental product, but I am thinking retrospectively, from the viewpoint of the consulting room. We discover in piecemeal fashion our patients' unconscious constructions and fantasies about gender in general and their own gender in particular, along with the psychodynamics borne of anxiety and defense that have helped to shape these, and I came to think in terms of the components of gender and sexuality over the course of years and in the context of my attempts, along with my patients, to understand shifting unconscious fantasies and transferences.

GENDER AS A SAME-SEX, CROSS-GENERATION CREATION IN BODY AND MIND

In this context of these multiple ingredients and individual psychodynamic creations of femininity and masculinity, it has seemed to me that two related creations of sex and gender especially take us beyond sexual difference. One concerns the multiple ways that the body is experienced, noticed, and fantasied about, and the other concerns the extent to which these fantasies and experiences seem to be organized around the generational rather than the sexual divide. My observation is that whether it begins from the presence or absence of the penis or from a non-biological fantasy system that organizes itself in terms of the differential relation to the phallus, the difference focus does not reflect experiential and clinical reality for many patients, perhaps especially feminine experiential reality and the bodily senses of sexuality and self that we discover in women. It is not news that presence or absence of the penis and phallocentrism are male-centered, but I also fully expect that, if we were to bring back to the psychosexuality of men what we have learned from women, we would find that such a narrow definition does not match masculine experiential or clinical reality either (see, e.g., Corbett, 2009; Fogel, 1998; Limentani, 1984).

Beginning with Horney (1924, 1926, 1932, 1933), several clinicians and theorists have pointed out that Freud's original perspective did not accurately portray the primary sexual and self-organization that emerges from a girl's own body configuration and her direct bodily experiences. We now call this primary femininity theory. Following Horney and Klein (1928), Mayer (1986), Bernstein (1990), Richards (1996), Elise (1997), and others have argued that there exist specifically feminine genital representations and experiences—openness, unseenness, diffuseness, a sense of internality or unboundedness—and female forms of genital (rather than "castration") anxieties, for example, fear of penetration, rupture, and diffusivity, that derive from what the girl has, rather than what she does not have. These more specifically female experiences are also sometimes seen to lead to more typical elements in female character or experiences of the other. Mayer, for example, notes that women tend to fear being emotionally closed over and to notice emotional closed-offness in men. By complement, following Kestenberg (1956a, 1956b, 1968), Fogel (1998), Elise (2001), and others suggest that men also have inner genital awareness or fears of penetration similar to women. I would add my own observation of patients for whom what we would consider severe and driven penis envy, desire for a penis, or even a fantasy penis may sometimes be found to defend against a much more profound, depressive sense of lack and incompleteness, not in comparison to men, but in comparison to other fully endowed females (e.g., women with breasts or fully functioning internal reproductive organs).

As critique, as theory, and in its closeness to clinical and developmental observation, the primary femininity hypothesis was a great advance. However, it is also limited. Because it begins as an argument with Freud, it does not really get away from centering gender on a male-female comparison. Moreover, it still for the most part retains an almost-exclusive focus on the external genitals—female genital experience and genital anxieties. It assumes, that is, that the external genitals are psychologically the criterial defining organs of sex and have, in women as in men, exclusive or near-exclusive primacy in bodily gender. Now, of course, we cannot overemphasize the importance of genital configuration and experience to bodily awareness and representation; to arousal, excitement, and desire; and to unconscious fantasies, not only about body but also about the self in the world. But for many women, certainly (and perhaps in corresponding fashion for men—we do not know), even when we want to stay close to the body and to body experiences themselves, other organs equally define biological femaleness and are experientially and in unconscious and conscious fantasy as important and intrinsically defining for them of their femininity and (female) sense of self.

Notman (2003) elaborates this point. Beginning developmentally, she points to the lack of breasts and subsequent breast development—visible to the little girl in comparison with her mother at least as early and as fully as the sexual genital difference. Our infant-centered gender/sexual theories have tended to refer to *the* breast. But from the point of view of the girl, and of women, it is the breasts, two of them, their size, their meaning, how they develop and when, their early function in the infant's life, and later, their responsiveness to nursing and sexual stimulation, that matter. Notman observes that when they develop, the girl's breasts are a new organ, and we might add that they become a different organ again when they are used for nursing. The inner bodily potential to become a mother—knowledge of the uterus, the sense that there is a great difference between a little girl who cannot get pregnant and a mother who can—are important to a girl from very early on (on this see Balsam, 1996, 2003, 2011), and as she gets older, the girl's knowledge of the inner bodily potential to become a mother becomes both further concretized and further enveloped in fantasy through the experiences of puberty and menstruation. For some women and girls, reproductive drives seem as potent and organizing as sexual drives, and we are as likely to find difficulties and disorders around reproductivity and fantasies of the reproductive body (the uterus, the ovaries, menstruation) as of genital sexuality in women.

A focus on the genital difference (especially as such a focus has been, with the exception of Kestenberg, mainly on the external genital, even if this genital has an opening to internality) misses all of these bodily experiences and their potential psychological concomitants, all of which are equally feminine, equally emergent from the body, and as developmentally and clinically central to what many women mean by and experience as their bodily femininity. In addition, suggests Notman, we sometimes find women centering their femininity around weight, whose connection to sexuality and gender can, we know, follow different paths in different women—dieting, exercising, in extreme cases bulimia and anorexia. We could add that facial hair, pubic hair, and bodily hairiness, among other bodily features, may also play a role in women's sense of femininity or its lack—facial hair "masculinizing" women, pubic hair giving them the body of an *adult* woman as opposed to that of a little girl. Women vary in the extent to which they organize their bodily femininity around the genital difference, or even around genital experience and its representations over these other aspects of body and reproductivity, and in the extent to which their prevalent animation of gender is bodily in the first place.

In *The Power of Feelings* I describe K. It was in thinking about K that I noticed how a woman could make bodily and even external genital configuration, but not sexual difference, central to her sense of femaleness.[11] For K, the most intensely charged aspects of gender were not primarily organized around the male/female polarity. Although this polarity was present in her fantasy life, her comparisons of herself to men were relatively not so salient, and they were centered mainly in conscious fantasies about men and women in the work world. Whether or not she had a penis was not so noticed, and her desires for men and fantasies about what a relationship to a man might bring her (whether sexual gratification, a sense of narcissistic completion or confirmation, rescue, etc.) were not that elaborated.

Yet, in both contradistinction to and confirmation of the classical theory, for K, feminine versus masculine was not so central, but organizing gender with reference to her genital body was. With great feeling and fantasy elaboration, K organized her bodily gender in terms of the little girl/mother polarity. She felt herself to be an inadequate little girl with inadequate little genitals. Her locus of comparison was not "the boy" but grown women, originally her mother, with adult genitals. She had images of this felt comparative inadequacy from as far back as early latency, and they were also active in early and middle adolescence.

Shame and disgust were the affective tonalities that characterized K's animation of gender and experience of her female body, whether she imagined herself as a little girl or as a grown woman. In one fantasy elaboration of body, K was an inadequate little girl with little-girl genitals, but both during development and currently, she also felt that grown women's bodies were intrinsically problematic. Pregnancy and menstruation, for example,

[11]The following paragraphs summarize my case description (1999b, pp. 84–86).

give women cramps, make them weak, sluggish, and heavy, and remind women that they are tied to these uncontrollable bodies.

Heterosexual relationships posed a conflictual solution to K's shame. A strong, masculine man could help her appreciate her adult feminine body and make her feel successfully feminine, but he also by his presence served as a reminder of her weakness and the general shamefulness and weakness of adult femininity. However, when she was involved with men whom she perceived as not so conventionally masculine, even though she was not so reminded by their presence of her own weakness, she felt inadequate as a heterosexual feminine woman, which was shameful in its own way. A further quandary for K was her conscious self-identification as a feminist, which made her, as she put it, "hate to think that women are weak."

K, then, was focused on external genital configuration as central to femininity, and in this sense she followed the original Freudian claim. However, her locus of comparison was not primarily the penis and sexual difference. She was preoccupied, rather, with the difference between having a little girl's or a grown woman's genitals. A *same sex/different generation* comparison located in the external genitals thus constituted K's prevalent animation of gender. Also according to the Freudian claim, dominant affective tonalities were involved in K's sense of difference, but for her the comparison elicited shame and disgust, not envy. Shame was prevalent when she thought of herself as having an inadequate little girl body in comparison to that of a fully formed woman, but the alternative was no better: when she fantasied the menstrual excretions, pregnancies, and sexual and maternal excess that come with the fully adult woman's body, she felt disgust and disdain for weakness, out-of-controlness, and vulnerability.

Individual women may parse the body and difference divide in other ways. For some women, the comparison and main constituents of gender may also be bodily and, as with K, generational, but in their case focused on the adult woman-little girl difference more fully in terms of reproductive internality. For one woman, a uterus, cervix, and internal vaginal opening—structured and elaborated insides—contrast with her own emptiness or internal nothingness. For another, the all-too-present maternal uterus, which has produced too many babies, is attacked through an attack on one's own all-too-present uterus, for instance, in multiple abortions (see Chapter 8; Pines, 1982, 1990). In such cases, body is internal and reproductive rather than external and genital, but the main locus of difference and relation remains same sex.

For still other women, the male-female difference may be primary but body secondary. These women organize gender, we might say, anaclitically rather than narcissistically, predominantly through internal objects that meet or do not meet felt needs, rather than through the body. I describe in *The Power of Feelings* (1999b) one woman who animates gender predominantly in light of the man she cannot *be*, in terms of affective organization and behavior (a projective fantasy about her father's and brother's sense of entitlement) and another who animates it predominantly in terms of the man she cannot *have* (a depressively toned longing for a divorced, and thereby lost and romanticized, father).

I am implying that, much as primary femininity theory is a major advance over the phallocentrism of the traditional sexual difference perspective, and much as it certainly describes the bodily sexual animation of gender for many women, even this *non-male-centered* sexual difference perspective bypasses two elements that I have found to be equally prevalent in sex/gender: first, difference, comparison, and relation that crosses generation but is single sex, and second, sexed-gendered body that is not centered on the external genitals. Thus, although male/female will certainly enter into any woman's construction of femininity, femininity for women always involves not only their relation to masculinity, but also (and sometimes with much more force) their relation to generational difference: to femininity as little girl or grown woman, mother or not mother, what mother has and little girl does not have.

For men also, I have now come to theorize masculinity not only as not-female, as I had emphasized in *The Reproduction of Mothering* (1978), and as would be consonant with Freud's centering sexual difference on the presence or absence of the penis, but also as involving the man/boy dichotomy. When the developing boy compares himself or fantasizes his masculinity, it is not only in relation to his female, vaginal ("castrated") mother (with breasts, Klein would add). Difference also inheres in his comparison of himself, with his little penis and his small size, to his male father, with a large penis and testicles, pubic hair, large size, and seeming personal power. In this comparison with grown men, humiliation and inadequacy, rather than castration, are the threat (similarly, our case reports suggest that male patients are as likely to feel inadequate and humiliated as they are to feel potentially castrated in relation to their male analysts). When a man's "masculinity" is threatened, it is as often because he feels like an inadequate and humiliated little boy vis-à-vis other (adult, masculine) men, as I name this, the Achilles complex, because he is being created by adult men as a subordinate masculinity, rather than because he feels feminized, or "castrated." In this context, I claim:

> I am suggesting that Freud was right, in "Analysis Terminable and Interminable," when he suggested that men's conflicts about passivity with regard to another man are psychological bedrock, but he was wrong to call this femininity: The superordinate-subordinate, male-male relationship is not reducible to a male-female relationship. (ch 9, p. 132)

BACK TO FREUD: CONCLUDING REFLECTIONS

If we return to Freud and the other classical theories, my clinical observations of same-sex/cross-generation components to femininity and masculinity are not a theoretical surprise. In both its simple and complete forms, the Oedipus complex, while instigated by and in the classical account resolved through castration anxiety or the desire for a penis, in fact makes generation as well as gender central. This dual focus on the psychic role of gender and generation has been especially theorized by Chasseguet-Smirgel (1984, 1986) and McDougall (1986), but the terms themselves mitigate against seeing that generation itself may be intrinsically gendered. Both boy and girl evaluate the inadequacy, as well as the vulnerability, of their organ in relation to the same-sex parent, even as they also notice and make something of their organ's difference from and capacity to satisfy the opposite-sex (or, in the becoming-gay case, the same-sex) parent. In fact, same-generation (sibling) difference, which is often conventionally alluded to in discussions of difference—"the little girl sees the little boy and knows that she wants what he has"—seems a lesser component in the cross-sex comparison for most people.

That same-sex/different-generation components would be central to femininity and masculinity could be predicted from Freud's originary theory. They are directly discussed (though, in comparison to female-male or mother-son, not much) in relation to father-son and could be easily extrapolated in terms of mother-daughter bodily relations, difference, and comparison as well. When we add Klein's account of the early Oedipus conflict and her view that idealization of the penis develops in both sexes as a defense against the child's sense of the power of the maternal breast, we can especially see classical roots for the girl's location in a non-phallocentric, same-sex/cross-generation complex that does not center on the external genitals.

Of course, all of these classical theories have required major modification and critique, as I have discussed throughout this chapter. Especially, psychoanalytic and feminist critics have pointed to the need to emphasize the primary meanings of the female body for women and girls and to challenge the near-complete inattention to maternality in all the classic accounts (with the two-line exception of Horney). It has been necessary to elaborate upon the intrinsic, non-phallocentric development of reproductivity and maternality in women and to rethink female sexuality in order to restore theoretically to women the undoubted clinical and experiential reality of female sexual passion and desire that cannot be elicited from Freud's aseptic account. But even with the need for these major modifications, the classical theories of the Oedipus complex that we inherit from Freud, Lampl-de Groot, Horney, Klein, and others, which include serious attention to generational object relations as well as to gendered body, provide more of a foundation for the rethinking of femininity and masculinity than the sexual difference perspective *tout court*.

I have suggested several problems with the sexual difference perspective. First, it universalizes what is clinically individual and variable, and it reduces to one component, through a structural linguistics rereading of Freud's emphasis on the presence or absence of the penis, the many constitutive components that go into anyone's femininity or masculinity. Second, this perspective ignores other non-external genital but equally prominent bodily observations, comparisons, experiences, and fantasies that construct bodily imaged masculinity and femininity. Third, these other forms of embodiment often arise from and lead to a difference perspective that emphasizes same-sex cross-generation difference.

My observations in this essay arise from the clinical consulting room, but they result in a theoretical critique and an alternative theory. Femininity and masculinity are created through comparison with the other sex, but they are equally created through the psychic processing of directly powerful bodily experience, through comparison with those of the same sex but of a different generation, and through the ways they are lived in the context of the entire psychic life of the individual.

Chapter 11

Homosexualities as compromise formations

As we reached the second millennium and began to approach the 100th anniversary of Freud's *Three Essays*, mainstream American psychoanalysis experienced a small upsurge in interest in and rethinking of homosexuality. In December 1998, I participated in an interdisciplinary forum on homophobia at the meetings of the American Psychoanalytic Association that drew perhaps 800 people to the large ballroom of the Waldorf Astoria (Hoffman et al., 2000). Two years later, I spoke on a well-attended panel on bisexuality, also at the American Psychoanalytic Association. The present paper, written in response to an invitation from Janine Chasseguet-Smirgel to contribute to an issue of the *Revue Française de Psychanalyse* on the homosexualities, grows out of my forward to the *Three Essays*, my presentations on these panels, and my noticing what I had not said in that foreword, specifically about bisexuality. There is also a nod to the French context for which I was writing.

Its title echoing "Heterosexuality as a Compromise Formation," this paper argues that the homosexualities must be understood as part of sexuality more generally, and that they are like in kind to the heterosexualities. Freud's *Three Essays* provide a starting point for nuanced psychoanalytic understandings of sexuality in all its complexity. I elaborate upon and modify, for the purposes of a discussion of sexuality, the description of constitutive components that I develop in *The Power of Feelings* and contemporaneous writings on gender.[1]

When it comes to sexuality, psychoanalysis—theory, clinical understanding, and treatment—has needed on the one hand to catch up with both the culture and its own clinical findings and on the other to return to Freud. That our reconsiderations arise in a cultural and political context does not vitiate or weaken them. French psychoanalysis, via Lacan and structuralism, was among the first to argue that when it comes to gender and

[1] An earlier version of this chapter appeared in *Revue Française de Psychanalyse*, 67, 2003, pp. 41–64. Reprinted with permission.

sexuality, we are always partially in the realm of culture. Our bodies, masculinity, and femininity are named linguistically. Our identities, fantasies, and desires are filtered through our parents' own linguistically infused fantasies, through cultural stories, and through institutions like marriage, parenthood, religion and politics.

We are also in the realm of clinical reality. Our previous universalizations and generalizations, both about what was "heterosexuality" and what was "homosexuality," and about the relations of these to pathology, founder. We come up against the finding that each clinically particular individual has his or her own personally individualized sexuality, whose description requires much more than a generalization about the sex of the object in relation to the self (Chodorow, 1992). We see from one hour to the next two patients, the homosexually identified of whom has a creative job and lives in a stable, loving, long-term relationship helping to care for the children from his partner's previous marriage and the other of whom has been heterosexually married five times, compulsively womanizes, is filled with barely contained and volatile anger, is unable to experience women as whole objects, and sees his job as an opportunity to compete with, defeat, and humiliate other men (Kernberg, 1976, makes a similar point, claiming that some "heterosexuals" function at borderline or narcissistic, preoedipal, part-object levels, and others at oedipal-genital levels).

In what follows, I argue that we cannot understand the homosexualities without addressing sexuality more generally. I will use Freud's contributions and those of a couple of other founding analysts, somewhat in the manner of an interpretive *après-coup*, to initiate my own account of what I believe sexuality to consist in. I will then draw on two clinical cases to illuminate my view that sexualities are individual, composed of multiple facets, and, finally, not necessarily explainable in any of our classical terms. Our understanding of this complexity and individuality is what allows us to treat those of varying sexualities.

Somewhere in the middle of the 20th century, psychoanalysts began to refer to and treat an entity called homosexuality, which was a form of pathology or illness. In the United States, some analysts, often buoyed by thinly veiled moralistic and religious underpinnings, engaged in "directive-suggestive" treatment, more or less browbeating and threatening their (mainly male) homosexual patients into becoming "heterosexual." Cure was considered to be achieved in purely behavioral terms—if a man had sexual intercourse with a woman—without regard for internal changes or changes in general psychological functioning (see Mitchell, 1978, 1981; Chapter 5, this volume). In France, it was thought that no one could keep gender and generation clear in their mind if they chose a same-sex object. Gender, by definition, meant opposite-sex object choice. Other psychoanalytic settings and theoretical approaches, in their writings and presentations at least, ignored sexual orientation altogether. Throughout the psychoanalytic world today, psychoanalytic organizations in several countries still conflate object choice and level of pathology, proscribing the training of opening gay and lesbian candidates.[2]

All of these activities reflect an extremely narrow and partial reading of Freud. On the one side, this reading misunderstands much of the *Three Essays on a Theory of Sexuality* and ignores the complete Oedipus complex that Freud later postulates to be developmentally normal in both girls and boys. It confuses "oedipal"-level psychic functioning (neurotic rather than psychotic, triangular rather than dyadic, the psychic capacity to recognize a relationship between the parents, whole-object rather than part-object fantasies and relations to others, "genital" rather than "pregenital") with one oedipal sexual outcome, and it presumes rather than documents the association between pathology and alternate object choices.

On the other side, this reading follows a normative rather than clinical implication, both found throughout Freud. That is, in contrast to his nuanced and complex account that I will describe in the following discussion, Freud also implies that the desired developmental outcome is heterosexual object choice with coitus, engaged in by an active male who identifies with his father and has resolved his castration anxiety and a passive female who identifies with her castrated mother, has resolved her penis envy, and has moved her organ of sexual pleasure from clitoris to vagina.[3]

Freud's legacy, then, is curiously double. On the one hand, Freud implies, especially in his later writings (1924, 1925, 1931), that there is a single normal femininity and masculinity tied to a particular oedipal resolution, object choice, and passive or active stance. On the other, his earlier *Three Essays on the Theory of Sexuality* are astoundingly radical and complex,

[2] 2011 note: This paper was originally published in 2003, but I believe that the claim is still accurate.

[3] Lewes (1988) portrays this brilliantly in tabular form. He shows that the various factors involved in the Oedipus complex (Is the identification with mother or father? Is the mother phallic or castrated? Is the aim active or passive? Is the sexual position active or passive? Is the mode of object choice anaclitic or narcissistic? Is the object mother, father, or self? Is the gender identity feminine or masculine?) lead to 12 possible outcomes. Of these, six are heterosexual, but among these six, only one outcome is "normal." The boy's heterosexuality must involve an active sexual position and instinctual aim, identify with his father, take a castrated woman as object, be anaclitic, and express a masculine gender stance. See also Rubin (1984), influenced by Foucault as well as by Freud, who pictorializes what she calls the "sex hierarchy"—the "charmed circle vs. the outer limits" of acceptable sex (p. 281). The charmed circle of sex is heterosexual, married, monogamous, procreative, noncommercial, in pairs, in a relationship, between members of the same generation, at home, with no pornography, using bodies only: "vanilla." The outer limits include sex that is homosexual, unmarried, promiscuous, non-procreative, commercial, alone or in groups, casual, cross-generational, in public places, pornographic, with manufactured objects, or sadomasochistic. Rubin also describes the historically and culturally changing hierarchy that results from "struggle over where to draw the line" (p. 282). For example, in recent times, in some countries, unmarried heterosexual and long-term monogamous homosexual relationships have entered the charmed circle.

and his "Psychogenesis of a Case of Homosexuality in a Woman" (1920b) claims that his patient was not neurotic. Freud here describes in her a completely normal Oedipus complex (taking her father as love object and identifying with mother) and postoedipal homosexuality. Freud hints that the problem with his patient's choice of object was as much her object's dubious morality as her object's gender.

We can use Freud's thinking and that of some of his colleagues to help our rethinking of the homosexualities—indeed, to initiate our capacity to speak in the plural of sexualities in the first place. Two topics in Freud best point us toward this rethinking. First, his extremely useful inversion-perversion distinction helps us to reconsider the pathology of homosexuality. Second, and intrinsically related, Freud's considerations on bisexuality allow us to see sexuality and gender in multiple and complex rather than monolithic and oversimplified ways.

In the *Three Essays*, Freud is careful to distinguish inversion from other "deviations" in "object choice" (i.e., children and animals), as well as inversion from perversion—"deviations" with respect to sexual aim. Inversion, Freud is clear, refers only to the sex of the choice of object in relation to the sex of the subject: An invert chooses a same-sex object. Freud is curious about, and concludes that we cannot explain, the genesis of inversion in the individual, but he does not otherwise imply that such a choice (in contrast to the choice of children or animals) is automatically problematic or perverse (involving, by definition, a non-genital aim). Freud, then, carves away the choice of opposite-sex object from the rest of the sexual aberrations, especially from those he calls perverse in aim and implicitly from those he considers perverse or problematic in object choice.

Typical of his challenge to cultural normativity, Freud's treatment moves toward normalizing the homosexualities and problematizing the heterosexualities. Both homosexuality and heterosexuality, he tells us, involve a "tyranny" of one object and aim, such that exclusive libidinal object choice serves defensive functions and requires more explanation than bisexuality, and a single-object choice is suspect: "In all of us throughout life, the libido normally oscillates between male and female objects. ... When the swing over is fundamental and final, we suspect the presence of some special factor" (1920b, p. 158). Thus, "the exclusive sexual interest felt by men for women is also a problem that needs elucidating and is not a self-evident fact based upon an attraction that is ultimately of a chemical nature" (1905b/1915, p. 146).

For Freud, the homosexualities and the heterosexualities meet on the terrain of bisexuality since everyone has both homosexual and heterosexual libidinal attachments in their unconscious. "Bisexual disposition is somehow concerned in inversion," Freud (1905b, pp. 143–144) tells us, and when you get a previously homosexual person to be interested in the opposite sex, he says, you are "restoring his full bisexual functions" (1920b, p.

151). But bisexuality is also involved in non-inverted, heterosexual, object choice, such that heterosexual object choice is just as restricted in its choice and aim as homosexual: "In addition to their manifest heterosexuality, a very considerable measure of latent or unconscious homosexuality can be detected in all normal people" (1920b, p. 170). Thus, we *call* people who choose or consciously desire partners of the same and opposite sex bisexual, but "every human being is bisexual in this sense and ... his libido is distributed, either in a manifest or a latent fashion, over objects of both sexes" (1937, p. 244).

Sexuality is not only a matter of sexual desire or object choice. It involves "mental sexual characteristics" (Freud, 1920b, p. 170)—what we might call gender identification or gender identity—as well, and the one does not predict the other. Challenging our stereotypes and our tendency to elide object choice with appropriate masculinity or femininity in "The Psychogenesis of a Case of Homosexuality in a Woman," Freud tells us:

> The literature of homosexuality usually fails to distinguish clearly enough between the questions of the choice of object on the one hand, and of the sexual characteristics and sexual attitude of the subject on the other, as though the answer to the former necessarily involved the answers to the latter. (p. 170)

Unlike subsequent analysts, when Freud tries to define the subject characteristics, masculinity and femininity, he does not assume that he knows what masculinity and femininity are. In his reasoning, if masculinity simply refers to the empirical characteristic of being male, and femininity to being female, then the definitions are tautological. So, he introduces in the *Three Essays* and takes with him throughout his writings the arbitrary definitions: Masculinity is active, femininity passive: "Everything that is strong and active male, and everything that is weak and passive female" (1937, p. 188).

But masculinity and femininity do not in any simple way go respectively with being anatomically male and female. Everyone, says Freud, has a mixture of both:

> In human beings pure masculinity or femininity is not to be found either in a psychological or a biological sense. Every individual displays a mixture of the character-traits belonging to his own and the opposite sex; and he shows a combination of activity and passivity whether or not these last character traits tally with his biological ones. (1905b, p. 220)

As Freud combines his considerations on gender character and identity with those on object choice, he becomes even more postmodernly gender-bending. He notes that homosexuality does not necessarily go with a "change-over in the subject's other mental qualities, instincts and character traits into those marking the opposite sex" (1905b, p. 142). A homosexual man, for example, *may* feel like a woman in search of a man, but *many* homosexual men choose feminine men as sexual objects and themselves are extremely masculine:

> There is, as it were, a compromise between an impulse that seeks for a man and one that seeks for a woman, while it remains a paramount condition that the objects' body (i.e., genitals) shall be masculine. Thus the sexual object is a kind of reflection of the subject's own bisexual nature. (p. 144)

A man, Freud notes, may have masculine personality characteristics and a masculine (i.e., active) orientation in sexual life but be homosexual, whereas another man may have a mainly feminine character, behave in love like a woman, and be heterosexual: "In men the most complete mental masculinity can be combined with inversion" (1905b, p. 142). We would have to say, concludes Freud, that

> The mystery of homosexuality is therefore by no means so simple as it is commonly depicted in popular expositions—"a feminine mind, bound therefore to love a man, but unhappily attached to a masculine body; a masculine mind, irresistibly attracted by women, but, alas! imprisoned in a feminine body." (1920b, p. 170)

"The choice of object" and "the sexual characteristics and sexual attitude of the subject" are not, any more than object and instinct, "soldered together."

From Freud, then, we learn, first, that everyone, whatever their conscious behavioral homosexuality or heterosexuality, is bisexual in object choice, if we look not just at manifest but at latent unconscious libidinal orientations. Second, everyone has the characteristics of both masculinity and femininity within them. Third, either a man or a woman can be predominantly masculine or feminine, if we see these in terms of activity and passivity. And fourth, there is no direct relation between the masculinity or femininity of the subject and the biological sex (or masculinity or femininity) of the libidinal object.

This multifaceted theory was fertile ground for Freud's colleagues and followers. Deutsch, Jones, Lampl-de Groot, and others emphasized in particular the girl's oedipal bisexual attitude toward mother and father, and Freud claimed that children of both sexes develop a "complete Oedipus complex." In "Womanliness as a Masquerade," Joan Riviere especially extends Freud, making a clinically grounded argument against both foundational gender and exclusive sexual orientation. She points to

> men and women ... who, while mainly heterosexual in their development, plainly display strong features of the other sex. This has been judged to be an expression of the bisexuality inherent in us all; and analysis has shown that what appears as homosexual or heterosexual character-traits, or sexual manifestation, is the end-result of the interplay of conflicts and not necessarily evidence of a radical or fundamental tendency. The difference between homosexual and heterosexual development results from differences in the degree of anxiety, with the corresponding effect this has on development. (1929, pp. 90–91)

Riviere thus emphasizes that all gender and sexual solutions are products of defensive layering and conflict resolution. As she puts it, subjective femininity in a woman and, presumably, masculinity in a man, are *both* the real thing *and* a masquerade.

You would think that this theoretical grounding would have led psychoanalysts to the forefront of cultural, political, and clinical questioning of rigid conceptions of normative gender and sexuality, but it is only in recent years, spurred by pressure from without, that such questioning and rethinking have developed. For example, when Kubie (1974) wrote of "the drive to be both sexes" in the early 1970s, he took the drive to be problematic since it cannot be satisfied. Today, by contrast, in the United States contemporary relational feminists like Aron (1995), Bassin (1996), Benjamin (1995), Fast (1984), Elise (1997), and Goldner (1991) take a more pro-bisexual view when it comes to the sex of the subject, arguing that some retention of gender overinclusiveness (fantasies of being both sexes or having characteristics of both sexes) is desirable and necessary. Narrow adherence to all the characteristics and identifications of one gender is defensive and rigid, what Sweetnam (1999) calls paranoid-schizoid gender. Rethinking of object choice has also been late in developing. Lewes (1988) and I (1992) claim that all oedipal outcomes are based on conflict, defense, and the management of trauma and anxiety—as I put it, that heterosexuality, as well as homosexuality, is a compromise formation. Following feminist arguments for differences among women and based on my clinical experience, I also argue in several writings that there are many femininities and masculinities, many heterosexualities and homosexualities.

But such extensions of Freud have not been widespread. As I note in "Heterosexuality as a Compromise Formation," most analysts historically have assumed that heterosexuality is normal, along with an innate masculinity or femininity that arises—even as it follows the tortuous paths of the complete Oedipus complex—directly from genital experience. In the face of incontrovertible evidence, theorized as a mainstay of psychoanalysis, that the sexual drive and desire have all to do with pleasure and little to do with reality, and that most heterosexual coitus is not for purposes of reproduction, these analysts maintain or imply that heterosexuality is normal because there must be some heterosexual coitus resulting in pregnancy for species continuity.

Although most analysts claim to follow Freud's hypothesis of innate bisexuality, which would implicitly distinguish homosexualities and heterosexualities not on the basis of choice of object in relation to subject but according to other clinical criteria, they do not, in my experience, mean his subtle, complex, and multilayered investigation. Freud notes:

> It must be born in mind that hitherto only a single type of invert has been submitted to psycho-analysis—persons whose sexual activity is in general stunted. ... The problem of inversion is a highly complex one and includes very various types of sexual activity and development ... all human beings are capable of making a homosexual object-choice and have in fact made one in their unconscious. (1905b/1915, p. 145)

But in later times, the hypothesis of bisexuality has been reduced to a sort of mantra, or shibboleth, substituting for further investigation of the great complexities of sexual orientation, sexual fantasy, sense of gender, character traits, and forms of pathology.

Before we can go more deeply into the homosexualities, we need to return to Freud's second important distinction, that between inversion and perversion. Perversion takes us to body parts, component drives, and the psychosexual developmental theory. As with his discussions of inversion, Freud is astoundingly radical. He argues that sexuality is about more than the genitals for anyone, and that all kinds of behaviors and fantasies are normal as long as (and here is where commentators have rested their case for the perversion intrinsic to inversion) they end up in normal "sexual union" (1905b, p. 150). He says "most of these extensions, or at any rate the less severe of them, are constituents which are rarely absent from the sexual life of healthy people" (p. 160). It is only when he discusses perversion, rather than in his discussion of inversion, that Freud uses the word *symptom* to describe what he is discussing: "If ... a perversion has the characteristics of exclusiveness and fixation—then we shall usually be justified in regarding it as a pathological symptom" (p. 160).

Freud's writings, then, invite us to see sexuality as composed of a number of different components, or ingredients. In reading Freud, however, I believe that psychoanalysis has made a category mistake, confusing the fact of these typical, even universal, contributions to individual sexuality with their specific manifestations in individuals. This confusion has led to a tacit comparison of a generalized normality to deviation as the only two possible developmental and psychopathological pathways. But gender and sexuality need to be discovered clinically and are individual and different for each person. Although we can find patterns that might characterize larger groups of people, and although we may need to have these patterns in the back of our minds as we do clinical work, everyone's sexuality will be its own unique final combination.

All sexualities, as I have argued previously, are compromise formations, such that the binary poles *heterosexuality* and *homosexuality* do not describe the specificity of any person's sexual desire and fantasy. Rather, the particular ingredients that are combined and recombined in each person's personal mixture of heterosexuality and homosexuality, masculinity and femininity, will be psychodynamically individual. Although, as Freud makes clear, there is no universal relation between gender and object choice, each individual constructs his or her own particularized personal fantasy of this relation. As an individual chooses a male or female sexual object (whose anatomical construction does not predict the personal fantasy construction of that object's gender or sexuality), she or he relates to that object with an unconscious sense, also personally particularized, of masculinity or femininity.

As a way of characterizing subjective states in which people feel themselves, consciously or, as we discover, in unconscious fantasy, to have physical or psychological traits of one sex or the other, a wish to be both sexes or the other sex, to be partly mother and partly father, or to have desires for people of both sexes, the concept of bisexuality can help us. But this does not distinguish "bisexuals" from the rest of us: Everyone has unconscious and conscious fantasies of being masculine or feminine, or partly some of each, and everyone has some people of the same and some of the other gender who are found desirable and some who are undesirable and not the object of fantasy.

My own clinical and theoretical inquiries yield several components of individual sexuality. These are universal components found in everyone, each particularized and combined to constitute any individual's sexuality.[4] First, and most centrally, we find *erotization*: bodily-experienced pleasures, lusts, and desires. Erotization includes body image, some way of experiencing one's own body, its attractiveness, its arousal, and its appetites. Actual, bodily erotization has been hard for psychoanalysis to conceptualize, as is evidenced in Freud's convoluted attempt in the *Three Essays* to describe the "highly obscure" "problem of sexual excitation" (1905b, pp. 204, 212). Ruth Stein (1998) suggests that you cannot put this primarily bodily experience into words, make it purely psychological, or capture it in terms of orientation or object choice. There is something ultimately private, ineffable, indescribable, and even mysterious about sexual and bodily Eros.

Erotization has something to do with *sexual practices*, that is, actual, behavioral sex—what someone does or likes to do with their own and the other's body. Some sexual practices arise out of desire or passion and bring pleasure, but some may not. This is partially because all kinds of internal

[4] My chapter here echoes and develops for sexuality the previous chapter's considerations on gender.

prohibitions, inhibitions, and cultural rules help to shape sexual practices and because many sexual practices may not be erotic at all. I do not have in mind here the question whether pain or aggression can be pleasurable, but rather, for example, a woman's pretending to have orgasms in intercourse to please men. Erotization also has something to do with bodily givens. Each person is born with or comes to develop his own particular given sensitivities, sensitivities that are individual and not automatically tied to sexed body, and each person has early bodily-emotional interactional experiences that he or she makes something of. These bodily sensitivities are beyond and developmentally before the conventional arousal and bodily-genital experience of oedipal sexuality that reacts to and fantasizes about a gendered and genitalized whole-object mother and father, which is a fairly late developmental achievement.

Sexuality includes an *internal world*, which we traditionally call "oedipal." This world filters introjectively and projectively mother, father, and their combination and helps to constitute both same- and cross-gender identifications, object fantasies, and object choices. This internal world may be whole or part-object. Again, psychoanalysis has often confused the universal and the particular in the matter of the internal oedipal world. Any experience with parents will be personally individual. As Freud notes, who is to say outside of clinical particularity how a mother experiences her "femininity" and thus what she conveys to a child about it, whether two apparently heterosexual parents are in fact the feminine and masculine partners in the primal scene, whether a father experiences his penis and sexuality as active or passive, and so forth? A girl's identification with her mother, or a boy's with his father, is never simple.

As with the sense of gender and gender identity, each person's sexuality takes on an *affective tonality*. Does the individual feel that her sexual desire is acceptable or not? Is his genital body to be ashamed of, attacked, inadequate, or weak? Part of this affective tonality concerns the relative significance of sexuality itself, which varies among individuals. Thus, we find clinically that among people of the "same" sexual orientation, there are enormous variations in how sexuality fits into the rest of life, and this is exactly where psychoanalysis began: We can only discover, in the individual case, how much and how a person's sexuality is tied into conflict, defenses, regression, the making and breaking of internal or external relationships, narcissism, or self-stabilization.

One of the main goals of the clinician, whether or not she is an ego psychologist, is to assess the relative autonomy of sexuality for the patient: In an earlier period, analysts were prone to the genetic fallacy and a lack of recognition of possibilities for secondary autonomy in the psychoanalytic treatment and understanding of homosexuality (see Mitchell, 1978, 1981). But by definition, all sexualities begin in conflict and defense, and we should not make the mistake of conflating this originary conflict and defense with pathology. We should also be aware, clinically, that even sexualities that may have begun in extreme conflict and pathology can come to function apart from these origins.

Surprisingly, *sexual object choice* needs to be conceptualized apart from erotization and the internal world. Sexual object choice concerns the conscious choice of partner. We tend to think, as does Freud, of whether the object is of the same or the other sex (I am putting aside Freud's attention to whether the object is adult or even human in the first place), but, as I argue in "Heterosexuality as a compromise formation," object choice is much more individual. As I note there, we are only glossing when we say that a woman is heterosexual since not every man suits a heterosexual woman's fancy, and vice versa. We know that object choice can be more or less fixed, that, for example, there are "primary lesbians" who have always and forever been attracted only to women, even when they were married, and "elective lesbians" who live a short or extended part of their lives in fulfilling and exciting heterosexual relationships, without any sense that these relationships at the time were sexually or psychically wrong, or who come out for political as much as for sexual reasons. There are women who consider themselves lesbian but are married because they fell in love with a *particular* man, even though, in general, they are attracted to women (Stein, 1997).

Sexual identity, a person's own preconsciously or consciously labeled sense of his or her sexual orientation, is separate from gender identity (the sense of self as male or female), and in the current period can even be separate from the actual behavioral or libidinal choice of object. Though this was not true throughout history and across cultures, people today are called upon culturally and politically to label themselves according to sexual orientation, and this itself becomes a constituent of sexuality. Beyond the already great complexities of sorting out sexuality, patients, as I describe in the following discussion, find themselves trying to "figure out" their orientation. In "sexual identity" or "sexual orientation," sexual object choice takes on a new, conscious, subjective meaning that brings with it further psychological conflicts and difficulties. It is not just a matter of the patient's or analyst's observing the nature of object choices, but of the patient's (and sometimes the analyst's) drive to categorize it.

Sexual orientation and identity take us to *culture*. The cultural meanings of self, sexuality, and gender are intertwined and begin to enter consciousness and unconscious fantasy from birth. These cultural meanings are at first filtered nonverbally through parental affect and fantasy, and they are later filtered linguistically and discursively through siblings, peers, and teachers, stories, movies, and TV. But all of these more conscious experiences take on personal emotional resonance through context, affect, fantasy, and relationship. Part of the tight link between sexuality and gender that I point to earlier (and that French psychoanalysis in particular, crossing Freud and

Lévi-Strauss, has made so central) results from cultural context, though the particulars of this link vary cross-culturally as well as individually. Our contemporary rethinking challenges the singularity of this link, pointing to different masculinities (Corbett, 1993) or the varieties of developmental pathways to lesbian object choice (Schuker, 1996), and wondering whether lesbians are more gay or more female—more like heterosexual women or like gay men.

Finally, sexuality has cultural as well as emotional and fantasy loading, as Freud also notes (Breuer and Freud, 1895, Freud, 1905b, 1908, and elsewhere). Culture enters into how parents handle and label the child's genitals, the stories told and read, the parents' fantasies about sexual and gendered body and self and sexual and gendered body and self of the child. As I note, in our culture today, a naming of one's sexual identity is a requirement that was not hitherto required. Psychoanalysis has itself led ordinary people to have different ways of thinking about their sexuality and gender.

Fantasy, in some ways, helps put all of this together. Person (1999) makes a persuasive case that sexual excitement or passion for any person is generated by a driving personal fantasy that is relatively early developed and unchangeable. Fantasy brings together, in each uniquely constructed case, erotization and body experience; sexual practices; body image; an internal world; affective tonality; relative autonomy or relative drivenness; object choice, orientation, and identity; the particular relations of subjective conscious and unconscious gender to sexual-body erotism and the sex of the choice of object; and a fantasy and affective filtering of culture. These fantasies may include aggression as well as lust—fantasies of power and domination or submission, the desire to harm or retaliate for humiliation, the management of anxiety about sexual performance through power, and so forth.

Here as elsewhere in our theory of mind, all of these generalized considerations are true for everyone. In our daily lives and fantasies, analyst as well as patient wrestles with the same components of sexuality. Nor is the therapist, however well analyzed, free from anxieties and preoccupations about sexuality—anxieties about erotic transference and countertransference, about our own body integrity and sexuality, about the complexities and content of our own fantasies and object choices. We also always have in mind, in our transference to the profession, how consequential and important sex is for psychoanalysis and how it has spilled well beyond the bounds of what we ordinarily think of as sexuality, to libido-Eros as a generative force in all life, to sublimation, to drive theory, to the metaphor of parental intercourse as a linking of minds, and so forth.

The multifaceted character of psychoanalytic understanding of sexuality enables and requires us to hear many different aspects of sexual object choice and sense of gender—multiplicity rather than a single sexuality. I cannot think of a patient for whom, in the broadest sense, attraction to and fantasies about men and women and aspects of self-identified (whether conscious or unconscious) masculinity and femininity are not part of the clinical picture. When these are rigid and defended, even if they follow normative gender and sexual patterns, we are in the arena of conflict and splitting. In the clinical consulting room are added the analyst's own countertransference movements of erotic position, sexuality, and sense of gender that arise in response to a patient's own shifting identities, fantasies, desires, and transferences.

By definition, the account I am developing takes issue with any simple single developmental model, though a staunch developmentalist could theorize the ensemble of these ingredients, or components, as a developmental line. Clinically, however, how these different components emerge varies, in ways that are also closely tied to transferential unfoldings. There is a spectrum of qualities of object relatedness, erotization, compulsiveness, drivenness, anxiety or envy about genital anatomy, imaging of gender, specificity versus broadness of object choice and sexual aim, denial or defense, character pathology or neurosis, conjoinings of fantasy and reparative goals, tied to different people's sexuality.

It is only in this context of the sexualities more generally that we can consider the homosexualities. To do so, I will describe one young man's treatment and compare him briefly to another. Both entered treatment in their late 20s; one is gay, the other straight (I bring in from the outset what I have called sexual *identity* as well as *object choice*: These young men would not refer to themselves as homosexual and heterosexual, as we psychoanalysts might be more likely to do). J, who is gay, came to treatment living on the edge, having occasional unsafe sex and in fact being drawn to unsafe sex. He was part of the gay bar scene, drinking much too much or getting high and then picking up men with whom to have sex. He was unevenly able to observe himself. When he first came to treatment, he was panicked about becoming HIV positive after engaging in unsafe sex, fearful of getting tested, fearful of doing it again, and worried about how he would tell his mother if he turned out to be HIV positive. He was jobless.

J did not strike me as a candidate for any kind of insight therapy or analysis. In addition to his drinking, smoking, and promiscuous drive to "get laid," he described a history of angry outbursts in childhood and after. As a young teenager, he had been sent to a psychiatrist after smashing things in the family home, and only 2 years before beginning treatment, drunk at a family holiday celebration, he had physically attacked his brother in a rage when his brother taunted him. He seemed to be someone who could not mentalize and who got rid of unpleasant affect through violence. Provocatively, in his first hour, J claimed that ever since he knew he was gay, he wanted to have sex with his father. He also normalized his drinking and promiscuity as typical of the gay world.

J's parents' marriage, often tension-filled, had a traditional division of labor. His mother was a stay-at-home mom who did everything in the house and for the children, and father provided. J's most recent job had been in his father's business, and he described his mother as his "best friend," whom he talked to almost every day—although he could not bring himself to tell her about the HIV risk. J described his own rages as part of a family pattern. His volatile father had occasionally lashed out at his mother, and all the siblings fought physically. As with his drinking and promiscuity, J's initial reaction was to normalize such violence, claiming that other families were also violent.

After our two initial meetings, really concerned about whether we could work together, I shared my concerns with J. I said that my sense of things, as he described them, was that he avoided feeling pain by drinking, smoking marijuana, and impulsive acting out (for instance, getting violent or getting picked up). I wasn't taking a side, telling him that he *should* give up drinking and drugs, but I did not know if he could or wanted to think about what was painful to him at this point. J's first transferential reaction was to turn me into a judgmental paternal policeman and to assure me that he would not come in drunk. I repeated that I wasn't meaning to be a policeman, but that we needed together to know what might help him, and he needed to know what kind of help I could give.

J turned next to worrying that perhaps he needed to see a gay man, who would know more what the gay world and its rapid sexual involvements were like. When I suggested to him that I did not think that therapy required people who were exactly the same, he—foreshadowing an organizing theme in his gender and sexual fantasies—recast me from straight to female, saying that, really, he was able to talk to women much more easily than to men. In response to my directness, the capacity to reflect that led J to seek treatment returned. We could thus begin to discover the role of "gayness" and "straightness" in J's mind, how these sexual, but not necessarily gendered, terms had become a tacit filter for much of J's view of the world and himself.

In J's treatment, we began by exploring his great resistance to looking for a job. The "success ethic," he claimed, was his father's, and he resented his father, who, in his view, had done nothing as a father except to be successful and provide financially. When I suggested to J that he was displacing his own wishes and desire to succeed onto his father, he could see it quite quickly. Although he continued to resent his father, J saw that what was keeping him back were his own fears of failure and great desires for success, which were themselves part of his own conflicted and consciously resisted definition of straight masculinity. He stopped undermining his job interviews and landed a good job in his field. A related early interaction involved J's talking about what his "straight" friends thought of some of his sexual choices and their approval or disapproval of parts of his lifestyle. Again, he came to see how he divided himself into "gay" and "straight" and tried to ward off through projection onto his friends what he experienced as his own "straight" reactions to his own "gay" desires.

J's "straight" self seemed to contain identifications with his father, both as positive ego ideal and as judging superego. In his identification with his father as an ego ideal, J came to recognize that he himself wanted a job. Moreover, his capacity to reflect seemed to develop as he could identify with parts of his father that were not violent and critically denigrating but were, rather, professionally successful. On the father as superego side, J also rebelled against his internal punitive straight father with too high expectations by not getting his taxes in on time and failing to keep his car insured. Father had in fact been harsh at different points in J's life. J remembered being hit when he got his homework wrong. As an adult, when he complained that his father was always criticizing him, J's father had said, "That's what fathers are for."

J described how he often woke up in bed, the morning after a pick-up, thinking, "Who *is* this I'm lying next to?!" As he projectively put it, neither his straight friends nor his father approved of J's sexual choices. But whereas his straight friends/self were on the surface supportive of his gayness, J's father does not approve of his gayness at all—perhaps, even, of libidinal sexuality itself. Or at least, if J has to be gay, he should make different, more attractive, sexual choices. The "Who is this?" then, turned out to be J's straight father in himself, asking why he has to be in bed with a man.

J traced his sexual interest in men to a time when his father had briefly left his family, when he was about seven. Though he had a couple of girlfriends in college and after, and the sex with them was unproblematic, he claimed that he could not really love them, that the "cerebral" part was missing. At the same time, J also worried that he was unable to love men, that the capacity to love was *itself* lacking in him. Thus, J was gay, but the fact of not being able to love did not seem to differentiate the sex of his partner.

J's mother played an entirely different role than his father in his sexual identity. The youngest child, he described still being very close to her, talking with her on the phone every day. In contrast to his father, his mother always loved J's non-straight side. She had been delighted that J liked to be outrageous, that he made jokes, that he felt oppositional to the straight world, that he was cool, and that he liked art and music. Before J got his job, but after we had explored somewhat his identification with his father's success ethic and his own identification with the judgments of his straight friends, J recognized his own worry that his interest in success was a betrayal of his mother.

Struck by this gay/straight division, I suggested that it was as though he thought that his gay self was his mother's son and his straight self his father's son. He lit up, and said "Yes! My mother is always saying, 'You're so funny! You're so witty! I'm so glad I have a gay son!'" Countertransferentially, I found myself somewhat disapprovingly thinking about how J's mother loves his gayness, loves everything about him, but would not love him to want people like her sexually.

But being cool and gay was itself a maternal superego demand. J described finding it difficult to work so hard to be cool, to make jokes, and to pretend not to care, when he cared desperately about what people thought about him. We learned that his compliance with this felt maternal expectation was, in fact, part of what had generated his acting out and incapacity to reflect when he first came into treatment. Although it was harder for him to look at his anger at his mother than at his father, J's self-destructiveness also began to seem to be tied to his relationship with his mother.

As I learned more about, and we began to explore, J's life-threatening attraction to having unsafe sex, he remembered an incident as a teenager when, after an argument with his mother, his response was to smash most of his carefully created art. I also speculated to myself that J's provocation during his first hour, about wanting to have sex with his father, was a transferential expression of this outrageousness which mother loves and of his anger at its demands: He would be in your face, and at the same time compliant, with this analyst-mother who wanted him to talk about all his most outrageous wishes and memories.

A particular hour illuminated further the role of J's mother and father in his homosexuality and gay and straight identities, as well as the complexity of the transference-countertransference interchange around sexuality. Like all homosexuals and heterosexuals, as I describe this chapter, J's erotization and object choice were particularized. J was attracted to "bears," and he liked to be penetrated. As someone who liked to be penetrated, he saw himself as feminine, referring to himself as the "mistress" of a man he had sex with who was living with another man.

During this particular hour, J came in puzzling further about his uncomfortable attraction to "bears," whom he shouldn't be attracted to, and his worry about what his "straight" friends, but also what "cool" gay people, will think of him. I wondered out loud if I was one of those straight people who would think these men were disgusting. He dismissed my query: He knows all about transference so he shouldn't worry, even though he does. I inquired further about what was on J's mind, all these "shouldn'ts." He responded, "Well, I like fat, hairy guys, but people will find it weird."

J continued to reflect. He doesn't know, but perhaps—and he hates to think it—he even thinks there is something wrong with being attracted to men at all, with being gay. He "shouldn't" think this and tried to dismiss the thought, saying that it is probably just because gays are a minority, because we live in a homophobic society. I brought him back to his own discomfort: What about fat, hairy guys? At this point, J got rather dreamy, saying it is hard to go right to the whys, but he thinks he is looking for a father. He thinks he likes feeling smaller, and somehow protected, by these big guys. He then thinks of deep voices, and, again, that he cannot help it, but he feels that there is something wrong with this attraction. But—immediately—there shouldn't be anything wrong.

J had been conscious all along about looking for an approving father, so I wanted to see what else we could find out if we went back to his discomfort with his sexual choices. He reflected, and then said, "Well, once my mother asked me what kind of guys I was attracted to, and I said big hairy guys. She said, 'That's great! So am I!'" I suggested, "So, you're like your mother here." J laughed and said, "Yeah, maybe it's genetic," and then went back to his projective "Why isn't it all right? Society ... " When I pointed to the displacement, he said, "Yeah, me. My mother's son and my father's son. We keep coming back to it. Sometimes I scare myself, that there's a part of me that thinks I shouldn't be gay. The father part. My father would think, why can't I at least be attracted to more attractive men?"

I suggested that his father represented what he wanted to be and his mother what he felt he was. He then, again rather dreamily, suggested that, though he did not know what to make of it, "Maybe it's because I was around her a lot, and not around my father." There was definitely some recognized sense of being like, almost one with, his mother. He continued, "Yeah, that's right. My mother represents who I am, and my father who I want to be. ... But I don't want to be those things! Also, the father in me would say, 'Just get on with it! Stop all this mulling around!' It's my mother who's been in therapy for years, my father wouldn't think of it! He'd be, 'Be violent and action-oriented!'" Here, J wrestles with the ambivalence of his father and mother identifications: Just as he has straight "be-a-man" standards, he also has the angry father to integrate.

The fluctuations of gender and sexual object choice and the ineffability of sexuality are clear in this emotionally intense hour, but they become even clearer if I describe my own countertransference feelings and thoughts. At one point, when J was reaching to describe why he was attracted to "big, hairy guys," this felt quite visceral and charged to me. I could feel the elusive difficulty of putting attraction into words, as I identified directly and immediately with an intense focus on the mystery of why I am attracted to particular men, and not to men in general. I found myself afterward wondering if I had lost, like his mother, my sense of our being of different genders. For the moment the "sex of the object," the attraction to men, as well as the mystery of erotization and fantasy, had cross-cut gender and generation and overridden the heterosexual-homosexual divide.

Another way to examine the homosexualities in relation to the multiple ingredients of sexuality is to compare J with D. In this even briefer look, I suggest that similar family, sexual, and gender fantasies do not necessarily correlate directly with sexual object choice. Of a similar culture and generational cohort, J and D both had short-cropped hair, were solid, fit, athletically built, and wore 20-something jeans and T-shirts. Gay J did not look any more feminine than straight D or have more feminine mannerisms (whatever that means!). If I had had to guess from first impressions, I might just as easily have thought that J was the active, masculine-identified side of a gay male pair; by complement, D was emphatically not macho. Like J, D had trouble finding "adult" men's work and went between menial jobs and unemployment for some time. Both described parental marriages with some tensions and intense, very involved relationships with maritally discontented, sometimes depressed mothers who were overly interested in their sons' lives. Like J, D reported talking to his mother almost every day and feeling just like her. Yet, straight D continually felt that he could not, and since childhood never could, capture his mother's attention or compete with her intense loyalty toward and excitement about his father. Gay J, by contrast, was involved with a mother who was exciting to and excited by him.

Where J's primary divide was gay/straight, D's was feminine/masculine. Like J, D saw his sexuality in relation to his mother, but in his case, there was a driving desire to figure out, by getting inside a woman, what she felt and, especially, what made her unhappy or unhappy. He wanted to know from within what it was to be a woman. Yet, despite being attractive to women and sexually successful, D also had the sense that women did not need him sexually. His dreams included sexually and physiologically bisexual women, complete without men.

Like J, D identified with women, sensed that he was like them, and (along the lines of my countertransference thought about how J's mother wanted him to like her in every way but sexually) thought that women did not need him sexually. But J's homosexuality and his attraction to men—even the same kinds of men that his mother liked—seemed, emotionally, to make him closer to his mother than heterosexual D's attempts through direct sexual connection with women to understand and be close to them. At the same time, D's erotic heterosexuality made maternally derived fantasies about women more threateningly liable to overwhelm him than was the case for J. Shortly after he had a dream that involved a sexual encounter between himself and me, D started spending time in gay bars, contemplating the action and imagining what it would be like to be picked up.

In relation to their fathers, J saw his father as traditionally masculine as well as straight. He focused on his father as a successful businessman with stern expectations of his son, whose pathology ran in the direction of violence and anger. D, by contrast, saw his equally successful businessman father as someone who did not live up to the traditional masculine role. Thus, straight D's masculine identifications with his father were much more bisexual, in terms of the "sexual characteristics and sexual attitude of the subject," than were gay J's masculine identifications with his father. D, moreover, expressed great longings to gain his father's attention and love, and he wished that his father would notice him more, but this did not lead to sexual interest in men. J and D, however, were similar in seeing any form of identification with or desire for their father as a betrayal of mother.

Thus, we find J, attracted to a particular kind of man and a particular position in the gay relationship, who has had a bit of sexual experience with women and who sees himself as having an outrageous, nonconforming "gay" side that is his mother's and like his mother, and a "straight," conventional side, which is his father's and like his father. In J's mind, mother liked her gay son, but father certainly did not. But father had qualities of being a masculine man that J very much wished he could have. J saw himself as feminine in bed, but he wanted to be a successful man in the workplace, and he was self-critical about his sexual desires. Among sexual object choice, sexual orientation-identity, and gender, J's subjective divide was gay-straight more than feminine-masculine, though each side was associated to a parent.

By contrast, D was straight (with Freud's reminder that no one is exclusively one or the other), but, given his oedipal and gendered family dynamics, we could not predict heterosexuality, rather than homosexuality, as his own particular compromise solution to conflicts, attachments, or identifications. My own countertransference and object role—in the one case identifying intensely with J trying to figure out why he was attracted to particular men, in the other a terrifyingly engulfing maternal figure for D—further illuminate for us how complicated this congeries of fantasies and behaviors we call sexuality really is.

In his "Psychogenesis of a Case of Homosexuality in a Woman" (1920b), Freud traces the familial and oedipal origins of his patient's homosexuality. He warns us, however, of the limitations of his account:

> So long as we trace the development from its final outcome backwards, the chain of events appears continuous, and we feel we have gained an insight which is completely satisfactory or even exhaustive. But if we proceed the reverse way, if we start from the premises inferred from the analysis and try to follow these up to the final result, then we no longer get the impression of an inevitable sequence of events which could not have been otherwise determined. We notice at once that there might have been another result, and that we might have been just as well able to understand and explain the latter. The synthesis is thus not so satisfactory as the analysis; in other words, from a knowledge of the premises we could not have foretold the nature of the result. (p. 167)

Similarly, in the cases of J and D, why identifications went one way and object choice and orientation the other was a matter of an individual psychic history of defenses and uneasy solutions. These arose in particular familial and cultural contexts, were not predictable, and were barely retrodictively explainable from oedipal constellation, family history, or preoedipal attachments and self-experiences. While J is what we would classically call "homosexual," which he himself calls "gay," and D is "heterosexual," which he himself calls "straight," we mean, finally, only in some general way the gender and genitals of the object in behavioral relation to those of the self.

When we explore these sexual orientations and identities analytically, we find the specificity of erotization and body image, the specificity of particular men or particular women as object, the particularity of the parental constellation and each parent's personality and relation to the person, and the conscious and unconscious fantasy effects of these, as well as the transferential ways that they are brought to the analytic relationship. We find the senses of shame, inadequacy, anger, or resentment at the self's desires, the contemporary need to wrestle with the gay-straight divide, and, finally, the salience of sexuality in the life more generally. We find the mysteries of lust and desire. We find complex individual fantasy creations, compromises among wishes, fears, desires, and prohibitions, that exhibit both stability and change. To understand the homosexualities, we need to understand the sexualities in general.

References

Adorno, T. W., Frenkel-Brunswik, E., Levinson, D. J., & Sanford, R. N. (1950). *The authoritarian personality*. New York: Norton.

Alexander, F. (1966). *Psychoanalytic pioneers*. New York: Basic Books.

Almond, B. (2010). *The monster within: The hidden side of motherhood*. Berkeley: University of California Press.

Angier, N. (2000, February 15). For women in astronomy—a glass ceiling in the sky. *New York Times*, p. F5.

Apfel, R. J., & Keylor, R. G. (2002). Psychoanalysis and infertility: Myths and realities. *International Journal of Psychoanalysis*, *83*, 85–104.

Applegarth, A. (1976). Some observations on work inhibitions in women. *Journal of the American Psychoanalytic Association*, *24*(Suppl.), 251–269.

Arlow, J. A. (1984). Disturbances of the sense of time—with special reference to the experience of timelessness. *Psychoanalytic Quarterly*, *53*, 13–37.

Aron, L. (1995). The internalized primal scene. *Psychoanalytic Dialogues*, *5*, 195–237.

Aron, L., & Harris, A. (Eds.). (2004). *Psychoanalytic Dialogues*, *14*(2). Special Issue: Symposium on What's American About American Psychoanalysis?

Bakan, D. (1968). *Disease, pain, and sacrifice: Toward a psychology of suffering*. Chicago: University of Chicago Press.

Balint, A. (1939). Love for the mother and mother-love. In M. Balint (Ed.), *Primary love and psycho-analytic technique* (pp. 91–108). New York: Liveright, 1965.

Balsam, R. (1996). The pregnant mother and the body image of the daughter. *Journal of the American Psychoanalytic Association*, *44*(Suppl.), 401–427.

Balsam, R. (2003). The vanished pregnant body. *Journal of the American Psychoanalytic Association*, *51*, 1153–1179.

Balsam, R. (2011). *Women's bodies in psychoanalysis*. London: Routledge.

Bassin, D. (1996). Beyond the he and the she: Toward the reconciliation of masculinity and femininity in the postoedipal female mind. *Journal of the American Psychoanalytic Association*, *44*(Suppl.), 157–190.

Bassin, D., Honey, M., & Kaplan, M. M. (Eds.). (1994). *Representations of motherhood*. New Haven, CT: Yale University Press.

Becker, H. (1986). *Writing for social scientists*. Chicago: University of Chicago Press.

Benedek, T. (1952). *Psychosexual functions in women*. New York: Ronald Press.

Benedek, T. (1956). Psychobiological aspects of mothering. *American Journal of Orthopsychiatry*, *26*, 272–278.

Benedek, T. (1959). Parenthood as a developmental phase. *Journal of the American Psychoanalytic Association*, *7*, 389–417.

Benedek, T. (1960). The organization of the reproductive drive. *International Journal of Psychoanalysis*, *41*, 1–15.

Benedek, T. (1973). *Psychoanalytic investigations*. New York: Quadrangle/New York Times Books.

Benjamin, J. (1988). *The bonds of love*. New York: Pantheon.

Benjamin, J. (1995). *Like subjects, love objects*. New Haven, CT: Yale University Press.

Bergmann, M. V. (1985). The effect of role reversal on delayed marriage and maternity. *Psychoanalytic Study of the Child*, *40*, 197–219.

Bernstein, D. (1990). Female genital anxieties, conflicts, and typical mastery modes. *International Journal of Psychoanalysis*, *71*, 151–165.

Bertin, C. (1982). *Marie Bonaparte: A life*. New York: Harcourt Brace Jovanovich.

Bibring, G. (1959). Some considerations of the psychobiological processes in pregnancy. *Psychoanalytic Study of the Child*, *14*, 113–121.

Bibring, G., Dwyer, T., Huntington, D., & Valenstein, A. (1961). A study of the psychological processes in pregnancy and of the earliest mother-child relationship. *Psychoanalytic Study of the Child*, *16*, 9–72.

Birkstead-Breen, D. (1999). Dana Birkstead-Breen on Melanie Klein: Holding the tension. In D. Bassin (Ed.), *Female sexuality: Contemporary engagements* (pp. 279–286). Northvale, NJ: Aronson.

Blum, H. P (Ed). (1976). *Journal of the American Psychoanalytic Association*, *24*(5) Supplement-Female Psychology.

Brady, M. (2006). Panel report: The riddle of masculinity. *Journal of the American Psychoanalytic Association*, *54*, 1195–1206.

Breuer, J., & Freud, S. (1893–1895). *Studies on hysteria*. In J. Strachey (Ed.), *The standard edition of the complete psychological works of Sigmund Freud* (Vol. 2, pp. 1–309). London: Hogarth Press, 1955.

Briggs, J. (1971). *Never in anger*. Cambridge, MA: Harvard University Press.

Britton, R., Feldman, M., & O'Shaughnessy, E. (1989). *The Oedipus complex today: Clinical implications*. London: Karnac.

Brown, N. O. (1959). *Life against death*. New York: Vintage.

Buechler, S. (1999). Searching for a passionate neutrality. *Contemporary Psychoanalysis*, *35*, 213–227.

Butler, J. (1990). *Gender trouble: Feminism and the subversion of identity*. New York: Routledge.

Butler, J. (2001, April). *Is kinship always (already) heterosexual?* Unpublished inaugural lecture, University of California, Berkeley, Center for the Study of Sexual Cultures. University of California, Berkeley.

Carotenuto, A. (1973). *A secret symmetry: Sabina Spielrein between Jung and Freud*. New York: Pantheon.

Castro, D. (2002, February 3). Letter to the editor. *New York Times Magazine*, p. E4.

Chasseguet-Smirgel, J. (Ed.), (1964). *Female sexuality: New psychoanalytic views*. Ann Arbor, MI: University of Michigan Press.

Chasseguet-Smirgel, J. (1976). Freud and female sexuality: The consideration of some blind spots in the exploration of the "Dark continent." *International Journal of Psychoanalysis, 57*, 275–286.

Chasseguet-Smirgel, J. (1984). *Creativity and perversion.* London: Free Association Books, 1985.

Chasseguet-Smirgel, J. (1986). *Sexuality and mind: The role of the father and mother in the psyche.* New York: New York University Press.

Chodorow, N. J. (1971). Being and doing: A cross-cultural examination of the socialization of males and females. In *Feminism and psychoanalytic theory* (pp. 23–44). New Haven, CT: Yale University Press, 1989.

Chodorow, N. J. (1974). Family structure and feminine personality. In *Feminism and psychoanalytic theory* (pp. 45–65). New Haven, CT: Yale University Press, 1989.

Chodorow, N. J. (1976). Oedipal asymmetries and heterosexual knots. In *Feminism and psychoanalytic theory* (pp. 66–78). New Haven, CT: Yale University Press.

Chodorow, N. J. (1978). *The reproduction of mothering* (2nd ed.). Berkeley: University of California Press, 1999.

Chodorow, N. J. (1979). Gender, relation and difference in psychoanalytic perspective. In *Feminism and psychoanalytic theory* (pp. 99–113). New Haven, CT: Yale University Press, 1989.

Chodorow, N. J. (1985). Beyond drive theory: Object relations and the limits of radical individualism. In *Feminism and psychoanalytic theory* (pp. 114–153). New Haven, CT: Yale University Press.

Chodorow, N. J. (1986a). Histoire et vie des premières femmes psychanalystes [History and life histories of early women psychoanalysts]. *Psychothérapies, 6*, 165–171.

Chodorow, N. J. (1986b). Toward a relational individualism: The mediation of self through psychoanalysis. In *Feminism and psychoanalytic theory* (pp. 154–162). New Haven, CT: Yale University Press, 1989.

Chodorow, N. J. (1986c). Varieties of leadership among early women psychoanalysts. In L. J. Dickstein & C. C. Nadelson (Eds.), *Women physicians in leadership roles* (pp. 45–54). Washington, DC: American Psychiatric Association.

Chodorow, N. J. (1987). Der beitrag der frauen zur psychoanalytischen bewegung und theorie [Women's contribution to the psychoanalytic movement and to psychoanalytic theory]. *Psyche: Zeitschrift für Psychoanalyse und Ihre Anwendungen, 41*(9), 800–831.

Chodorow, N. J. (1989a). *Feminism and psychoanalytic theory.* New Haven, CT: Yale University Press.

Chodorow, N. J. (1989b). Seventies questions for thirties women: Gender and generation in a study of early women psychoanalysts. In *Feminism and psychoanalytic theory* (pp. 199–218). New Haven, CT: Yale University Press.

Chodorow, N. J. (1991a). Rethinking Freud on women. In *Femininities, masculinities, sexualities: Freud and beyond* (pp. 1–32). Lexington, KY: University Press of Kentucky, 1994.

Chodorow, N. J. (1991b). Where have all the eminent women psychoanalysts gone? Like the bubbles in champagne, they rose to the top and disappeared. In J. N. Blau & N. Goodman (Eds.), *Social roles and social institutions: Essays in honor of Rose Laub Coser* (pp. 167–194). Boulder, CO: Westview Press.

Chodorow, N. J. (1992). Heterosexuality as a compromise formation. In *Femininities, masculinities, sexualities: Freud and beyond* (pp. 33–69). Lexington, KY: University Press of Kentucky, 1994.

Chodorow, N. J. (1994). *Femininities, masculinities, sexualities: Freud and beyond.* Lexington, KY: University Press of Kentucky.

Chodorow, N. J. (1996a). Reflections on the authority of the past in psychoanalytic thinking. *Psychoanalytic Quarterly*, *65*, 32–51.

Chodorow, N. J. (1996b). Theoretical gender and clinical gender: Epistemological reflections on the psychology of women. *Journal of the American Psychoanalytic Association*, *44*(Suppl.), 215–223.

Chodorow, N. J. (1998). The enemy outside: Thoughts on the psychodynamics of extreme violence with special attention to men and masculinity. *Journal of Psychoanalysis of Culture and Society*, *3*(1), 25–38.

Chodorow, N. J. (1999a). From subjectivity in general to subjective gender in particular. Introductory essay to Melanie Klein's "Mourning and Its Relation to Manic-Depressive States." In D. Bassin (Ed.), *Female sexuality: Contemporary engagements* (pp. 241–250). Northvale, NJ: Aronson.

Chodorow, N. J. (1999b). *The power of feelings: Personal meaning in psychoanalysis, gender, and culture.* New Haven, CT: Yale University Press.

Chodorow, N. J. (1999c). Preface to the second edition. In *The reproduction of mothering* (pp. vii–xvii). Berkeley: University of California Press.

Chodorow, N. J. (1999d). La psychanalyse et les femmes psychanalystes [Psychoanalysis and women psychoanalysts]. In S. de Mijolla-Mellor (Ed.), *Les femmes dans l'histoire de la psychanalyse* [*Women in the history of psychoanalysis*] (pp. 11–32). Paris: L'Espirit du Temps.

Chodorow, N. J. (2000a). Foreword. In *Three essays on the theory of sexuality* by Sigmund Freud (pp. vii–xviii). New York: Basic Books.

Chodorow, N. J. (2000b). Reflections on the reproduction of mothering—Twenty years later. *Studies in Gender and Sexuality*, *1*(4), 337–348.

Chodorow, N. J. (2001). Melanie Klein (1882–1960). In *International encyclopedia of the social and behavioral sciences* (pp. 8111–8113). Oxford, UK: Elsevier Science.

Chodorow, N. J. (2002a). Born into a world at war: Listening for affect and personal meaning. *American Imago*, *59*, 297–315.

Chodorow, N. J. (2002b). From the front of the classroom to behind the couch and back again. In J. Raphael-Leff (Ed.), *Between sessions and beyond the couch* (pp. 163–165). Colchester, UK: CPS Psychoanalytic Publications.

Chodorow, N. J. (2002c). Glass ceilings, sticky floors, and concrete walls: Internal and external barriers to women's work and achievement. In B. Seelig, R. Paul, & C. Levy (Eds.), *Constructing and deconstructing women's power* (pp. 18–28). London: Karnac.

Chodorow, N. J. (2002d). Prejudice exposed: On Stephen Mitchell's pioneering investigations of the psychoanalytic treatment and mistreatment of homosexuality. *Studies in Gender and Sexuality, 3*(1), 61–72.

Chodorow, N. J. (2003a). From behind the couch: Uncertainty and indeterminacy in psychoanalytic theory and practice. *Common Knowledge*, *9*, 463–487.

Chodorow, N. J. (2003b). Hate, humiliation and masculinity. In S. Varvin & V. Volkan (Eds.), *Violence or dialogue? Psychoanalytic insights on terror and terrorism* (pp. 94–107). London: International Psychoanalytic Press.

Chodorow, N. J. (2003c). Les homosexualités comme formations de compromis: La complexité théorique et clinique d'une description et d'une compréhension des homosexualités (Homosexualities as compromise formations: Theoretical and clinical complexity in portraying and understanding homosexualities). *Revue Française de Psychanalyse, 1*, 41–64.

Chodorow, N. J. (2003d). The psychoanalytic vision of Hans Loewald. *International Journal of Psychoanalysis, 84*, 897–913.

Chodorow, N. J. (2003e). "Too late": Ambivalence about motherhood, choice, and time. *Journal of the American Psychoanalytic Association, 51*, 1181–1198.

Chodorow, N. J. (2004a). The American independent tradition: Loewald, Erikson, and the (possible) rise of intersubjective ego psychology. *Psychoanalytic Dialogues, 14*, 207–232.

Chodorow, N. J. (2004b). Beyond sexual difference: Clinical individuality and same-sex cross-generation relations in the creation of feminine and masculine. In I. Matthis (Ed.), *Dialogues on sexuality, gender, and psychoanalysis* (pp. 181–203). London: Karnac.

Chodorow, N. J. (2004c). Psychoanalysis and women: A personal thirty-five-year retrospect. In J. A. Winer & J. A. Anderson (Eds.), *The annual of psychoanalysis, vol. 32: Psychoanalysis and women* (pp. 101–129). Hillsdale, NJ: Analytic Press.

Chodorow, N. J. (2005). Gender on the modern-postmodern and classical-relational divide: untangling history and epistemology. *Journal of the American Psychoanalytic Association, 53*(4), 1097–1118.

Chodorow, N. J. (2007a). Reflections on Loewald's "Internalization, separation, mourning, and the superego." *Psychoanalytic Quarterly, 76*(4), 1135–1151.

Chodorow, N. J. (2007b). Review essay: James McLaughlin's *The healer's bent: Solitude and dialogue in the clinical encounter*. *Psychoanalytic Quarterly, 76*, 617–629.

Chodorow, N. J. (2009). A different universe: Reading Loewald through "On the therapeutic action of psychoanalysis." *Psychoanalytic Quarterly, 78*(4), 983–1011.

Chodorow, N. J., & Contratto, S. (1982). The fantasy of the perfect mother. In *Feminism and psychoanalytic theory* (pp. 79–96). New Haven, CT: Yale University Press, 1989.

Contratto, S. (1980). Maternal sexuality and asexual motherhood. *Signs, 5*, 766–782.

Contratto, S. (1987). Father presence in women's psychological development. In G. M. Platt, J. Rabow, & M. Goldman (Eds.), *Advances in psychoanalytic sociology* (pp. 138–157). Malabar, FL: Krieger.

Cooper, S. H. (2000). *Objects of hope: Exploring possibility and limit in psychoanalysis*. Hillsdale, NJ: Analytic Press.

Corbett, K. (1993). The mystery of homosexuality. *Psychoanalytic Dialogues, 10*, 345–357.

Corbett, K. (2001). Faggot = Loser. *Studies in Gender and Sexuality*, 2, 3–28.

Corbett, K. (2009). *Boyhoods: Rethinking masculinities.* New Haven, CT: Yale University Press.

Coser, R. L. (1981). Where have all the women gone? Like the sediment of a good wine, they have sunk to the bottom. In C. F. Epstein & R. L. Coser (Eds.), *Access to power: Cross-national studies of women and elites* (pp. 16–33). London, Sydney, and Boston: George Allen and Unwin.

Davis, A. (1937). *Deep south: A social anthropological study of caste and class.* Chicago: University of Chicago Press.

Davis, A., & Dollard, Y. (1940). *Children of bondage.* Washington, DC: American Council on Education.

de Marneffe, D. (1997). Bodies and words: A study of young children's genital and gender knowledge. *Gender and Psychoanalysis, 2*, 3–33.

de Marneffe, D. (2004). *Maternal desire: On children, love, and the inner life.* New York: Little, Brown.

Deutsch, H. (1973). *Confrontations with myself: An epilogue.* New York: Norton.

Dimen, M. (2003). *Sexuality, intimacy, power.* Hillsdale, NJ: Analytic Press.

Dinnerstein, D. (1976). *The mermaid and the minotaur.* New York: Harper & Row.

Dollard, Y. (1941). *Caste and class in a southern town.* New Haven, CT: Yale University Press.

Editorial Desk. (2001, September 12). The war against America: An unfathomable attack. *New York Times*, p. A26.

Elise, D. (1997). Primary femininity, bisexuality, and the female ego ideal: A re-examination of female developmental theory. *Psychoanalytic Quarterly, 66*, 489–517.

Elise, D. (2001). Unlawful penetration: Male fears of psychic penetration. *Psychoanalytic Dialogues, 11*, 499–531.

Elovitz, P. H., & Lentz, R. (2005). Nancy J. Chodorow: Psychoanalyst and gender theorist, featured interview. *Clio's Psyche, 11*(4), 113, 134–143.

Epstein, S. (1991). Sexuality and identity: The contribution of object-relations theory to a constructionist sociology. *Theory and Society, 20*, 825–873.

Erikson, E. (1950). *Childhood and society.* New York: Norton.

Fanon, F. (1963). *The wretched of the earth.* New York: Grove Press.

Fanon, F. (1967). *Black skin, white masks.* New York: Grove Press.

Fast, I. (1984). *Gender identity: A differentiation model.* Hillsdale, NJ: Erlbaum.

Felski, R. (1994). Modernism and modernity: Engendering literary history. In L. Rado (Ed.), *Rereading modernism: New directions in feminist criticism* (pp. 191–208). New York: Garland.

Flax, J. (1990). *Thinking fragments: Psychoanalysis, feminism, and postmodernism in the contemporary west.* Berkeley: University of California Press.

Fliegel, Z. O. (1986). Women's development in analytic theory. In J. L. Alpert (Ed.), *Psychoanalysis and women: Contemporary reappraisals* (pp. 3–31). Hillsdale, NJ: Analytic Press.

Fogel, G. I. (1998). Interiority and inner genital space in men: What else can be lost in castration. *Psychoanalytic Quarterly, 67*, 662–697.

Fogel, G. I. (2006). Riddles of masculinity: Gender, bisexuality, and thirdness. *Journal of the American Psychoanalytic Association, 54*, 1139–1163.

Fogel, G., Lane, F. M., & Liebert, R. S. (Eds.). (1986). *The psychology of men: Psychoanalytic perspectives.* New York: Basic Books.

Foley, H. (Ed.). (1999). *The Homeric hymn to Demeter*. Princeton, NJ: Princeton University Press.

Freud, S. (1900–1901). *The interpretation of dreams*. In J. Strachey (Ed.), *The standard edition of the complete psychological works of Sigmund Freud* (Vol. 4, pp. ix–627; Vol. 5, pp. 629–686). London: Hogarth Press, 1953.

Freud, S. (1905a). Fragment of an analysis of a case of hysteria ("Dora"). In J. Strachey (Ed.), *The standard edition of the complete psychological works of Sigmund Freud* (Vol. 7, pp. 7–122). London: Hogarth Press, 1953.

Freud, S. (1905b). *Three essays on the theory of sexuality*. In J. Strachey (Ed.), *The standard edition of the complete psychological works of Sigmund Freud* (Vol. 7, pp. 130–243). London: Hogarth Press, 1953.

Freud, S. (1908). "Civilized" sexual morality and modern nervous illness. In J. Strachey (Ed.), *The standard edition of the complete psychological works of Sigmund Freud* (Vol. 9, pp. 181–204). London: Hogarth Press, 1959.

Freud, S. (1913). *Totem and taboo: Some points of agreement between the mental lives of savages and neurotics*. In J. Strachey (Ed.), *The standard edition of the complete psychological works of Sigmund Freud* (Vol. 13, pp. vii–162). London: Hogarth Press, 1955.

Freud, S. (1914). On narcissism: An introduction. In J. Strachey (Ed.), *The standard edition of the complete psychological works of Sigmund Freud* (Vol. 14, pp. 67–102). London: Hogarth Press, 1957.

Freud, S. (1917). Mourning and melancholia. In J. Strachey (Ed.), *The standard edition of the complete psychological works of Sigmund Freud* (Vol. 14, pp. 237–258). London: Hogarth Press, 1957.

Freud, S. (1920a). Beyond the pleasure principle. In J. Strachey (Ed.), *The standard edition of the complete psychological works of Sigmund Freud* (Vol. 18, pp. 1–64). London: Hogarth Press, 1955.

Freud, S. (1920b). The psychogenesis of a case of homosexuality in a woman. In J. Strachey (Ed.), *The standard edition of the complete psychological works of Sigmund Freud* (Vol. 8, pp. 145–172). London: Hogarth Press, 1960.

Freud, S. (1921). Group psychology and the analysis of the ego. In J. Strachey (Ed.), *The standard edition of the complete psychological works of Sigmund Freud* (Vol. 18, pp. 69–144). London: Hogarth Press, 1955.

Freud, S. (1923). The infantile genital organization. In J. Strachey (Ed.), *The standard edition of the complete psychological works of Sigmund Freud* (Vol. 19, pp. 139–146). London: Hogarth Press, 1961.

Freud, S. (1924). The dissolution of the Oedipus complex. In J. Strachey (Ed.), *The standard edition of the complete psychological works of Sigmund Freud* (Vol. 19, pp. 173–179). London: Hogarth Press, 1961.

Freud, S. (1925). Some psychical consequences of the anatomical distinction between the sexes. In J. Strachey (Ed.), *The standard edition of the complete psychological works of Sigmund Freud* (Vol. 19, pp. 248–258). London: Hogarth Press, 1961.

Freud, S. (1930). *Civilization and its discontents*. In J. Strachey (Ed.), *The standard edition of the complete psychological works of Sigmund Freud* (Vol. 21, pp. 57–145). London: Hogarth Press, 1961.

Freud, S. (1931). Female sexuality. In J. Strachey (Ed.), *The standard edition of the complete psychological works of Sigmund Freud* (Vol. 21, pp. 225–243). London: Hogarth Press, 1961.

Freud, S. (1933). New introductory lectures on psycho-analysis. In J. Strachey (Ed.), *The standard edition of the complete psychological works of Sigmund Freud* (Vol. 22, pp. 1–267). London: Hogarth Press, 1964.

Freud, S. (1937). Analysis terminable and interminable. In J. Strachey (Ed.), *The standard edition of the complete psychological works of Sigmund Freud* (Vol. 23, pp. 209–254). London: Hogarth Press, 1964.

Garfinkel, H. (1967). *Studies in ethnomethodology*. Englewood Cliffs, NJ: Prentice-Hall.

Gediman, H. K. (2001). Review of the book *Female sexuality: Contemporary engagements* by Donna Bassin. *Psychoanalytic Psychology, 18*, 602–611.

Gediman, H. K. (2005). Premodern, modern, and postmodern perspectives on sex and gender mixes. *Journal of the American Psychoanalytic Association, 53*, 1059–1078.

Gilligan, J. (1996). *Violence: Reflections on a national epidemic*. New York: G. P. Putnam's Sons.

Goldberg, A. (2002). American pragmatism and American psychoanalysis. *Psychoanalytic Quarterly, 71*, 235–250.

Goldner, V. (1991). Toward a critical relational theory of gender. *Psychoanalytic Dialogues, 1*, 249–272.

Goldner, V. (2003). Ironic gender/authentic sex. *Studies in Gender and Sexuality, 4*, 113–139.

Gregor, T. (1985). *Anxious pleasures: The sexual lives of an Amazonian people*. Chicago: University of Chicago Press.

Haraway, D. (1988). Situated knowledges: The science question in feminism and the privilege of partial perspective. *Feminist Studies, 14*(3), 575–599.

Harris, A. (1997). Aggression, envy, and ambition: Circulating tensions in women's psychic life. *Gender and Psychoanalysis, 2*, 291–325.

Harris, A. (2005a). *Gender as soft assembly*. Hillsdale, NJ: Analytic Press.

Harris, A. (2005b). Gender in linear and nonlinear history. *Journal of the American Psychoanalytic Association, 53*, 1079–1095.

Hartmann, H. (1964). *Essays on ego psychology*. New York: International Universities Press.

Heenan, C., Chodorow, N. J., Van Mens-Verhulst, J., Orbach, S., Duindam, V., & Spruijt, E., Burack, C., et al. (2002). *The reproduction of mothering*: A reappraisal. *Feminism and Psychology, 12*(1), 5–53.

Heller, T. C., Sosna, M., & Wellbery, D. E. (Eds.). (1986). *Reconstructing individualism: Autonomy, individuality, and the self in Western thought*. Stanford, CA: Stanford University Press.

Herdt, G. (1981). *Guardians of the flutes*. Chicago: University of Chicago Press.

Hoffman, I. Z. (1998). *Ritual and spontaneity in the psychoanalytic process: A dialectical-constructivist view*. Hillsdale, NJ: Analytic Press.

Hoffman, L. G., Hevesi, A. G., Lynch, P. E., Gomes, P. J., Chodorow, N. J., Roughton, R. E., et al. (2000). Homophobia: Analysis of a "permissible" prejudice: A public forum of the American Psychoanalytic Association and the American Psychoanalytic Foundation. *Journal of Gay and Lesbian Psychotherapy, 4*(1), 5–53.

Holtzman, D., & Kulish, N. (1996). Nevermore: The hymen and the loss of virginity. *Journal of the American Psychoanalytic Association, 44*(Suppl.), 303–332.

Holtzman, D., & Kulish, N. (2000). The feminization of the female oedipal complex: Part I. A reconsideration of the significance of separation issues. *Journal of the American Psychoanalytic Association*, *48*, 1413–1437.

Horkheimer, M. (1936). *Critical theory*. New York: Herder & Herder.

Horkheimer, M., & Adorno, T. W. (1947). *Dialectic of enlightenment*. New York: Seabury Press.

Horney, K. (1924). On the genesis of the castration complex in women. In *Feminine psychology* (pp. 37–53). New York: Norton, 1967.

Horney, K. (1926). The flight from womanhood. In *Feminine psychology* (pp. 54–70). New York: Norton, 1967.

Horney, K. (1932). The dread of woman. In *Feminine psychology* (pp. 133–146). New York: Norton, 1967.

Horney, K. (1933). The denial of the vagina. In *Feminine psychology* (pp. 147–161). New York: Norton, 1967.

Horney, K. (1967). *Feminine psychology.* New York: Norton.

Isay, R. (1989). *Becoming homosexual: Gay men and their development*. New York: Farrar, Strauss & Giroux.

Jordan, J., Kaplan, A., Miller, J. B., Stiver, I., & Surrey, J. (1991). *Women's growth in relation*. New York: Guilford Press.

Keller, E. F. (1987). The gender/science system: Or is sex to gender as nature is to science? *Hypatia*, *2*, 37–50.

Kernberg, O. (1976). Mature love: Prerequisites and characteristics. In *Object relations theory and clinical psycho-analysis* (pp. 215–239). New York: Aronson.

Kestenberg, J. S. (1956a). On the development of maternal feelings in early childhood: Observations and reflections. *Psychoanalytic Study of the Child*, *11*, 257–291.

Kestenberg, J. S. (1956b). Vicissitudes of female sexuality. *Journal of the American Psychoanalytic Association*, *4*, 453–476.

Kestenberg, J. S. (1968). Outside and inside, male and female. *Journal of the American Psychoanalytic Association*, *16*, 457–520.

Kestenberg, J. S. (1976). Regression and reintegration in pregnancy. *Journal of the American Psychoanalytic Association*, *24*(Suppl.), 213–250.

Klein, G. (1973). Two theories or one? *Bulletin of the Menninger Clinic*, *37*, 102–132.

Klein, M. (1928). Early stages of the Oedipus conflict. In *Love, guilt and reparation and other works 1921–1945* (pp. 186–198). New York: Delta, 1975.

Klein, M. (1932). *The psycho-analysis of children*. New York: Delta, 1975.

Klein, M. (1935). A contribution to the psychogenesis of manic-depressive states. In *Love, guilt and reparation and other works 1921–1945* (pp. 262–289). New York: Delta, 1975.

Klein, M. (1937). Love, guilt and reparation. In *Love, guilt and reparation and other works 1921–1945* (pp. 306–343). New York: Delta, 1975.

Klein, M. (1940). Mourning and its relation to manic-depressive states. In *Love, guilt and reparation and other works 1921–1945* (pp. 344–369). New York: Delta, 1975.

Klein, M. (1945). The Oedipus complex in the light of early anxieties. In *Love, guilt and reparation and other works 1921–1945* (pp. 370–419). New York: Delta, 1975.

Klein, M. (1946). Notes on schizoid mechanisms. In *Envy and gratitude and other works 1946–1963* (pp. 1–24). London: Hogarth Press, 1975.

Klein, M. (1955). The psycho-analytic play technique: Its history and significance. In *Envy and gratitude and other works 1946–1963* (pp. 122–140). New York: Delta, 1975.

Klein, M. (1957). Envy and gratitude. In *Envy and gratitude and other works 1946–1963* (pp. 176–235). New York: Delta, 1975.

Kris, A. (1984). The conflicts of ambivalence. *Psychoanalytic Study of the Child, 39*, 213–234.

Kris, A. (1985). Resistance in convergent and divergent conflicts. *Psychoanalytic Quarterly, 54*, 537–568.

Kristeva, J. (1979). Women's time. In T. Moi (Ed.), *The Kristeva reader* (pp. 187–213). New York: Columbia University Press, 1986.

Kristof, N. (2002, May 7). Behind the terrorists. *New York Times*, p. A31.

Kubie, L. (1974). The drive to become both sexes. *Psychoanalytic Quarterly, 43*, 349–426.

Kulish, N., & Holtzman, D. (1998). Persephone, the loss of virginity and the female oedipal complex. *International Journal of Psychoanalysis, 79*, 57–71.

Kulish, N., & Holtzman, D. (2008). *A story of her own: The female Oedipus complex reexamined and renamed.* Northvale, NJ: Aronson.

Lampl-De Groot, J. (1927). The evolution of the Oedipus complex in women. In *The development of the mind: Psychoanalytic papers on clinical and theoretical problems* (pp. 3–18). New York: International Universities Press.

Langer, M. (1992). *Motherhood and sexuality.* New York: Guilford.

Laplanche, J. (1997). The theory of seduction and the problem of the other. *International Journal of Psychoanalysis, 78*, 653–666.

Laslett, B. (1996). The gendering of social theory: Sociology and its discontents. *Contemporary Sociology, 25*, 305–309.

Leuzinger-Bohleber, M. (2001). The "Medea" fantasy: An unconscious determinant of psychogenic sterility. *International Journal of Psychoanalysis, 82*, 323–345.

Levy, R. (1973). *Tahitians: Mind and experience in the Society Islands.* Chicago: University of Chicago Press.

Levy, S. T. (2004). From the editor: Splendid isolation. *Journal of the American Psychoanalytic Association, 52*, 971–973.

Lewes, K. (1988). *The psychoanalytic theory of male homosexuality.* New York: Simon & Schuster.

Limentani, A. (1984). To the limits of heterosexuality: The vagina-man. In D. Breen (Ed.), *The gender conundrum: Contemporary psychoanalytic perspectives on femininity and masculinity* (pp. 273–285). New York: Routledge, 1993.

Loewald, H. W. (1951). Ego and reality. In *Papers on psychoanalysis* (pp. 3–20). New Haven, CT: Yale University Press, 1980.

Loewald, H. W. (1978). Primary process, secondary process, and language. In *Papers on psychoanalysis* (pp. 178–206). New Haven, CT: Yale University Press, 1980.

Loewald, H. W. (1979). The waning of the Oedipus complex. In *Papers on psychoanalysis* (pp. 384–404). New Haven, CT: Yale University Press.

Lorber, J., Coser, R. L., Rossi, A. S., & Chodorow, N. J. (1981). On *The reproduction of mothering*: A methodological debate. *Signs*, 6(3), 482–514.

Marcus, S. (1975). Introduction. In J. Strachey (Ed.), *Three essays on the theory of sexuality by Sigmund Freud* (pp. xix–xli). New York: Basic Books.

Martin, K. A. (1996). *Puberty, sexuality, and the self.* New York: Routledge.

Matthis, I. (Ed.). (2004). *Dialogues on gender, sexuality, and psychoanalysis.* London: Karnac.

Mayer, E. L. (1986). "Everybody must be just like me": Observations on female castration anxiety. *International Journal of Psychoanalysis*, 66, 331–347.

Mayer, E. L. (1995). The phallic castration complex and primary femininity: Paired developmental lines toward female gender identity. *Journal of the American Psychoanalytic Association*, *43*, 17–38.

McDougall, J. (1986). *Theatres of the mind: Illusion and truth on the psychoanalytic stage.* London: Free Association Books.

Mead, M. (1935). *Sex and temperament in three primitive societies.* New York: William Morrow.

Meisel, P., & Kendrick, W. (Eds.). (1985). *Bloomsbury/Freud: The letters of James and Alix Strachey 1924–1925.* New York: Basic Books.

Miller, J. B. (Ed.). (1973). *Psychoanalysis and women.* New York: Penguin.

Miller, J. B. (1976). *Toward a new psychology of women.* Boston: Beacon Press.

Mitchell, J. (1971). *Woman's estate.* New York: Pantheon.

Mitchell, J. (1974). *Psychoanalysis and feminism.* New York: Pantheon.

Mitchell, J. (2004). The difference between gender and sexual difference. In I. Matthis (Ed.), *Dialogues on sexuality, gender, and psychoanalysis* (pp. 67–78). London: Karnac.

Mitchell, J., & Rose, J. (Eds.). (1982). *Feminine sexuality: Jacques Lacan and the école Freudienne.* London: Macmillan.

Mitchell, S. A. (1978). Psychodynamics, homosexuality, and the question of pathology. *Psychiatry*, *41*, 254–263.

Mitchell, S. A. (1981). The psychoanalytic treatment of homosexuality: Some technical considerations. *International Review of Psychoanalysis*, *8*, 63–80.

Mitchell, S. A. (1993). *Hope and dread in psychoanalysis.* New York: Basic Books.

Mitchell, S. A. (2000). *Relationality: From attachment to intersubjectivity.* Hillsdale, NJ: Analytic Press.

Mitchell, S. A., & Aron, L. (Eds.). (1999). *Relational psychoanalysis: The emergence of a tradition.* Hillsdale, NJ: Analytic Press.

Moulton, R. (1986). Professional success: A conflict for women. In J. L. Alpert (Ed.), *Psychoanalysis and women* (pp. 161–181). Hillsdale, NJ: Analytic Press.

Nadelson, C. C., & Notman, M. T. (Eds.). (1982). *The woman patient, vol. 2: Concepts of femininity and the life cycle.* New York: Plenum.

Nadelson, T. (2005). *Trained to kill: Soldiers at war.* Baltimore, MD: Johns Hopkins University Press.

Nagel, T. (1986). *The view from nowhere.* New York: Oxford University Press.

Notman, M. T. (2003). The female body and its meanings. *Psychoanalytic Inquiry*, *23*, 572–591.

Notman, M. T., & Lester, E. P. (1988). Pregnancy: Theoretical considerations. *Psychoanalytic Inquiry*, *8*, 139–159.

Notman, M. T., & Nadelson, C. C. (Eds.). (1978). *The woman patient, vol. 1: Sexual and reproductive aspects of women's health care.* New York: Plenum.

Notman, M. T., & Nadelson, C. C. (Eds.). (1982). *The woman patient, vol. 3: Aggression, adaptation, and psychotherapy.* New York: Plenum.

Orgel, S. (1965). On time and timelessness. *Journal of the American Psychoanalytic Association, 13*, 102–121.

Ortner, S. B. (1974). Is female to male as nature is to culture? In M. Z. Rosaldo & L. Lamphere (Eds.), *Woman, culture and society* (pp. 67–88). Stanford: Stanford University Press.

Person, E. S. (1999). *The sexual century*. New Haven, CT: Yale University Press.

Person, E. S. (2005). As the wheel turns: A centennial reflection on Freud's *Three essays on the theory of sexuality*. *Journal of the American Psychoanalytic Association*, *53*, 1257–1282.

Person, E. S. (2006). Masculinities, plural. *Journal of the American Psychoanalytic Association*, *54*, 1165–1185.

Pines, D. (1982). The relevance of early psychic development to pregnancy and abortion. In *A woman's unconscious use of her body* (pp. 97–115). New Haven, CT: Yale University Press, 1993.

Pines, D. (1990). Pregnancy, miscarriage and abortion. In *A woman's unconscious use of her body* (pp. 116–133). New Haven, CT: Yale University Press, 1993.

Pines, D. (1993). *A woman's unconscious use of her body*. New Haven, CT: Yale University Press.

Raphael-Leff, J. (1993). *Pregnancy: The inside story*. London: Sheldon Press.

Reich, W. (1946). *The mass psychology of fascism* (T. P. Wolfe, Trans., 3rd ed.). New York: Orgone Institute Press.

Rich, A. (1980). Compulsory heterosexuality and lesbian existence. *Signs*, *5*, 631–660.

Richards, A. K. (1996). Primary femininity and female genital anxiety. *Journal of the American Psychoanalytic Association*, *44*(Suppl.), 261–281.

Riviere, J. (1929). Womanliness as a masquerade. In *The inner world and Joan Riviere: Collected papers 1920–1958* (pp. 90–101). London: Karnac.

Roazen, P. (1971). *Freud and his followers*. New York: Knopf.

Roazen, P. (1985). *Helene Deutsch: A psychoanalyst's life*. New York: Anchor/Doubleday.

Roiphe, H., & Galenson, E. (1981). *Infantile origins of sexual identity*. New York: International Universities Press.

Rosaldo, M. Z. (1974). Woman, culture, and society: A theoretical overview. In M. Z. Rosaldo & L. Lamphere (Eds.), *Woman, culture and society* (pp. 17–42). Stanford: Stanford University Press.

Rothstein, A. (1984). *The narcissistic pursuit of perfection*. New York: International Universities Press.

Rubin, G. (1975). The traffic in women: Notes on the "political economy" of sex. In R. Reiter (Ed.), *Toward an anthropology of women* (pp. 157–210). New York: Monthly Review Press.

Rubin, G. (1984). Thinking sex: Notes for a radical theory of the politics of sexuality. In C. Vance (Ed.), *Pleasure and danger: Exploring female sexuality* (pp. 267–319). New York: Simon and Schuster.

Ruddick, S. (1989). *Maternal thinking: Toward a politics of peace*. New York: Ballantine.

Schafer, R. (1974). Problems in Freud's psychology of women. *Journal of the American Psychoanalytic Association*, 22, 459–485.

Schuker, E. (1996). Toward further analytic understanding of lesbian patients. *Journal of the American Psychoanalytic Association*, *44*(Suppl.), 485–508.

Scott, J. (1988). *Gender and the politics of history.* New York: Columbia University Press.
Sherfey, M. J. (1966). The evolution and nature of female sexuality in relation to psychoanalytic theory. *Journal of the American Psychoanalytic Association, 14*, 28–128.
Slater, P. (1967). *The glory of Hera.* Boston: Beacon.
Smelser, N. J. (1998). *The social edges of psychoanalysis.* Berkeley: University of California Press.
Sprengnether, M. (1990). *The spectral mother: Freud, feminism, and psychoanalysis.* Ithaca, NY: Cornell University Press.
Stein, A. (1989). Three models of sexuality: Drives, identities and practices. *Sociological Theory, 7*, 1–13.
Stein, A. (1997). *Sex and sensibility: Stories of a lesbian generation.* Berkeley: University of California Press.
Stein, R. (1998). The poignant, the excessive and the enigmatic in sexuality. *International Journal of Psychoanalysis, 79*, 253–268.
Stein, R. (2002). Evil as love and liberation. *Psychoanalytic Dialogues, 12*, 393–420.
Stein, R. (2009). *For love of the father: A psychoanalytic study of religious terrorism.* Stanford, CA: Stanford University Press.
Stimpson, C. R. (2005). A new look at core gender and gender role identity in women: Commentary. *Journal of the American Psychoanalytic Association, 53*, 1119–1131.
Stoller, R. (1965). The sense of maleness. *Psychoanalytic Quarterly, 34*, 207–218.
Stoller, R. (1968). The sense of femaleness. *Psychoanalytic Quarterly, 37*, 42–55.
Stoller, R. (1976). Primary femininity. *Journal of the American Psychoanalytic Association, 24*(5, Suppl.), 59–78.
Strouse, J. (1974). *Women and analysis.* New York: Grossman.
Sweetnam, A. (1996). The changing contexts of gender: Between fixed and fluid experience. *Psychoanalytic Dialogues, 6*, 437–459.
Sweetnam, A. (1999). Sexual sensations and gender experience: The psychological positions and the erotic third. *Psychoanalytic Dialogues, 9*, 327–348.
Taylor, C. (1989). *Sources of the self: The making of modern identity.* Cambridge, MA: Harvard University Press.
Thompson, C. M. (1971). *On women.* New York: Signet.
Thompson, N. L. (1987). Helene Deutsch: A life in theory. *Psychoanalytic Quarterly, 56*, 317–353.
Tyson, F. (1996). Female psychology: An introduction. *Journal of the American Psychoanalytic Association, 44*(Suppl.), 11–20.
Volkan, V. D. (1997). *Bloodlines: From ethnic pride to ethnic terrorism.* New York: Farrar, Straus & Giroux.
Whiting, B., & Whiting, J. M. (1975). *Children of six cultures: A psychocultural analysis.* Cambridge, MA: Harvard University Press.
Whiting, J. M. W., Kluckhohn, R., & Anthony, A. (1958). The function of male initiation ceremonies at puberty. In E. E. Maccoby, T. M. Newcomb, & E. L. Hartley (Eds.), *Readings in social psychology* (pp. 359–370). New York: Holt.
Williams, C. (1989). *Gender differences at work: Women and men in nontraditional occupations.* Berkeley: University of California Press.

Williams, C. (1992). The glass escalator: Hidden advantages for men in the "female" professions. *Social Problems*, *39*, 253–267.
Williams, C. (1995). *Still a man's world: Men who do "women's work."* Berkeley: University of California Press.
Winnicott, D. W. (1971). *Playing and reality*. New York: Basic Books.
Yanof, J. A. (2000). Barbie and the tree of life: The multiple functions of gender. *Journal of the American Psychoanalytic Association*, *48*, 1439–1465.
Yanof, J. A. (2007, June 7). *The changing sands of gender: Thoughts about gender in psychoanalysis*. Paper presented at Boston Psychoanalytic Institute.
Young-Bruehl, E. (1988). *Anna Freud*. New York: Summit Books.

Index

A

H

I

J

K

L

N

O

Y